Architecting Enterprise Solutions with UNIX Networking

ISBN 0-13-792706-1

9 780137 927067

90000

Hewlett-Packard Professional Books

Architecting Enterprise Solutions with UNIX Networking

John Blommers

http://www.hp.com/go/retailbooks

Prentice Hall PTR
Upper Saddle River, New Jersey 07458
http://www.prenhall.com

Library of Congress Cataloging-in Publication-Data

Blommers, John.
    Architecting enterprise solutions with UNIX networking / John
    Blommers.
        p.   cm. -- (Hewlett-Packard professional books)
    Includes bibliographical references and index.
    ISBN 0-13-792706-1 (paper)
    1. UNIX (Computer file)   2. Operating systems (Computers)
3. Computer network architecture.   I. Title. II. Series.
QA76.76.063B595   1998   98-38706
005.4'32--dc21   CIP

Acquisitions Editor: *John Anderson*
Editorial/Production Supervision: *James D. Gwyn*
Cover Design Director: *Jerry Votta*
Manufacturing Manager: *Alexis Heydt*
Marketing Manager: *Miles Williams*
Editorial Assistant: *Linda Ramagnano*
Manager, Hewlett-Packard Press: *Patricia Pekary*
Editor, Hewlett-Packard Press: *Susan Wright*

© 1999 by Hewlett-Packard Company

Published by Prentice-Hall PTR
Prentice-Hall, Inc.
A Simon & Schuster Company
Upper Saddle River, New Jersey 07458

Prentice Hall books are widely used by corporations and government agencies for training, marketing, and resale. The publisher offers discounts on this book when ordered in bulk quantities. For more information, contact: Corporate Sales Department, Phone: 800-382-3419; FAX: 201-236-7141; E-mail: corpsales@prenhall.com. Or write: Corp. Sales Dept., Prentice Hall PTR, 1 Lake Street, Upper Saddle River, NJ   07458

FrameMaker, Photoshop, Premier, Page Mill, and PostScript are trademarks of Adobe Systems. BONeS and Amazon.com are trademarks of Alta Group. APC is a trademark of American Power Corp. Macintosh, Apple-Talk, NextStep, OpenStep, Rhapsody, Home Page, ClarisWorks, AutoCAD, and Blues Brothers are trademarks of Apple Computer. Cisco is a trademark of Cisco Systems. QuickCam is a trademark of Connectix. WordPerfect is a trademark of Corel. CU-SeeMe is a trademark of Cornell University. DECNet is a trademark of Digital Equipment Corp. Raptor is a trademark of Eagle. HP-UX, HPPA, PA-RISC, VUE, LaserJet, PCL, SharedX, and SoftBench are trademarks of Hewlett-Packard. FlashPix is a trademark of Kodak. Windows is a trademark of the Microsoft Corporation. Navigator and JavaScript are trademarks of Netscape Communications. NetWare, IntraNetWare, Smalltalk and Ricochet are trademarks of Novell. SAP is a trademark of SAP AG. Starbucks is a trademark of Starbucks Coffee. Wabi, Java, and Wingz are trademarks of Sun Computers, Inc. All products or services mentioned in this book are trademarks or service marks of their respective companies or organizations.

Printed in the United States of America
10   9   8   7   6   5   4   3   2   1

ISBN 0-13-792706-1

Prentice-Hall International (UK) Limited, *London*
Prentice-Hall of Australia Pty. Limited, *Sydney*
Prentice-Hall Canada Inc., *Toronto*
Prentice-Hall Hispanoamericana, S.A., *Mexico*
Prentice-Hall of India Private Limited, *New Delhi*
Prentice-Hall of Japan, Inc., *Tokyo*
Simon & Schuster Asia Pte. Ltd., *Singapore*
Editora Prentice-Hall do Brasil, Ltda., *Rio de Janeiro*

Contents

Contents v

11 Integration Using X-Windows 187

12 Managing UNIX Networks. 203

List of Tables

List of Tables

List of Figures

List of Figures

Preface

This book is about UNIX and the corporate network. It's about architecting enterprise-wide computing solutions for finance, engineering, and manufacturing. It's about integrating desktop computer applications and UNIX systems. It's about using UNIX networking to create scalable open systems.

The author is a 15-year veteran with Hewlett–Packard Consulting and has had the pleasure of recommending, developing, and implementing HP UNIX (HP–UX) and network solutions for HP customers. This book may lean a degree or two toward HP products, but so great is HP's (and the author's) commitment to open systems that the reader will find all the information between these covers to be widely applicable.

Architected enterprise networked computing solutions have long been a strength of UNIX. This O/S has always enjoyed multivendor support. Robust implementations suited for commercial applications abound. The hardware that UNIX runs on is scalable; you can buy a low-cost workstation or a powerful high-availability networked cluster. Inherent support for multiple protocol stacks and services makes UNIX a major player in desktop integration solutions. With such depth and breadth, it is no wonder that architecting UNIX networks can be so challenging.

Now consider yourself in the following situation: You are preparing to meet your boss, the CIO (chief information officer), about the company's plans to install UNIX servers across the enterprise network. When the meeting is over, it will rest on your shoulders exactly how to architect the solution so that your team can implement it. Into the meeting you go, intent on plumbing the depths of all that this portends. Fresh coffee is poured, and you settle down to the interviewing task at hand.

You learn that your company has chosen a new client–server application to be implemented across your corporate network. Serious UNIX iron will run the database engines and application servers. Desktop computers will run the client software. Your job is to develop an architectural blueprint that will be used to implement the new application. The CIO wants a solution that is "able"–scalable, maintainable, upgradable, supportable, and reliable. A disaster recovery plan has to be developed, presented, and implemented. Naturally, the UNIX and desktop computers, the network printers, and existing productivity software such as Email collaboration tools all have to work together. You indicate that a comprehensive IP numbering plan has to be worked out, too, and, by the way, it's also time to design and implement a company-wide DNS system to support all these applications and systems. The CIO nods in understanding. You take another sip of coffee.

So far, so good, you think. But the company president wants customers to be able to send in orders and messages via the Internet. And why don't we put up a web site to let customers and prospects search for and download product information and download software updates, too? The CIO passes the buck to you. Then you're reminded that company orders are growing 30% annually. The training department wants to put in a UNIX video server so that they can deliver training clips via the network to any employee in the company.

In the back of your mind, you ponder. You take another sip. Can the UNIX servers and the network handle it all? How much expansion can a UNIX network accommodate? What if the UNIX boxes run out of capacity? How can the IP and DNS configurations be worked out for the multihomed UNIX servers and the IP routers? You swallow another mouthful of coffee to stop the pain growing inside your head.

The CIO sums up: we need a complete UNIX network architecture drawn up for a review session next week. The architecture needs to specify topology, configuration, security, performance, and functionality. You agree, drain your coffee mug, and exit to ponder your next move.

Back in the sanctum sanctorum of your work space, one thing is clear. This is not a simple IP numbering problem. It's not jut about desktop computers using DHCP, WINS, or DNS. And performance won't be achieved simply by dropping ATM switches into the data center. Meeting reliability goals using multiple LAN adapters, backup servers, mirrored disks, and distributed DNS servers is a tricky business, too. In short, architecture is not simply a matter of forcing together a bunch of point solutions until you stumble across one that looks like it will work. You glance up at your bookshelf for a reference about UNIX and networking architecture... .

If this is a situation you've been in, then this book will help you with the necessary architecture. We introduce desktop operating system integration issues with UNIX. Two- and three-tier architectures are covered. Special features of IP and DNS are explained in context. And we go into high-availability design methods. You will see example architectures for UNIX networking solutions in industries such as wireless, cable TV, manufacturing, utilities, and engineering. Applications such as SAP, Oracle Financials, Digital Video, X-Windows, NFS, and WWW are covered. We analyze these architectures, applications, and solutions for scalability, reliability, performance, manageability, and weakness.

Enjoy the read!

Sincerely,

John Blommers

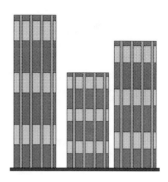

CHAPTER 1

Principles of Architecture and Design

Introduction

The multitier application won't run significantly faster when the database engines are beefed up. Increasing the speed and number of application servers doesn't improve user response time very much either. Even increasing the network bandwidth gives only modest performance gains. What is going on here? This system has an architecture problem.

The best UNIX networking architects design their solutions by taking advantage of sound, time-tested methodologies and principles. Any solution must be based on a thorough requirements analysis, a process that discovers needs and purposes. Functional specifications derive from this, and implied functionality follows naturally. When point solutions already exist, brainstorming them may yield a partial or total solution that meets all the requirements. A complete understanding of UNIX and networking principles is a prerequisite for architecture and design to proceed.

An individual can produce an architecture and design, and a structured walk through can be performed by the same person. A team review of peers, subject matter experts, and even clients is a valuable process for gaining solid acceptance of the requirements, while validating the basic architecture and design at a high level. Several alternative architectures and designs may be developed, and a structured decision analysis can identify the best one.

What-if analysis is used to test the design on paper. The process invents changes in the design and tests its functionality, scalability, durability, flexibility, reliability, and suitability. For example, we may invent a scenario with ten times the number of users specified originally. A paper analysis may suggest small changes to the architecture and design to accommodate this possibility.

Many solutions result in failed implementations because no implementation plan was included. A distributed UNIX product that manages a country-spanning SS7 network via a standard IP data network must specify the connectivity, response time, throughput, and configuration of its components. In addition, an implementation process must be defined. Any solution must be supportable under disastrous conditions. A disaster recovery plan should be devised to support the continued operation of the solution. This plan is part of the solution delivered to the client.

Finally, a capacity plan assists in the implementation of the solution to ensure that it will perform under the anticipated loads. At a minimum this will be a cookbook of standard engineered design configurations and specifications. The Universal Building Code in the United States is an example. When conditions are expected to deviate from the cookbook designs, then a capacity planning process should be specified to ensure that the solution meets these requirements. See Figure 1-1.

Requirements Analysis

Requirements analysis determines what the design is needed for. We are aided by a standard set of questions, a questionnaire, to support a consistent methodology. Some standard questions might be as follows:

> Where are the users located?
> What services does the user need?
> Who are the users?
> How many users will be active at the busy hour?
> What are the user work habits?
> What is the business cycle?
> Are data pushed or pulled?
> What are the data types?
> What reliability is needed?
> What functions are needed?

To help compile a comprehensive set of questions, keep in mind the six basic questions: "who, what, where, when, why, and how." Ask open-ended questions versus closed-ended questions. A closed ended question is typically answered with a yes or no reply and gives very little new information. An open-ended question might be "What aspects of remote access worry you?" and result in a flood of unexpected quality information.

Leave no stone unturned. Interview a wide range of users, clients, managers, vendors, and support staff. Try to set up remote telephone (or Email-based) interviews to get representation from all sections of the company, not just the

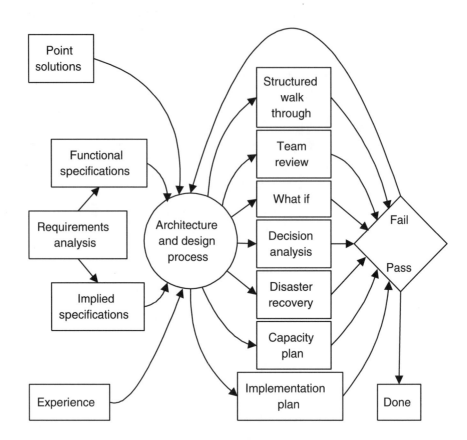

Figure 1-1   Product design process diagram

The product design process shows how information flows from the initial specifications to the final validated design. We begin with our inputs and develop an architecture to support them. The architecture is a high-level depiction or model of what parts and processes are needed. The design that follows is a detailed breakdown of all these parts and processes, how they interoperate, what standards to use, what components should be chosen, and what parameters should be assigned to the building blocks. The implementation process consists of installation, configuration, testing, and acceptance (the "Done" step shown above). As an analogy, in the construction industry we have architects, civil engineers, and construction workers.

central site. Probe with each of these questions along a wide range of dimensions to get the broadest possible results. A suggested beginning list of such dimensions is given below, and you should try to add more dimensions as appropriate to the client business:

Each of the seven layers of the OSI model
Performance metrics
Reliability
Complexity
Ease of use
Maintainability
Cost
Time to implement
Geographic coverage
Speed issues
COTS versus custom developed

Consider the suitability of architectural elements distributed functionality, such as client, server, application server, database, and multiple tiers. Avoid accepting point solutions as requirements. Don't accept a statement like "we need an SAP solution" or "we need an Email system" because it's loaded with presumptions. Look under the hood for the true requirements. Also avoid a requirement statement like "select among SAP, Oracle Financials, Baan, and PeopleSoft" or "help us choose between NFS, Novell Netware, LAN Manager, and DFS."

From a purist's perspective, when making choices, requirements such as "should be open" and "must be standards based" and "shall be available from multiple suppliers" are implied. Architectures with open interchangeable components are preferred from a procurement viewpoint because competitive pressures keep prices in line. For a simple requirement like a file and print server, an NFS point solution is preferred because it is available from many vendors, is bundled with many UNIX and Linux variants, and runs on most hardware platforms (PA-RISC, Intel, PowerPC, Alpha, Sparc, and SGI). Oh, if only all requirements were so simply matched to a solution.

Functional Specifications

Requirements are translated, transformed, or mapped to functionality. The mapping does not result in a product or component list. Perhaps some examples going from requirement to functional specification are in order (see Table 1-1).

Table 1-1   Requirements and specifications

Requirement	Functional Specification Extracted from Requirement
Send a message with file attachments	Email, collaboration package, file archival, and compression package
Read-only access to financial data from any location on the network	X-Windows client, Web, and Java
Remote connection to corporate network	PPP, frame relay, wireless, FAX
Run program on legacy host remotely	SNA gateway
Remote printing	Web printing, network printer, UNIX, RIP protocol
Low client administration	X-terminal, diskless computer, network computer, Macintosh, NetPC

Implied functionality is a trickier matter. The client may have some implied functions in mind as being so obvious that they are not stated at all. Naturally, these have to be discovered early, because they will eventually come out in the form of a surprise. If they do come out later, you will wind up saying "oops" in front of the client. This is not a good credibility builder.

Some examples of implied functionality are in order. Without exception, TCP/IP is the implied transport and network protocol of choice. As a UNIX bigot, the author also believes that UNIX is the implied operating system of choice, certainly for the server side of a solution. Video applications imply UDP/IP and reserved available bandwidth to carry the traffic. Group file sharing implies a file server. Email for a large and varying user community implies a directory service. A low-administrative client system implies limited flexibility for the user and more work at a point of central control. Open implies UNIX, Rich Text File format, NFS, X-Windows, TCP/IP, DNS, RFC compliance, IEEE compliance, SMTP, MIME, Java, C and C++, and Ethernet. In an ideal world, there are plenty of fully functional open solutions to go around. In our world, we are often forced to adopt a proprietary, closed, or single-vendor solution.

Canvasing for Point Solutions

Solution developers and end users prefer preexisting solutions or commercial off-the-shelf (COTS) products over customized or totally proprietary solutions. For sufficiently complex requirements, such as those dictated by a combination of government legislation, system complexity, and client needs, the marketplace does not have a total solution. This is where systems integrators earn their bread and butter. They canvas the marketplace for point solutions that meet most of the requirements and then integrate them. They search for integration tools and methodologies and apply their own expertise to making the glue that holds the diverse products together.

When no point solution can meet the requirements, lumping together several point solutions may achieve the goal. Alternatively, it may be prudent to find a product that meets the requirements as best as possible, setting aside those requirements that are not met and rationalizing that they were not that important anyway. A more rigorous approach to this is to select requirements that are "must haves" and designate the rest as "wants." From the point solutions that satisfy the "must haves," choose among the wants according to how important they are and how well they meet the requirement. The highest-scoring solution is chosen.

Few are willing to take a vendor's data sheet at face value and choose a product sight unseen. If several contending solutions are available, there are two ways to evaluate them; sequentially or in parallel. Sequential evaluation lets you select the most likely solution if it is tested first and passes. If there is doubt, move on to the subsequent solutions. This approach can take longer, but might not. A parallel evaluation takes more workers. The evaluation approach is often called a pilot, prototype, or benchmark phase. Lessons are learned and applied to the architecture and design of the final solution.

Note that accepting a point solution implies that an underlying architecture from the vendor has been accepted. The best solutions are those whose architectures are similar, interoperable, and interchangeable. The worst solutions are those with a proprietary architecture, because you lose all the advantages of choice, flexibility, and cost.

Whichever architecture you choose, remember that it must be able to scale well. This is by no means cut and dried. For example, specifications for an Email system may indicate that it can accommodate 100,000 users. However, the limits of the architecture may mean that, for all practical purposes, on practical computer hardware and existing networks, the limit is 500 users per server before performance degrades to unacceptable levels. The pilot may have been limited to only a few hundred users on one server, and the problem won't be encountered until the implementation is well underway and it is realized that 200 servers in total will be needed.

How do we go about finding our point solutions in the first place?

Magazine annual buyers guides
Magazine web page product evaluation search engines
Web search engines
Internet news groups (search first, then post a question)
Product category web pages
Magazine ad index
Go through your personal paper file of clippings
Search your hard drive for forgotten PDF files
Consult your personal people network
Hire a consultant

Structured Walk Through

The structured walk through is a process that compares the original requirements with the final design. The architecture and design details get a thorough review. But what's so structured about it? The process keeps the walk through on track. The process is driven by standard questions and it is not a back-stabbing session. This is a genuine opportunity to help improve quality. A step-by-step gap analysis is done for each requirement. The gap analysis is a four step-process itself:

1. State the requirement as it is.

2. Note the actual as-is feature in the architecture or design.

3. Compare the two and state the differences—the gap.

4. Recommend how to close the gap.

The structured walk-through process is meant to verify the strengths of the design and discover any weaknesses that are not immediately obvious. Detecting unspecified and implied requirements is one of the goals. Revealing any omissions at this stage is cheaper than fixing them later. Architectural flaws might be exposed. And given the quality of the participants, their combined skill will very likely result in an embarrassingly rich amount of analysis and fixes. At the end of the session, complete documentation of all findings gives the architects and designers total recall of the walk through.

In preparation for the structured walk through, a standard list of questions and objectives is developed or leveraged from previous walk throughs. Some of these might be as follows:

> For each requirement, point out where the solution meets it.
> For each part of the solution, where is the requirement?
> Do any of the architecture's point solutions not coexist?
> Are the requirements self consistent and not in conflict?
> Review any calculation.
> Check all stated assumptions.
> Verify that the approach to integration can be done.
> Are the proposed configurations correct and valid?
> Are there product version dependencies?

> Will the performance goals be met?
>
> What are the failure modes?
>
> Are the resources required to implement the solution available

The structured walk-through meeting is an excellent time to remember that hindsight has 20–20 vision and to recall weaknesses in architecture, design, or implementation from past experiences. For example, the Network File System (NFS) was designed for use on high-speed, low latency LANs, where it works very well. But NFS did not perform well over low-speed, high-latency WANs. The only recourse to using NFS over WANs is to tweak the tunable parameters that NFS clients and IP routers provide to mitigate the problem. NFS is thus relegated to a tweaking approach to improve its performance because its architecture does not cope with a factor-of-ten change in operating conditions. Indeed, one major reason for the development of the Distributed File System (DFS) was to overcome exactly these architectural limits.

If there is even the slightest indication that a design requires the use of polling, it is flirting with the enemy of scalability. No process should poll for status. Rather, a process should block on an event and let the operating system send it a signal to resume execution. A close relative to polling is the chatty protocol, and chatty protocols don't allow for large implementations. Note that the design of IP, TCP, and DNS contain no chatty components, and these protocols form the backbone of the Internet. This is indeed grand testimony for scalability.

Other implementation problems from the past include IP's 32-bit network address, 8-bit CPU addressing models, 16- and 32-bit operating systems, installers that can't install software on file systems with more than 2 gigabytes free, 32-bit pointers and addresses that can only address 4 gigabytes of virtual or physical memory, applications that can't handle physical memory over 64 megabytes, and the 32-bit counters in SNMP version 1. In each case, the fundamental design and implementation of these examples had to be totally redone to overcome their limitations. Thus, IP version 6 proposes 128-bit addresses, the latest chips and operating systems use 64-bit addressing and wide data paths, and file systems are using 64 bits to measure file size.

Remember to think outside the box.

Team Review

The team review, as the name says, is conducted by the technical staff working on the architecture and design. The structured walk through is attended by a diverse group, including clients, users, vendors, and team members. The review is a friendly, helpful process where egos are checked at the door. There is great value from the group's experience and from the variety in personalties and viewpoints. The team may opt to do a structured walk through as well. The meeting size should not be allowed to grow because we want to limit the overhead of many-to-many interactions. Remote collaboration by the team is quite acceptable and reasonable when they are given a few tools to facilitate it. A shared electronic whiteboard and an audio conference setup often suffice. The review can be taken off site to limit interruptions, especially if pagers and cell phones are stored in a container that is RF-proof. A VPN wireless link between the group's laptops and the main office can provide access to information needed by the group.

Decision Analysis

Decision analysis is a structured tool for making correct repeatable decisions. In our case, we want to pick from a set of alternative solutions. Begin by identifying all the features that are absolutely required. These are the "must haves." Eliminate from further consideration any solutions that don't meet this obvious criterion. Now identify the "wants," features that would be nice but we can live without. Consider how valuable or important the "wants" and "must haves" are and weigh them on a scale, with the most important a 10 and the least important a 1. Next rate how well each solution meets that feature on a scale from 0 to 10. Multiply each solution's score by its importance, and sum up all these weighted scores by solution. The solution with the highest-weighted score is the best solution.

Given that solution A is better than solution B, we might be tempted to choose it out of hand and be done with the matter. Still, solution B isn't that much worse. Isn't there a way to make a compelling case for one over the other? The answer is that we can do a risk analysis using decision analysis.

We need to create a list of risks associated with solutions A and B, each establish their importance on a scale of 1 to 10, assess the probability of each risk, calculate the weighted risk, and add them up to find the most risky solution. (see Figure 1-2).

Feature	Importance	Solution A		Solution B		Solution C	
		Score	Weighted	Score	Weighted	Score	Weighted
Cheap	10	9	90	4	40	5	50
Fast	6	5	30	10	60	5	30
Flexible	3	10	30	8	24	5	15
Reliable	1	4	4	6	6	5	5
Rating			**154**		130		100

Figure 1-2   Decision analysis tabular format
A decision analysis for choosing between the three solutions A, B, and C. The arithmetic for applying the solution scores reveals that solution A is by far the superior choice. Solution B isn't that much worse than solution A, but we can dispense with solution C altogether.

What-if Analysis

What-if or risk analysis is used to test the architecture, design, and solution (see Figure 1-3). The idea is to grab hold of each piece and yank at it, figuratively speaking, to see what happens. We may wonder what happens if we try to send a 10-megabyte file over the Email system we have been designing. The specification called for 1 megabyte and we know it can handle 2 megabytes. By following good engineering principles, we doubled the specification! What if we send a 100-megabyte file. A gigabyte? The point of this thinking is that it may expose some fundamental design limit we didn't think much about while we were focused on the work at hand. Some other questions: What if

		Solution A		Solution B	
Risk	Importance	Probability	Weighted	Probability	Weighted
Limited supply	8	10	80	5	40
Vendor stability	10	8	80	3	30
Unproven	5	5	25	2	10
Poor support	6	4	24	10	60
Total risk			**209**		140

Figure 1-3   Risk analysis tabular format

The risk analysis reveals that solution A is significantly more risky than solution B, so we will in fact chose solution B over solution A, even though solution A is the better fit to the requirements.

A new requirement is added late in the cycle?

A requirement is deleted?

A "standard" changes?

Component Y becomes unreliable?

The capacity plan is based on wrong assumptions?

A data link fails?

Solution B becomes unavailable or changes in version 2.0?

Solution A gets a new bug in version 3.0?

Solution A is broken in version 4.0?

Disaster Recovery Planning

For a solution to be deployed successfully, it has to be maintainable, survivable, and reliable over its lifetime. As organizations become dependent on a given UNIX networking solution, so does business stop when the solution breaks down. To avoid the effects of disaster, a solution must be accompanied by a set of disaster recovery planning guidelines. A plan with a little more meat than "back up often" is appropriate.

Disaster recovery planning, or the more palatable term business continuity planning, has three major facets: solution, environment, and business. The solution itself is at risk from some clearly defined disasters that the architects, designers, and implementers can foresee and address. Thus they specify that file server incremental backups be scheduled automatically to a DLT array every 4 hours during the prime shift. The physical and logical environment into which the solution is integrated is less defined. Therefore, the installers and implementation team should assess the environment and extend the disaster recovery plan appropriately. Thus they will specify that the file server's UPS with 30-minute sustaining power be backed up with a diesel generator, knowing full well that the AC power at a manufacturing site is subject to summer outages lasting several hours. The business that implements the solution in turn has its own unique disaster scenarios. Thus they will specify that an additional printer will be available within 30 minutes of a printer failure, given the importance of printing up job orders in a timely manner.

Capacity Planning

An architecture, design, and implementation plan is incomplete without an accompanying capacity plan. A capacity plan includes the necessary analysis to ensure that the implemented solution will provide the specified functionality at the required level of performance under reasonable worst-case conditions. There is nothing worse than implementing a wonderful solution only to have it roll over dead on its side shortly after installation. Capacity planning helps reduce the risk of unacceptable performance.

Capacity planning is used to help size the various components of the target implementation. For computers, we need to size RAM, the number and configuration of the disks, the number of processors, the processor speed, and the number LAN adapters. For the network, we need to choose media speeds, router memory, the number of clients per shared media segment, the bandwidth for the WAN links, and the number of clients per server. Most importantly from a user perspective, we need to establish the end-to-end response time for the design under the load conditions defined by the customer.

Several methodologies can be used to do capacity planning. Benchmarking is a favorite. A synthetic workload is applied to a representative test configuration in a lab. Hardware and software instrumentation measure how well the LAN and systems perform. Lessons learned are fed back into the design. Benchmarking requires considerable resources: time, equipment, personnel, equipment, facilities, and expertise. It is not practical to benchmark every design, nor is it practical to stage a complete design for benchmarking. There are too many variables.

Mathematical methods can be used to leverage benchmark data. Queuing analysis or simulation methods can be applied to very large systems and networks to predict their behavior. Once a model is built, it can modified in the modeling tool any number of times until it's right—without any real hardware being staged. Workloads can be added and altered at a whim. Endless what-if analysis can be performed. Think of this as a theoretical stress test. This work can be leveraged, too. When the consultant's next customer engagement arrives, past work experience increases their productivity.

Models can be handmade using math scratchpads like Mathcad. Very nice discrete event simulation tools are also on the market. Detailed accurate models of networks and systems can be built, and arbitrary loads can be placed on them to determine resource utilization and response time. Resource bottlenecks are very easy to find with these tools. Vendors of simulation tools include the Alta Group, CACI, Mil3, and Zitel.

Three terms should be clarified: model, methodology, and tool. A *model* describes how much detail is used from the architecture and design. How simplified have we made the model? Einstein said that "things should be as simple as possible but no simpler." Less detail makes the model more usable, faster to evaluate, less costly to develop, less accurate, and more convenient. *Methodologies* for analyzing models include the method of averages, queuing theory, approximation analysis, and discrete event simulation (see Figure 1-4.) *Tools* for implementing a model include calculators, spreadsheets, math scratchpads, special software products with closed form analytic solutions for systems and networks, and discrete event

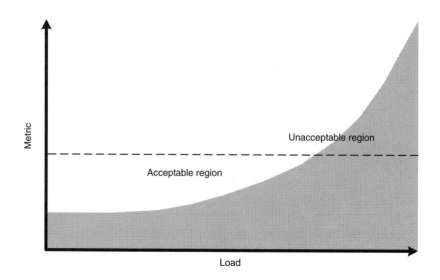

Figure 1-4   Knee in the response time curve
A simulated system and network stress test might result in this response time curve. Knowing where the knee in the curve is allows us to set user expectations.

simulation engines complete with graphical user interfaces, component libraries, and report generators.

References

Kepner, Charles H. and Tregoe, Benjamin B., *The New Rational Manager*. Princeton, NJ: Princeton Research Press, 1981, ISBN: 8101 901017.

A fine and very readable article by Kara Kapczynski entitled "The World of the Technical Architect" is recommended reading. It's on the Internet at

http://www.sun.com/sunworldonline/swol-03-1998/swol-03-itarchitect.html

CHAPTER 2

Multitier Architectures

Introduction

A powerful concept in network and systems architecture is to break up the functionality of an application into several levels called *tiers*. The degenerate case is the single-tier solution—everybody has a system on their desktop that meets all their business needs. Of course this is neither practical, economical, maintainable, nor desirable. Another example is the single computer that runs both batch and interactive applications, with thousands of fairly dumb terminals located around the "network." At least two tiers are needed for a scalable noncentralized architecture.

The two-tier solution is known as the classic client–server solution. Examples include telnet, FTP, NFS, and X-Windows. Multiple clients access a central server where shared resources are located. Scalability can be achieved by adding more servers. Note that a simple web client may download from one web server an HTML document that references images located on several other web servers. This is still a two-tier scenario with multiple servers and a single client.

Three-tier solutions offer even greater scalability. This is demonstrated by the German company SAP and its SAP/R3 business software. The three tiers are the client, the application server, and the database server.

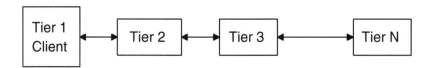

Figure 2-1   Generalized n-tier architecture communications pattern
There are more instantiations at tier 1 than at tier 2, more at tier 2 than at tier 3, and so on. There is nothing that requires a client to dedicate itself to a specific tier 2 application server. By generalizing this principle for all tiers, a very robust hierarchy is possible.

Four tier solutions are less frequently found in the field but they're impressive in their capability. A shining example is the meta search engine. The user operates a web client and posts a request to the meta search engine at tier two. The meta search engine formulates requests to a number of web search engines and summarizes the results for the user. The web search engines at tier three accept the search parameters and in turn makes queries to their database server at tier four.

In general, each tier does some local processing and conducts non-trivial transactions with the next tier over a network connection.

To appreciate the performance implications of a multiple tier architecture, consider the simplest transaction - a single packet request and a single packet reply. Each packet experiences a network delay as it moves between tiers. Each tier system does some processing when it receives a request packet, adding another delay. See Figure 2-1   .

Two-tier Architectures

Client–server is the classic two-tier architecture. Common industry-standard client–server applications are telnet, file transfer protocol (FTP), X-Windows, network file system (NFS), and hypertext transport protocol (HTTP). Clients usually send a request to a server and receive a response. This exchange of packets over the network is called a *transaction*.

The transaction will involve client-side and server-side processing. Client-side processing involves interacting with the user, putting up forms, drawing graphics, validating information, exchanging data with the server, and displaying the results for the user. Server-side processing involves exchanging data with the client, doing calculations, looking up information, and saving information.

Servers are placed on networks to be shared by many clients distributed over the enterprise network. (The author will avoid the terms intranet and extranet.) This places a time-varying load on the server that follows the business cycle. When the server becomes busy, users will detect a degradation in transaction response time. Users learn to associate poor

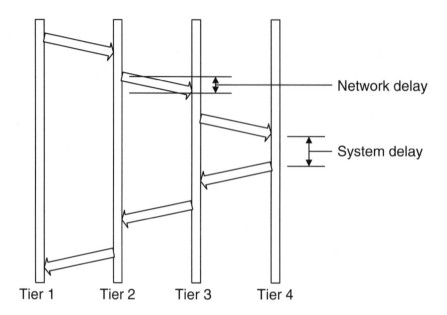

Figure 2-2   Four-tier performance properties
Performance issues with a four tier architecture are depicted here as a series of time delays. The greater the slope of the arrow the longer the network delay. The greater the vertical gap between entering and departing packets the longer that tier is taking to process the transaction.

response time with busy servers, and will complain about the server any time they are unhappy about it. See Figure 2-2.

Since client–server transactions pass packets over local area networks (LANs) and very possibly over wide area networks (WANs), it follows that network latency contributes to the total transaction response time. See Figure 2-3. Transactions that require a lot of packet exchanges will naturally experience much more network latency. LAN-connected client–server systems benefit from the relatively high speed of 10 Mbps (megabits per second) or 100-Mbps LANs and perform well for complex transactions. But connected over relatively slow WAN links, complex client–server transactions may incur intolerably high latencies. As before, users learn to blame the network for poor transaction response time.

In addition to server- and network-side performance, client-side performance is also a component of total system performance. For example, a RAM-starved client with a slow disk drive may be responsible for more latency then the server and network combined. This is an implementation issue with the client. Server and network performance issues can be addressed with some architectural principles.

When the performance of a single server becomes a limiting factor to expansion, than multiple servers can be distributed across the network. Besides the obvious benefit of multiplying server horsepower, we have the flexibility to place the additional servers at optimum locations on the network. Load balancing technologies may be deployed to help the client locate the "best" server at the time.

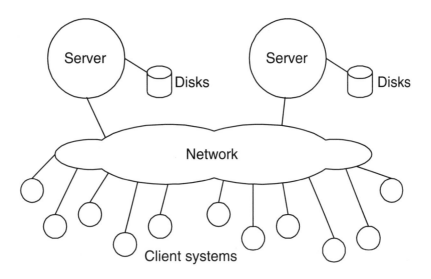

Figure 2-3   Two-tier client–server architecture
Client–server two tier architectures scale by increasing the number of servers to increase computational capacity. Clients use the best server, which may or may not be nearest. Network congestion may cause clients to prefer an alternative server. Depending on the application, data accessed by the servers might need to be replicated and synchronized periodically so that all users have data.

Three-tier Architectures

When networked applications are implemented in three tiers they can perform better and scale better than their two tier equivalents. The usual client system is still there, making requests to its application server, which in turn makes requests to its database server. An example is the SAP Company's SAP/R3 suite of business applications. See Figure 2-4.

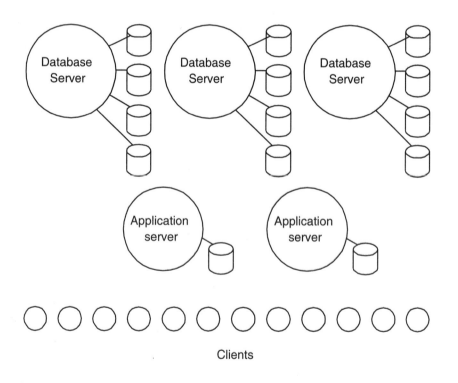

Clients

Figure 2-4 Three-tier architecture diagram

A classic three-tier architecture depicting a multitude of clients at tier 1, two application servers with a local disk at tier 2, and three database servers at tier 3. The network connections have been omitted for clarity.

The client system still performs the duties of interacting with the user, reading values from fields in a GUI, doing simple data checking, and displaying data returned by the application server. Since there will generally be multiple application severs that need not all be identical in functionality or performance, the better clients are able to transparently choose the appropriate application server. At a minimum, the user is able to choose one, usually just by clicking the appropriate icon on the desktop.

The application server at tier 2 is where much of the functionality resides. The application accepts the client request and does whatever computations and data lookups are appropriate. The necessary data may be in RAM, on local disks, or available from a database engine. The interaction with the database server may be very simple or quite complex. Many data may be passed between the two before the results are ready to be sent back to the client. Application servers may be provisioned as necessary and situated appropriately on the network to achieve the desired performance levels.

Many real-world implementations of three-tier architectures have a database server at tier 3. As before, there are generally several tier 3 servers in the design. The databases that they manage need not be identical, so the application servers can take advantage of this, keeping multiple databases occupied concurrently on their behalf to increase performance. Database engines may be provisioned as necessary and situated appropriately on the network to achieve the desired performance goals.

Network traffic between tiers 1 and 2 tends to be relatively light compared to that between tiers 2 and 3. The high-volume traffic between client and server in two-tier architectures now occurs between the top tiers in three-tier architectures. This means that a lot more client systems can be supported over relatively slow WAN links. Because of the high data volumes between the application and database servers, these systems are usually located on the same high-speed LAN: 100-Mbps FDDI, 100-BASE-T, or 155-Mbps ATM.

Four-tier Architectures

The best way to exemplify the four-tier architecture is to visit the web metacrawler site on the Internet. Its URL is *http://www.metacrawler.com*,

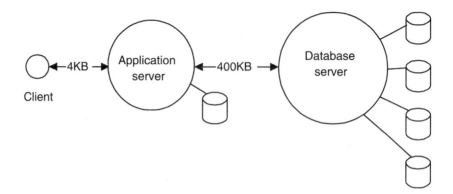

Figure 2-5   Three-tier application data volumes
Three tier applications generally exchange modest amounts of data between the client
and the application server and considerable amounts between the application server
and the database server. The 4KB (Kilobytes) and 400KB may be taken as typical for
one transaction.

and the user can concurrently search multiple web search engines by simply
entering search parameters into the metacrawler.

A typical web search engine may be considered a three-tier solution as
shown in Figure 2-5. The user is tier 1, the web server is tier 2, and the
database engine is tier 3. Given a list of search engines, the user would
normally go from one to the next, enter the search criteria, and wade through
the results. Since each search engine has its own GUI for data entry and a
unique method for constructing the search, this can be a difficult error-prone
and time-consuming task. Many search engines will return the same links.

The metacrawler adds value by constructing HTML requests appropriate to
each search engine that it drives, by issuing the search requests in parallel,
removing duplicate hits, and presenting HTML results in one output screen.
The user is spared a great deal of drudgery, time, and inconvenience.

The search engines are not aware of the metacrawler per se. The failure of
one or more search engines does not break the system. Random
communication failures between the metacrawler and the search engines
doesn't break anything. The solution is quite robust. See Figure 2-6.

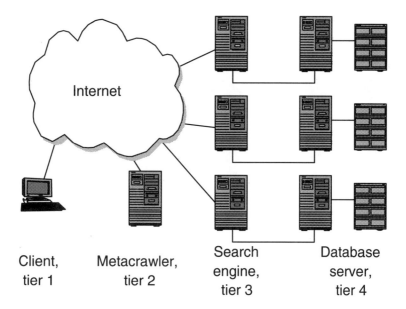

Client,   Metacrawler,   Search   Database
tier 1   tier 2   engine,   server,
                               tier 3   tier 4

Figure 2-6   The metacrawler's four tiers
The metacrawler exemplifies a four-tier architecture. It empowers a single client to concurrently search multiple Internet search engines and save time, avoid duplicate "hits," benefit from multiple and unique databases, and transparently ignores extremely slow or inoperative search engines.

Another example of a multi-tier architecture is the web proxy and socks solution. Clients inside a private enterprise network can reach the Internet via a web proxy system, which in turn uses the socks server on the corporate firewall to reach web servers on the Internet. The client is tier 1, the web proxy server is tier 2, the socks server is tier 3, and the target web server is tier 4. This arrangement provides Internet connectivity through a firewall (where the socks server runs) for clients without a socksified IP stack. Unfortunatcly, thc packct dclays through this many ticrs can noticably increase the response time for interactive queries.

For completeness, please refer to Figure 2-7 for the OSI seven-layer view of client–server architecture.

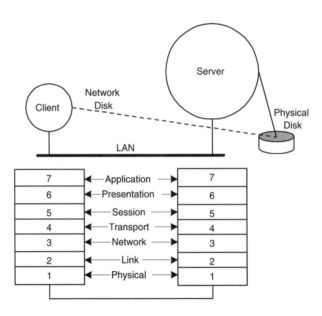

Figure 2-7   Client–server from the OSI viewpoint
This is the simplest client–server system. The client has no disk drive and depends on the server for its configuration, operating system, applications, file sharing, and print services. This architecture applies to the original HP-UX diskless nodes, X-terminals, and, more recently, to the network computer, the NetPC, and the thin client.
Plus la change, plus la meme chose.

References

Edwards, Jeri, *3-Tier Client/Server at Work*. New York: Wiley Computer Publishing, John Wiley & Sons, Inc., 1997, ISBN: 0-471-184.

CHAPTER 3

High-availability
Issues

Introduction

H igh availability is a term associated with mission-critical systems with 24×7×365 uptime requirements. The design for such solutions has to include a reliability analysis to verify that the choice and configuration of highly reliable components, redundant subsystems, and spares provisioning meet the specified availability. Figures like 99.9% availability are commonly specified. Additional nines after the decimal point come at greater expense.

Continual reevaluation of system reliability is recommended. Operational uptime and failure statistics should be viewed in the light of statistical variability and start-up failure phenomena. Growth and change in a system may affect the overall reliability without notice.

This chapter reviews the mathematics necessary to design high availability systems. Reliable network designs will be reviewed. System clustering principles will be explained and fail-over issues examined. Load balancing and the HP Network Connection Policy Manager will be introduced as one solution for achieving high availability. Finally, the X-Windows XDMCP approach to load balancing is examined.

Essential Reliability Mathematics

A quick review of serial and parallel component reliability is appropriate here. Serial components are like links in a chain. One link failure equals one chain failure. A client–server network with one LAN and one server will fail if either LAN or server fails. The failure rate of the system equals the sum of the failure rates of the series-connected parts. For parallel-connected components, all of them have to fail for the system to fail. The probability of systems failure is the product of the component failure probabilities. Before pressing on with some formulas and examples, some helpful information is given in Table 3-1.

Table 3-1   A list of useful constants

Quantity	Description
24	Number of hours in one day
365	Number of days in one standard year
1,440	Number of minutes in one day
3,600	Number of seconds in one hour
8,760	Number of hours in a standard year
86,400	Number of seconds in one day
525,600	Number of minutes in a standard year
31,536,000	Number of seconds in a standard year

For computer systems, a failure of the CPU, memory, disk, or LAN adapter is a systems failure. For a network, a failure of the local LAN hub, local router, WAN circuit, remote router, remote LAN, or the remote server is a systems failure as far as the local users are concerned.

One way to improve the reliability of a system is to use highly reliable parts. But some quick arithmetic may reveal that a collection of such parts results in unacceptable reliability. Redundancy is the usual way to compensate for this. LANs are made more reliable by using a second backup link between the hubs. Routers have dual power supplies. Servers use RAID and mirroring technology. WANs have multiple physically diverse circuits. Computers have multiple processors. Data centers have multiple application servers. Publishing shops have printer pools.

A major assumption or requirement is imposed on us. The mathematics assumes that failures are independent of each other. If a spindle fails in a RAID, the reason for the failure is supposed to be localized to the spindle. A power failure might knock out all the routers at a site, so they have independent UPS units.

Now that we are familiar with the basic concepts of reliability engineering, let's review the metrics. Mean time before failure (MTBF) is the average time between failures. The reciprocal of MTBF is the failure rate measured in failures per unit time. Mean time to repair (MTTR) is the average time it takes to restore service. *P* is the probability that a system or device is up. Reliability is a percentage calculated from the following formula:

$$P = \frac{MTBF}{MTBF + MTTR}$$

$$reliability = 100 \times P$$

To put numbers into the formulas, consider a simple hypothetical UNIX TCP/IP network consisting of a serial WAN link and a remote UNIX server. Historically, we know that we can expect a failure once a year lasting 12 hours for the WAN link. The server suffers two failures a year, and the average repair time is 4 hours. The failure rate of this serially connected system is the sum of the WAN and server failure rates, which add up to three failures per year. The MTBF is the reciprocal of the failure rate or 1/3 year per failure.

Now the MTTR is different for the devices. We know the server is twice as likely as the WAN to fail, so the composite MTBF could be the weighted average with a weight of 2/3 for the server and 1/3 for the WAN link. The composite MTBF is given by

$$MTBF = \frac{2}{3} \times 4 + \frac{1}{3} \times 12 = \frac{20}{3} \text{ hours}$$

We are almost ready to calculate the reliability, but the MTBF has units of years per failure and the MTTR has units of hours. Converting the 1/3 year to hours using Table 3-1 for reference gives us 2910 hours. The reliability of the system is

$$\frac{2910}{2910 + \left(\frac{20}{3}\right)} \times 100 = 99.7714$$

Suppose that this is not acceptable. We decide to put in three parallel WAN links with the same properties.

$$P1 = \frac{MTBF1}{MTTR1 + MTBF1}$$

$$P2 = \frac{MTBF2}{MTTR2 + MTBF2}$$

$$P3 = \frac{MTBF3}{MTTR3 + MTBF3}$$

$$MTTR = MTTR1 + MTTR2 + MTTR3$$

$$MTBF = \frac{MTTR}{(1 - P1) \times (1 - P2) \times (1 - P3)}$$

For three parallel devices, the new MTTR and MTBF are given by the above formulas, where P1, P2, and P3 are the probabilities that the three devices are up. On a bad day all three devices will fail, and all of them will have to be repaired, one after the other.

The WAN links have MTTR = 0.5 day and MTBF = 365 days. Three in parallel have an MTTR = 1.5 days, an MTBF = 585926836.5 days, and a probability of being up of P = 0.999999997439953, which is virtually a perfect data link. The reliability of the triple WAN and the UNIX file server approaches that of the file server alone.

To evaluate the reliability of a system, where do the MTBF and MTTR figures come from? In the design phase, the equipment vendor can provide them for hardware and the network service provider knows their service record and will be able to give some sort of guarantee. Conversely it is practical to use the reliability mathematics to specify how reliable the various components of a system must be in order achieve some total reliability.

High-availability Network Design Principles

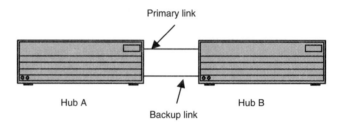

Primary link

Hub A

Backup link

Hub B

Figure 3-1   Backup links between hubs
Primary and backup links between hubs increase the reliability of the LAN. A link may fail because a cable breaks, a transceiver goes dead, or it is inadvertently disconnected. Both hubs monitor the primary link for integrity and when the link fails, both hubs switch almost at the same time to the backup link. This redundancy is transparent to upper-layer protocols such as IP.

LANs can be made more reliable by using the backup link between hubs (see Figure 3-1). Normally, the primary-to-primary link is active, and the backup-to-backup link is on standby. A failure of the primary link brings up the backup link transparently for the devices connected to these hubs.

Bridge and switch devices may be connected in a mesh topology to provide redundancy. By using the IEEE802.1 spanning tree feature, the devices convert the mesh topology to a tree topology by removing any remaining loops in the mesh. The spanning tree protocol monitors the tree and will reactivate devices when its peer fails. As a practical matter, if the installer fails to activate the spanning tree protocol, the resulting meshes will immediately loop traffic continuously around, resulting in extremely high utilization and red faces.

Ethernet switches may also be connected using multiple trunk lines that can be load balanced. This increases reliability by providing additional paths and

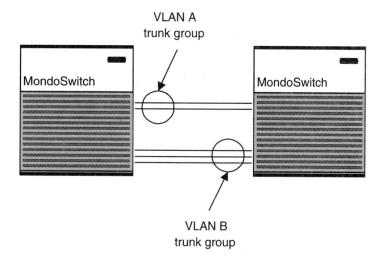

VLAN A
trunk group

MondoSwitch

MondoSwitch

VLAN B
trunk group

Figure 3-2   VLAN trunk groups
Two switches and two VLANs are depicted with trunk groups joining the VLANs.
Trunk group A has two 100-BASE-T segments that join VLAN A between switches.
Trunk group B has three 100-BASE-T segments that join VLAN B between the
switches. In addition to increasing the aggregate bandwidth between the switches, the
multiple-segment trunks increase reliability. This physical layer redundancy is transparent to any network layer protocols.

all the paths are actually carrying useful data, unlike the spanning tree
protocol. See Figure 3-2.

WANs can be made more reliable by adding additional links between sites.
The poor construction worker with the back hoe that digs up both lines
cannot be faulted because the designer failed to provide diversity routing.
But some interesting IP routing problems can pop up. Suppose that we have
two independent routers on a site, one for each WAN circuit. This means that
there are two routes that might be chosen by a local client. IP stacks
generally perform simple routing decisions. If the target network is directly
connected to one of the client's network interfaces, the packet is sent directly
to the destination system. Otherwise, the client consults the routing table to
see if there is an entry for the target network and, if so, forwards the packet

to that system. Otherwise the client sends the packet to the default route, if one is configured.

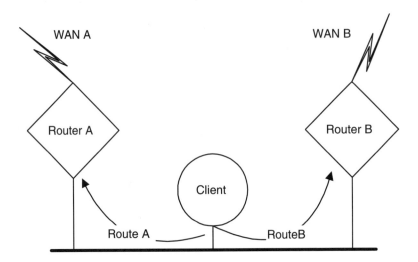

Figure 3-3   Dual router high availability network design
A high-availability network design with two distinct IP routers and two distinct WAN lines provides two routes that a client may choose. If one of the routers fails, the client benefits by switching to the other router. There is no standard method for doing this, so a range of methods is given in the text.

It is common practice to configure a default route into all IP addressable devices. With some exceptions, only one default route is available. The exception is an IP stack that will "ping" successive default routes to find a working router. But the goal of providing a reliable IP backbone is difficult to meet if specific routes must be hard coded into network devices. For if router A in Figure 3-3 goes down, and the client has hard coded routes for some destination networks that point to router A, the client can't reach the target network even though it could, if it knows about router B. What to do? See Table 3-2 for solutions.

Table 3-2   Dealing with multiple IP routes

Solution	Explanation
Proxy ARP	Configure all local IP routers to respond to ARP requests for networks the local LAN can't reach with its own MAC address. Local systems have the default subnet mask. Nodes must ARP to reach any system, and the first router to reply will become the router for that connection.
Multiple default routes	Purchase an IP stack that supports multiple default routes and configure in the IP addresses of both router A and B.
RIP	Purchase an IP stack that supports a routing protocol like RIP that listens on its network adapters for RIP broadcast packets from routers and other participating devices. This is common for UNIX systems running the *routed* daemon process
ICMP	Routers and other IP devices may send ICMP redirects to clients that updates their routing tables with more direct routes to certain destinations. This assumes the router with the down WAN is itself running properly.
Manual reconfiguration	Advise the user that the default route must be changed to the alternate router's IP address. A three-finger salute may be required to restart some client systems.
One router	Install one router with a single LAN adapter to avoid confusion. Provision two WAN cards in the router to handle the two WAN circuits.
Random route	One less than stellar solution is to configure half the clients with default route A and the other half with default route B.

Focusing our attention to the enterprise level, we need to design the company WAN backbone to be bulletproof. This speaks to the reliable redundant diverse IP backbone concept (see Figure 3-4).

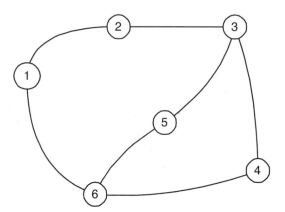

Figure 3-4   Reliable IP backbone architecture
This reliable IP backbone has six hub sites, each with at least two links to other hub sites. Note that between any two hub sites a path can be found that doesn't exceed two hops. Normally, this backbone offers low latency. A single link failure will not partition this network. Two link failures, say 2–3 and 1–6 will leave sites 1 and 2 on one partition and sites 3 through 6 on a second partition. But many two-link failures will leave the entire network functioning.

Assuming for the moment that the backbone is made up of point-to-point leased circuits, we need to build redundant links between quite a few hub sites so that one or more failures will not result in a partitioned network. Very large networks can be built this way. A hub site is has least two WAN links to other sites and is part of the reliable IP backbone. For performance reasons, there should be no more than two WAN links between hub sites. An engineering analysis may determine that more than two links can meet performance objectives, but let's stay with two for this discussion. Given that frame relay is often preferred over point-to-point leased lines, a private network may be designed with the same logical topology as given in Figure 3-4. See Figure 3-5. The reliability of the frame relay network is squarely on the shoulders of the network service provider, but the PVCs are still point-to-point, and reliability issues are about connectivity and economics. Let's look at a frame relay network with PVCs that mirror the point-to-point design in Figure 3-4. Suppose site 1 goes down completely and site 2 needs to

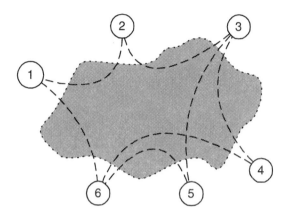

Figure 3-5   Reliable frame relay network design

This frame relay network has the same logical structure as the point-to-point circuit of Figure 3-4. It is based on the same performance guidelines and suffers from the same reliability issues. As with point-point circuits, each PVC is purchased from the service provider. Consequently, a fully meshed topology is not usually cost effective. Often, a hub and spoke topology is adopted, with the hub located at a data center and the spokes located at all the remote sites.

communicate with site 6. The PVC to and from site 1 would be the best choice. Now site 2 will have to use the PVC to site 3, which in turn can choose a route to either site 4 or 5, both of which connect to site 6. The network can still be segmented by failures at multiple sites.

Alternative ways to provide reliable communications take advantage of alternative, generally slower media. Dial-up technologies are popular because no cost is associated with the service, other than the on-site equipment when it's not in use. See Table 3-3 for information about backup communications links.

Table 3-3   Backup communications links

Backup Type	Description
ISDN	ISDN speeds range from 64 to 1544 Kbps. A data call can be initiated in about 2 seconds.
Wireless	Microwave and spread spectrum RF technology can provide short-range connectivity. VSAT services are available with Internet connectivity. CDPD and microcellular services like Ricochet approach 19.2 to 28.8Kbps speeds.
Dial-up PPP	One or more dial-up modem connections can be "bonded" (multilink PPP) for greater throughput, taking advantage of POTS.
Alternative carrier	Using services from two network providers can provide redundancy and independence of failure modes.
Cable modem	Emerging technology targeted at the home user that uses a cable modem, a type of router with an Ethernet adapter for the home, and a coax cable connecting to the cable service provider, which in turn provides Internet connectivity
VPN	Virtual private networks are using either a proprietary point-to-point tunneling protocol (PPTP) or a secure IP protocol to create a secure, encrypted, virtual, private network across the Internet itself.

System Clustering Principles

UNIX systems may be grouped to increase their reliability. Resources like disk drives are shared to make this work. MC/ServiceGuard for HP-UX can cluster individual systems. The systems monitor each other's heartbeat to detect a system failure. An Ethernet, FDDI, or ATM dedicated LAN segment carries the heartbeat.

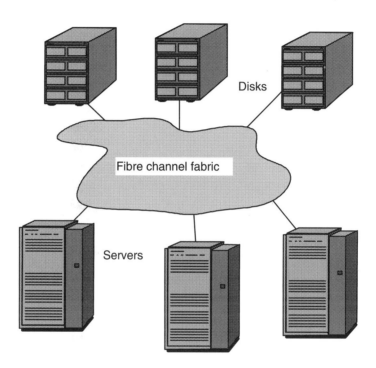

Figure 3-6   Fibre channel mass storage architecture
Three UNIX systems and three disk arrays are shown clustered in a high availability configuration. Each system has access to the three disk arrays. Clustering software is responsible for controlling shared file access by multiple systems, mirroring, striping, logical volume management, buffering, and security.

Technologies like fibre channel (Figure 3-6) are imminently suited for sharing disks among members of a cluster. The fabric provides reliable, nonblocking, high-speed paths between disks and systems.

Fail-over Issues

High-availability configurations are not a plug-and-play proposition. The devil's in the details, as they say. The following paragraphs introduce some of the issues.

Applications should be tested with the clustering technology and certified or brought into compliance with the clustering environment. To assume that the clustering will "automagically" provide transparent redundant hardware underneath the application is folly. Compliant applications must be retested when the version of the UNIX operating system increases, the clustering software is updated, or the application itself goes to the next revision.

The time it takes to perform a complete fail-over should be checked during an acceptance test. For very large file systems, with many open files, with large file system buffer caches, with many applications, and with networked applications and remote clients over slow network links, fail-over may take longer than a simple bench test would suggest.

Data-center staff need full training for fail-over situations on the specific applications being used. Standard operating procedures may not be appropriate in a fail-over state. The training may come partially from the vendor, but the specific configuration, applications, and business needs may dictate that local training be developed. For example, if one system goes down, then the total CPU capacity remaining may not meet peak demand at the busy hour, and some form of load shedding has to be addressed.

Domain name server (DNS) support for the compute environment has to be part of the fail-over strategy. The fail-over clustering technology may assign the domain name, IP address, and network adapter MAC addresses of the failed system to its backup system so transparently that DNS need not be involved. When the clustering technology leaves IP addresses alone, then the backup server's IP address should be mapped to the name of the official server so that new client connections are directed to the backup. A tie-in to the DNS database is needed in this case.

The notion of a data center leads companies to place all their eggs in one basket. Naturally, the IT group keeps a vigilant eye on this basket. Still, the advantages of a second data center include the ability to switch all users to the alternative data center when their home data center becomes unavailable due to scheduled downtime or an unscheduled disaster.

Load Balancing

In a high availability environment the additional redundant equipment is preferably used for productive purposes. Equipment doing no useful work in standby mode is an expensive form of insurance. Load-balancing techniques make the most of these extra resources by giving users the best and most consistent response time possible.

The system disk mirror drivers distribute the reads across the mirrors by alternating from one to the other on successive operations. If the 80–20 rule holds, then 80% of the I/O operations are reads that benefit from alternating disks. Ideally, this succeeds in equalizing utilization of the disks, which theory says minimizes the variation in user response time. This works because read operations don't make changes to the data on the disk, so alternating the reads is OK. Write operations must be posted to all disks in the mirror of course.

To keep a pool of servers load balanced, a "hacked DNS" may hand out IP addresses in round robin-fashion as name resolution requests arrive. This technique is somewhat blind because, if one of four servers is already quite busy, it will still get about 25% of the new connection requests. HP's Network Connection Policy Manager overcomes this limitation by contacting agents on each computer in the logical cluster to monitor key resources like CPU utilization, free memory, disk I/O rates, and network activity. The Policy Manager is an authoritative DNS server and returns the IP address of the best system.

Many high availability environments run multiple servers with unique names and IP addressees. These systems often have multiple network adapters connected to several subnets to enhance the reliability of their communications. These adapters all have a unique IP address, and the DNS is usually configured to return the complete list of IP addresses, since the same server name maps to multiple IP addresses. The standard implementations of DNS will try to return an IP address closest to the requester. A DNS-aware application will take advantage of this list of IP addresses by trying them in succession until a working IP address is found. FTP and telnet are examples of DNS-aware applications.

Three-tier applications like SAP have clients capable of sending requests to the best application server at the moment. This is specific for the SAP application, and if the application server is used for other applications, these won't benefit.

Another load-balancing method used in industry assigns a user to one of several systems based on the load the that user is expected to place on the system. A front-end application tracks the number of user loads by application and transaction and assigns a new user to the system with the least expected load. The state of the systems is not actually checked; only the assumed loads are used.

HP-UX running on multi-CPU HP9000 systems intrinsically load balances the CPUs. Some limitations are inherent here. If a process ties itself to one of the processors, this limits the system's ability to load balance. If there are more processors than processes, then the remaining processors won't improve application performance.

At the network level, IP routers can load balance WAN links. Multiple physical circuits can be grouped into one logical circuit. The routers at either end try to keep each physical circuit equally loaded in both directions. The OSPF routing protocol is a standard that has the same ability over arbitrary topologies. If multiple paths to a target network are available and if the cost metrics are equal, then participating routers will load balance among them.

HP Network Connection Policy Manager (NCPM)

NCPM load balances server systems by controlling the IP address DNS returns to client lookups (Figure 3-7). NCPM agents run on each server and monitor system resources that are of particular interest to the clients. The agents can be configured to monitor any kind of system resource that a script is able to return information about. The NCPM acts like an authoritative name server for the load-balanced systems. As long as client systems use DNS name lookups when connecting to the servers, NCPM will return the IP address of the server with the best fit at that time. The load balancing is therefore very dynamic. Load balancing can be based on the following server metrics:

CPU percent free
5, 10, and 15-minute load average
Disk storage free
Disk I/O rate
RAM available
VM activity
LAN activity
Number of users
Number of FTP connections
Number of concurrent software "builds" in progress
Number of processors in the system
Version of the operating system
Availability of a particular software package

NCPM comes preconfigured with a standard list of system resources. The agents can be extended with user-written scripts to return special information more appropriate to the clients. In the list above, the version of the operating system is listed. In a mixed-server environment (say running HP-UX 10.20 and 11.0), the client may want to choose just from HP-UX 11.0 systems without having to create a separate server pool for each version of HP-UX.

NCPM helps maintain the illusion of 100% uptime for the server group. As practical minded people, we know systems have to be taken down for system maintenance, say once a month. NCPM lets the system administrator mark a particular system as unavailable to the group so that new client requests are deflected to the remaining systems. When the last client has disconnected, the machine can be serviced. The users really don't notice that there is one less available server, and business goes on as usual, perhaps a little more slowly. When service is restored NCPM, is advised and new connection requests are directed to the restored system once more, transparent to the users. In this environment, users are discouraged from connecting to systems using their IP address, but nothing will prevent them doing so. Inverse DNS

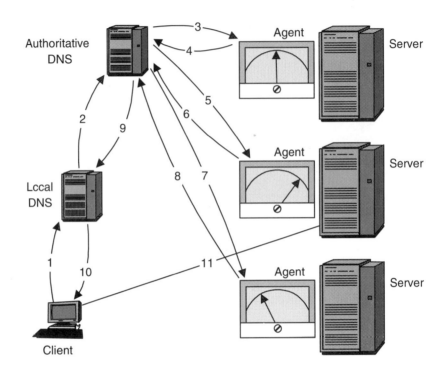

Figure 3-7   Load balancing with HP NCPM

Load balancing with the HP Network Connection Policy Manager. (1) Client sends DNS lookup for server to local DNS. (2) Local DNS consults authoritative DNS, where NCPM resides. (3–8) NCPM checks with each agent and determines the best server IP address. (9) NCPM returns this IP address to the local DNS. (10) Local DNS returns IP address to client. (11) Client connects to the best server IP address.

lookups are problematic since all systems in the server group have the same name in DNS.

XDMCP

X-Windows Display Manager Control Protocol (XDMCP) provides a wonderfully easy to use and powerful feature—a menu choice of UNIX systems and their current load factor. The user picks a system, which then displays a login X-window. The user logs in and enjoys the complete X-Windows environment on that UNIX system.

XDMCP is a simple tool that gives the user easy access to a group of UNIX systems intended to give the user a highly available environment. XDMCP is configured on the X-terminal or X-terminal emulation software. Three modes of operation are available, as shown in Table 3-4. The broadcast

Table 3-4   Three XDMCP modes of operation

Mode	Description
Broadcast	The X-terminal broadcasts an XDMCP query. All systems on the local IP subnet running an *xdm, dtlogin,* or *vuelogin* daemon process will reply to the X-terminal, which lists the responding system in a selection window.
Direct	The X-terminal is configured to contact a system directly. This system will put up a login X-window immediately to authenticate the user.
Indirect	The X-terminal passively waits for a system to cast a login window onto it. Usually, the system is configured with a file holding the names of the X-terminals.

mode lists each system's load factor, usually the 1-, 5-, and 15-minute load average. The load factor is defined as the average number of processes in the run queue for 1, 5, or 15 minutes. The 1-minute load factor reflects the most current CPU utilization, while the 15-minute load factor is a long-term indicator. Note that for a small system a load factor of 10 may be considered high, while for a large system a load factor of 10 may normally give users good performance.

Broadcast mode sends a MAC-level broadcast with the subnet's IP broadcast address, and this packet will be stopped by the local routers per normal IP standards. Users must be on the same subnet as the servers to use broadcast mode. The other modes don't suffer from this inconvenience.

A High-availability Exercise

We have seen how adding additional network adapters and using routing protocols can be used to build fault-tolerant solutions. Consider now a very simple network that provides a client system with access to a server that has a 10-Mbps Ethernet and a fast Ethernet adapter (Figure 3-8). Assume that the client uses DNS to look up the server IP address and that the DNS system itself is always available. What can possibly go wrong with this design?

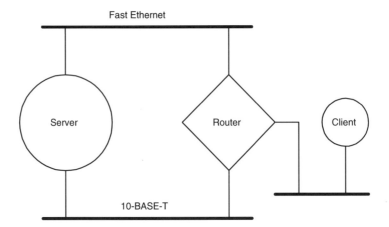

Figure 3-8   An unreliable dual adapter server network
This very simple network may not function after a single LAN failure occurs. The server and router should be running a route discovery protocol to remove downed subnets from the routing tables. The client applications should be DNS aware, and the DNS should provide a list of all IP addresses associated with each multihomed system, the server and router in this example.

Under normal operating conditions, the client will contact the server using the name "Server," and the DNS will return an IP address. We don't know in this case which of the two possible server IP addresses DNS will return. Suppose that it's the fast Ethernet adapter's IP address. That's good, because it's the faster adapter. When the server sends back a reply, which adapter will it choose to send it on? This depends on the server's routing table. Let's assume that it's the fast Ethernet adapter.

Suppose that the fast Ethernet adapter on either the router or the server goes down. The client still tries to communicate using the server's fast Ethernet IP address. Since this isn't reachable now, the router will fail to deliver the packet to the server. Had the client application been written to be DNS aware, it would have been able to try the second IP address associated with the hostname "Server" and would have succeeded in communicating with the server on its 10 BASE-T adapter. Unfortunately, if the server still tries to use the fast Ethernet adapter to reply, we're still in trouble.

It is clear that our highly reliable solution needs additional help in the IP routing department. The server and the router need to run a routing discovery protocol so that when the fast Ethernet LAN becomes unavailable all references to it are removed from their routing tables.

Note that Chapter 7 covers additional methods for creating highly available clusters.

References

Dhillon, Balbir S., *Reliability Engineering in Systems Design and Operation*. New York: Van Nostrand Reinhold Company, 1983, ISBN: 0-442-27213-8.

Roberts, Norman H., *Mathematical Methods in Reliabiity Engineering*. New York: McGraw-Hill Book Company, 1964, Library of Congress Catalog Card Number 63-22526.

Weygant, Peter S., *Clusters for High Availability, A Primer of HP-UX Solutions*. New York: Hewlett–Packard Professional Books, Prentice Hall, 1996, ISBN 0-13-494758-4.

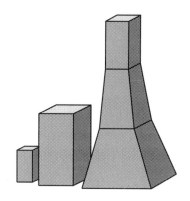

CHAPTER 4

Performance Scaling Principles

Introduction

C onventional wisdom offers plenty of insight into how to make UNIX networks bigger and faster and more capable. Just add more of what you have. Certainly, one can experience a lot of success with this methodology. But how far can you push this? A small Email server may handle all 100 users in a small business. If the company grows to 150 users, no doubt the same system can handle the load, albeit somewhat more slowly. How about 200 users? No sweat - double the memory to 256 Megabytes and add a second 4-Gigabyte disk. How far can this strategy take us? Can one Email server be built to handle, say, Hewlett–Packard's 140,000+ employees plus all the additional traffic from HP's business partners and customers?

The question that this chapter will help you remember to ask is "how do you know how scalable your solution is?" If it uses NIS (Network Information Service), is there some unknown upper limit to its size? Do you know the maximum number of unique user IDs a that system can support? Does the high-availability solution you've specified scale to a sufficiently high number of nodes and has the vendor tested it? Suppose that your on-line service may have to support 10 million users? Are you comfortable with this? What if your new satellite-based backbone may have to support 50 million earth stations.

The point is that doubling or quadrupling resources does not necessarily result in a doubling or quadrupling of performance. You can't attach a rocket booster to a Volkswagen to increase the bug's top speed. Performance does not necessarily scale linearly with the amount of resources thrown at the solution. For example, a faster CPU will produce greater application performance. But overall performance depends on code localization, system bus speed, the hit rate on the level I and level II caches, the size of these caches, the degree of pipelining in the CPU, the effectiveness of the super-scalar architecture, and I/O efficiency

Yet many of these limiting factors are beyond the control of the designer. What can be controlled are the number of servers, the number and speed of the network adapters, the number and speed of the disks, the speed and number of CPUs, the amount of RAM, the number of TCP sockets, system bus speed, the size of the level II cache, and the overall clock speed.

In a networked environment, replacing the 10-BASE-T LAN adapter with 100-BASE-T or 100-VG-AnyLAN or FDDI may not give a corresponding 10× increase in throughput. This never happens. To see why, consider that throughput can be calculated by dividing the amount of data moved by the sum of delays encountered during its movement. Using bytes to measure data and seconds to measure delay, suppose that CPUDelay, LANDelay, and DiskDelay are encountered while moving DataMoved bytes of data. The following formula defines throughput in bytes per second:

$$\text{Throughput} = \frac{\text{DataMoved}}{\text{CPUDelay} + \text{LANDelay} + \text{DiskDelay}}$$

Even if LANDelay is reduced to 1/10 by going from 10- to 100-Mbps network adapters, the other delays prevent the throughput from increasing by 10. All three delays will have to be reduced to 1/10 to get a 10 throughput increase.

More Servers

An essential feature of a scalable architecture is intrinsic support for multiple-server systems. This allows an installation to begin small with just one server and grow considerably over time, keep the existing hardware, take advantage of equipment upgrades, and even distribute the hardware across multiple business locations.

For example, a single NFS server may suffice initially, but as usage grows it may become prudent to add more servers and partition the data among them. See Figure 4-1 for an example. Database servers may be harder to replicate because the underlying schema, table allocation, and user interface definitions may have to be changed, which is far more difficult than our simple NFS example.

Similar server scaling is commonly used to ramp up web servers, SAP application servers, compute servers such as render farms, Email servers, and software development build farms. Load-balancing methods will

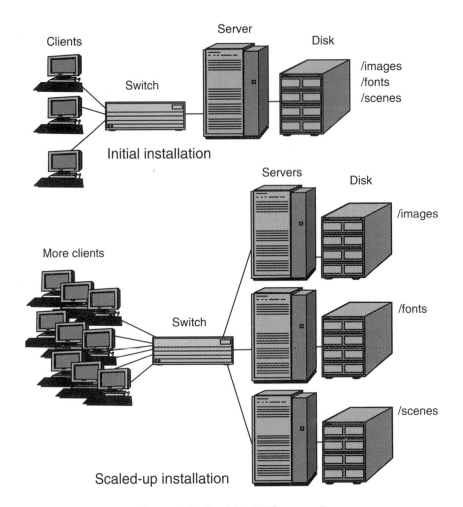

Figure 4-1 Scalable NFS server farm
A small NFS server supports its small user base quite happily, but over time the single
server performance degrades. Two additional NFS servers are added, and the data are
repartitioned to balance the load. We conveniently neglect the LAN as a potential
bottleneck in this illustration.

improve the user experience and make best use of the increased resources. It
would be embarrassing to add servers only to find one or more of them
idling.

Scalable architectures need to include provisions for an arbitrary number of servers, located on any subnet, separated by arbitrary networks and connected by circuits with arbitrary speed and utilization. For example, suppose that an Email server can handle 20,000 users. But we have five sites located at remote locations with T-1 WAN circuits connecting them. Each site has 20,000 users. Naturally, we want to place an Email server at each site. But the Email system must have an easy to administer directory service so that users don't have to remember where remote users are located. The overhead associated with this service must be low or scalability will suffer.

As the number of Email users increases, the incidence of users sending mail to sizable distribution lists will rise. An Email system that recognized that multiple users share the same mail server will not replicate the message during transmission, but send it once to their common mail server and link copies to their in-boxes. This is especially beneficial as users send larger and larger messages, usually because they discover that they can send file attachments. In general, the scalability features of applications are a major success factor in server replication strategies.

More Network Adapters

Adding network adapters to a system can increase the aggregate network throughput if the single adapter becomes saturated or if the system architecture can't drive the adapter at full media speed. This is a widely used capability to increase the performance of NFS servers, whose NFS IOPS rating is bottlenecked when only a single Ethernet adapter is used.

Each network adapter must be configured with an IP address on a distinct IP subnet. This is necessary for correct routing to occur. By default, an HP-UX system will route across its interfaces, where the necessary fragmentation and reassembly will occur. This lets you make an HP-UX system with multiple media LAN adapters act as a media converter. For example, an FDDI segment and several Ethernet segments can be connected using an HP-UX system to double as a router. The different MTU sizes are accommodated via the fragmentation and reassembly.

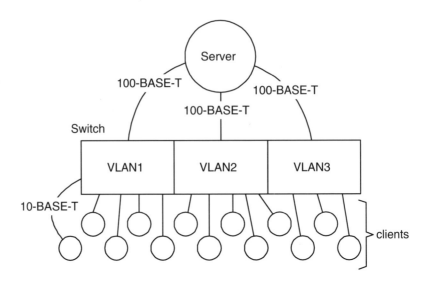

Figure 4-2   VLAN traffic control between clients and a server
A fairly large community of 10-BASE-T clients can reliably access a single server
without contention using an Ethernet switch configured as three VLANs. The server
has three full duplex 100-BASE-T adapters theoretically capable of 600Mbps. Load
balancing is relatively crude here, but high traffic clients can be manually configured
onto different VLANs to spread them evenly across the three subnets.

To scale an Ethernet LAN, Ethernet switches have become exceedingly
popular. To regain control over the broadcast domain, regulate connectivity,
and increase performance, Ethernet switches may be configured into
multiple virtual LANs (VLAN), as shown in Figure 4-2. Systems may be
assigned to one or more VLANs on the basis of

> MAC address
> Protocol type
> Port number

Large switched topologies may require multiple connections called trunk
groups among the switches to join together the VLANs.

An additional LAN adapter in the server may prove to be beneficial to isolate
high traffic volumes from client systems. Consider an SAP installation with
one LAN segment devoted to clients, one for printing, and one for the

database server (Figure 4-3). The client segment will have low utilization. The printer segment has one traffic source and possibly a dozen or so JetDirect printers. Such a segment can be driven to high utilization without serious effects. And the FDDI segment dedicated to the database server moves potentially high data volumes at 100 Mbps. The SAP application server will have three LAN adapters in this scenario. A VLAN solution may be attractive here.

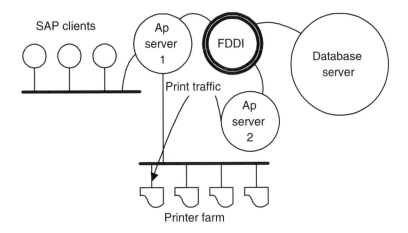

Figure 4-3   Controlling SAP print traffic contention
Adding just one additional Ethernet adapter to the SAP application server provides an outlet for the often intense printer traffic that would potentially degrade client response time during peak print periods. The application server may be running OpenSpool and the other application servers (not shown here) may route print data across the FDDI ring via the application server to the printer farm.

More Disks

Adding more disk drives is an obvious way to increase storage capacity. As long as there are available addresses on the SCSI, bus expansion is trivial. Performance penalties may be associated with the additional I/O that the new drives will place on the bus. A new SCSI bus adapter will solve this problem if a slot is available for it and the new disk drives can be attached there.

Beyond simply adding disks, planning the way a database will be laid out across these disks is essential if maximum performance is to be obtained. Some scheme to place storage in such a way as to balance the I/O evenly across the disks will maximize performance. The more independent disk spindles available, the more I/Os per second that can be handled. Even if storage capacity is not the issue, adding more disk spindles to improve performance may justify it. Indeed, there are many ways to organize the bytes on a group of disk drives:

>Mirroring a pair of disks for reliability and performance
>RAID (redundant array of independent disks) for reliability and performance
>Striping logical tracks across multiple disk mechanisms for speed
>LVM (logical volume manager) for flexibility in extending volumes
>JFS (journal file system) for fast crash recovery and data integrity
>Raw disk partitions for speed (avoids UNIX file system)

At this writing (spring of 1998), 18-Gbyte mechanisms are the largest available. Large disk arrays such as those from EMC Corporation can be internally configured to terabyte capacities and come with gigabytes of buffer RAM as part of the product. The UNIX buffer caches are meant for improving the performance on systems with slower disks, and there is a low- and high-water mark for dynamic buffer cache. The cache can be filled quite quickly with data on fast processors. But since all modern SCSI disk drives carry on-board cache memory, it often makes sense to enable *asynch* I/O on the UNIX disk driver. This means that the controller signals the CPU that it wrote the data to the disk, when in fact it is merely holding the data in its cache for eventual writing to disk.

SCSI buses may have 8 to 16 addresses, including the controller, depending on whether it is SCSI I, II, or III. They may be fast, wide, ultra, and ultra 2 SCSI. See Table 4-1. This gives bus speeds of 5, 10, 20, 40, or 80 MBps (megabytes per second). Note that at some point, the addition of SCSI buses to a system will reach a point of performance saturation as aggregate data rates approach that of the system bus. The original HP9000 HP-PB I/O architecture is making way for the new faster HSC I/O system as a result of pressures for higher-performing storage subsystems (see Figure 4-4).

Table 4-1 SCSI bus characteristics

SCSI Name	Bus Width in Bits	Burst Transfer Rate in Megabytes per Second
SCSI-1	8	5
Fast SCSI	8	10
Wide SCSI	16	10
Fast Wide SCSI	16	20
Ultra SCSI	8	20
Wide Ultra SCSI	16	40
Ultra 2 SCSI	8	40
Wide Ultra 2 SCSI	16	80

Hewlett–Packard manufactures a range of high-performance HP-UX systems that have high-speed buses that interconnect the CPUs, memory, and I/O subsystems. On the K-class systems the memory-processor bus has a 960MBps speed, which is about 20 times greater than that found on typical desktop computers. The 802.3 LAN adapter, single-ended SCSI, Fast/Wide/ Differential SCSI, parallel Centronics ports, plus all the optional HSC and HP-PB adapters share some of this bandwidth. The point is that the disk I/O subsystem is one part of a larger system of high-speed buses, and they will interact to some degree that will affect scalability.

More CPUs

Adding CPUs to a computer is a time honored method for increasing system horsepower. Even Wintel and Macintosh computers can support from four to

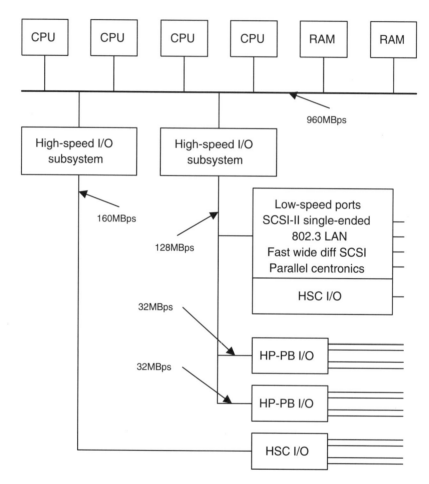

Figure 4-4   K-class HP9000 architecture
The backplane of a K-class HP-UX machine showing the peak data rates in megbytes
per second. The sustained rates are a little lower. Note the HSC I/O bus adapter at the
bottom of the diagram makes 160 MBps available to four HSC adapters, well in ex-
cess of what the four HP-PB adapters can deliver. The lesson is that adding disk to a
system to improve performance must be done with the I/O structure of the server in
mind.

eight processors in certain configurations. HP-UX systems have symmetric
multiprocessing (SMP) capabilities that extend the traditional UNIX

multiprogramming multitasking features across multiple CPUs in a balanced symmetric fashion. The HP-UX kernel does not always run on the same CPU, and kernel threads are essential for implementing concurrent instantiations of kernel code on several CPUs.

Despite the best efforts of the HP-UX operating system, the aggregate performance for an n-processor system is usually somewhat less than n times that of a uniprocessor. Power increases nonlinearly with the number of CPUs, as shown in Figure 4-5. (Note that the concept of clustered systems is not quite the same thing as multiprocessing.)

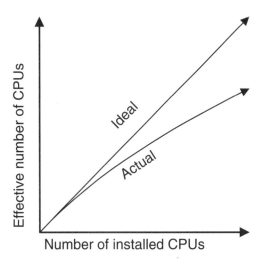

Figure 4-5   Total system performance versus processor count
Adding processors to a system such as an Enterprise Parallel Server (EPS) will increase performance along a curve that's linear initially, but which turns downward as internal system interactions compete for shared resources such as memory, system bus bandwidth, disk, and network I/O. The more interaction that the CPU has with its environment, the faster the curve bends downward.

HP-UX will attempt to load balance the CPUs under normal operating conditions. SMP is essential for good scalability. Application software can take advantage of multiple processors by invoking multiple processes or using multiple threads of execution that are capable of running almost independently. A simple serially executing shell script runs just one process at a time and can't take advantage of multiple CPUs. If the tasks in the script can be parallelized, however, real gains are possible. Consider a three-line shell script that runs serially:

```
task1 p1 p2
task2 p3 p4 p5 p6
task3 p7 p8 p9
```

If each task is independent of the other tasks, then simply running each task in the background will allow each task to run on a separate CPU:

```
task1 p1 p2 &
task2 p3 p4 p5 p6 &
task3 p7 p8 p9 &
```

Of course, multiple users logged into a multiprocessor system will think that they died and went to heaven, since their tasks are usually mutually exclusive and can run on separate processors.

At any rate, simply plugging in a second processor does not immediately ensure twice the performance, especially if the processes currently running on a troubled system exhibit some of these problems:

Wait states are built into the applications.
Applications block each other for resources.
Programs wait for resources a lot of the time.
Spinlocks or other foolish polling methods waste CPU cycles.
Starvation for other resources occurs.

For example, reconsider the little script above. If each of the tasks listed generates serious disk I/O, and they all manipulate data on the same disk, then the disk drive may become the bottleneck and we don't see three times the performance after all.

IP routers often include a central CPU and a CPU per network adapter. The more adapters there are, the more the processing power. This is valuable when the router has to perform many CPU-intense functions, such as SNMP requests, OSPF update calculations, serial line compression and decompression, packet fragmentation, packet filtering, and queue management.

More RAM

There is a saying in the computer industry. To make a computer run faster,

> first add more memory,
> then get faster disks, and,
> finally, upgrade the processor.

Adding memory is effective because it allows program code and data to stay in memory. The CPU level I data and instruction caches and the level II caches stay full. It reduces disk I/O due to swapping. Note that UNIX code (text) is usually marked readonly, so it doesn't modify itself, and consequently it's not necessary to swap code to the swap area; it can be read back directly from the executable file (marked as busy) on the file system or from the buffer cache (especially if the application's sticky bit is set.) Adding memory is also a quick fix for "memory leaks" that can render an application unusable after only hours or days of use.

HP-UX detects the amount of physical memory as the system boots. Kernel tunable parameters can affect how much of this memory is allocated to specific table areas, resources, the number of users, disk caching, network memory, and a hundred other parameters.

Memory may also be dedicated to a memory resident "disk" area. Frequently, accessed data are placed here. A common trick is to place the Netscape browser cache on RAM disk. RAM may also be used to create a shared memory area, usually locked down to prevent swapping, through which significant amounts of data may be moved between programs. The HP OmniBack cell controller can use it to move data between the disk agent and the media agent to maximize backup throughput when both agents are on the same computer. Memory is also used to hold messages to support interprocess communications (IPC).

IP routers also benefit from extra RAM, especially when a large number of network adapters with significant speed differences is installed. Serious buffering is necessary to accommodate the line speed differences and the bursty nature of IP traffic, so extra memory helps avoid packet loss.

More Sockets

Programs that communicate over a TCP/IP network generally use sockets provided through an API such as the Berkeley sockets on UNIX, Winsock on Wintel, and Open Transport on Macintosh. These interoperable APIs allow two programs to open a full duplex, reliable, flow-controlled virtual circuit over the network. The performance or functionality of a single virtual circuit may not be sufficient for some reason, and the programmer may choose to code the application to open multiple sockets between two end points in an effort to improve throughput.

Netscape Navigator 3.x allowed the user to change the number of concurrent connections from 1 to 4 to give the user a chance to improve performance. Many web pages contain GIF or JPG images, and these can be downloaded concurrently instead of serially if more sockets are made available. But why would it be faster to try to download four images at once, rather than four images in sequence?

The answer lies in the dynamics of TCP. Each new image download is done over a new TCP connection. The setup requires the exchange of three TCP SYN/ACK packets before any data can be sent. That's three network round-trip times of delay before data can be sent. But TCP's slow-start feature slows down data transmission for the first few packet exchanges until the connection is running wide open, by which time a modest image has already been sent without the potential benefit of TCP's streaming mode.

A TCP connection subject to packet loss will also perform poorly, since the TCP retransmission timers have to expire before data transmission can resume, and then the slow-start mechanism has to complete before full TCP streaming can resume. Applications that open multiple TCP connections and time out on just one of them may continue to stream data on the remaining connections. This increases performance and reliability as well.

Even without packet loss and slow-start problems, some TCP connections may not be able to sustain data rates approaching media speeds. At very high media speeds and with insufficiently large send and receive TCP buffers, full streaming may not be possible. Multiple TCP connections driven by a multithreaded process or by multiple forked processes may overcome this limitation by taking advantage of concurrency (one socket per thread or process).

The limitations of TCP cited above may be taken as an indication that the implementation calls for UDP. The application has to guarantee delivery in the presence of packet loss and deal with flow control issues.

We conclude that an architecture will be much more scalable by allowing for multiple sockets for data communications.

Greater Network Media Speed

When the network is the bottleneck, make the network faster. Is 10-BASE-T not fast enough? No problem, we have 100-BASE-T. Still not fast enough? No problem, we have 100-VG-AnyLAN. Still not fast enough? 155 Mbps ATM is here. Still not fast enough? Gigabit Ethernet is here. For the WAN, we can start with a dial-up 33.6 Kbps V.34 modems at the low end to T-3 45 Mbps lines in the mid-range to 155 Mbps ATM at the high end. See Figure 4-2.

Table 4-2   Network media speeds

Speed	Media Description
33.6 Kbps	V.34 dial-up modem, raw speed before compression
56 Kbps	X2, K56Flex, V.90 dial-up modem, DS0 carrier, ISDN
128 Kbps	2B ISDN, two DS0 carriers
256 Kbps and up	Fractional T-1 increments
1.544 Mbps	Full T-1
4 Mbps	IEEE802.4 Token Ring LAN
10 Mbps	Ethernet, 10-BASE-T LAN
16 Mpbs	IEEE802.4 Token Ring LAN

Table 4-2   Network media speeds (Continued)

Speed	Media Description
25 Mbps	IBM ATM over twisted pair
45 Mbps	T3 point-to-point carrier
100 Mpbs	100-BASE-T, 100-VG-AnyLAN, FDDI, ATM TAXI
1062 Mbps	100 MBps Fibre channel
155 Mbps	ATM OC3
622 Mbps	ATM
1 Gbps	Gigabit Ethernet

Raw media clock speed is not the same as throughput, of course. Media clock speed is an upper limit, like the speed of light in physics. Various latencies in the operating system, program resource contention, drivers, the system bus, the network adapters, shared media contention, the network routers, WAN utilization, and the applications will reduce throughput. So will interframe gaps, protocol headers, and handshaking. Nothing is sacred anymore.

It is not uncommon to find that a system isn't capable of driving the network medium into saturation, especially the first release of the hardware. But consider the system and I/O bus speeds. A desktop computer with a lowly 33-MHz, 64-bit system bus can push 2112 Gbits/sec peak between components, but the PCI adapter backplane may not be able to drive a 100 Mbps fast Ethernet adapter into saturation on a continuous basis.

Higher media speeds can be used to create a performance hierarchy to increase total throughput. A high media speed at the high level of the architecture supports a large number of lower-speed clients. The hierarchical switched Ethernet LAN takes advantage of increased media speed. See Figure 4-6.

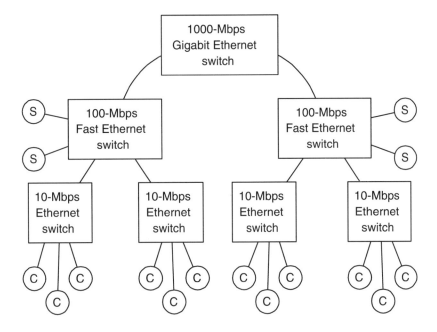

Figure 4-6   10-BASE-T, 100-BASE-T, and 1000BaseSX switch hierarchy
This LAN takes advantage of increasing media speeds to create a high-performance
hierarchy of Ethernet switches connecting 10-Mbps clients and 100-Mbps servers.
The Gigabit Ethernet switch at the top of the hierarchy forms a high-speed backbone.
The uplink speed from the 10-Mbps switches is 100 Mbps, and the uplink speed of
the 100 Mbps switches is 1000 Mbps. Servers may be connected directly to the Gigabit switch via 1000BaseSX adapters available for the HP9000 Enterprise Servers.

Parallel LAN Links

A single 100-BASE-T adapter does not often provide sufficient bandwidth
into a file server. After all, even a disk drive on a lowly 20 MBps SCSI bus
has 160 Mbits/sec peak throughput, far greater than fast Ethernet. A solution
is to aggregate multiple LAN adapters.

An example is HP's Auto-Port Aggregation software for HP9000 Enterprise
servers, which can aggregate up to four full-duplex 100-BASE-T adapters

and which interoperates with Cisco's Port Aggregation Protocol (PAgP) on Cisco switches (where it's called Fast EtherChannel) and with HP 1600 and 8000 switches to provide feature such as

> Discovery of PAgP capable links
> Autoconfiguration with PAgP links
> Load balancing (really a form of address balancing)
> Automatic fail-over

A single IP address is assigned to the aggregated fast Ethernet adapters in the HP9000 server. Note that the current implementation and testing limits this technology to aggregating up to four FDX adapters, which provides 800 Mbits/sec of throughput. Doubtless, future features will increase this number and include 1000BaseSX Gigabit Ethernet adapters as well.

Bigger Level II Cache

Very fast processors may become starved for instructions when the memory subsystem can't keep up with the CPU. Enter the level II cache. Desktop systems do with 256 Kbytes and larger systems require several megabytes. The more localized the code is, the more likely it will all fit in the cache and the greater the application performance that results. A good compiler will arrange code to increase the chances of this happening. Predictive prefetching of the CPU will also keep the level II cache filled. Note that backside level II caches that connect directly to the CPU avoid the system bus entirely and seriously improve performance.

Higher CPU Clock Speed

All else being equal, the system with the higher clocking CPU will outperform the system with a slower CPU. Doubling CPU clock speed will not usually double performance. For localized code, CPU-intense applications like 3D rendering, ray tracing, discrete event simulation, and numerical analysis take the machine with the faster CPU anyway.

Wider Data Paths

Data buses can move data faster simply by increasing the number of bytes that they can move in a single clock cycle. This is a well-known feature that gives the 16-bit-wide SCSI bus its ×2 advantage over standard 8-bit SCSI. Graphics accelerator adapters with internal 128-bit paths tend to be faster than their 64-bit brethren. Computers with 64-bit instructions may outperform those with 32-bit instructions provided the compilers, system libraries, UNIX kernel, and applications all take advantage of them. HP-UX 11.0 is a 64-bit O/S for 64-bit HPPA hardware.

Higher System Bus Speed

While clearly not a tunable parameter, the speed and width of the system bus and the I/O buses can be chosen at implementation time. A board swap or a box swap is required to increase bus speed. For computationally intense CPU-bound applications, the speed of the system bus is critical, since this is the path between the memory, level II cache, and the CPU. For I/O-intensive applications, the bandwidth of the path to the I/O adapters and the fan out (the number of network adapters that can plug into the I/O adapter) are the bottlenecks.

The Megahertz Wars

CPU chips are rated in megahertz (MHz) but, as we've seen, faster clock speeds don't "automagically" translate into faster application performance. So why is it that an HP-UX UNIX system with a 200-MHz HPPA (Hewlett–Packard Precision Architecture) CPU is faster than an Intel Pentium II clocking at the same speed? For a hint, see Figure 4-7). How come an Apple G3 Macintosh with a 266- MHz-type 750 CPU outperforms an Intel Pentium II PC clocking at 400 MHz in the Byte benchmark? Who can explain why a Mathematica benchmark runs faster under Linux than a Wintel O/S on the

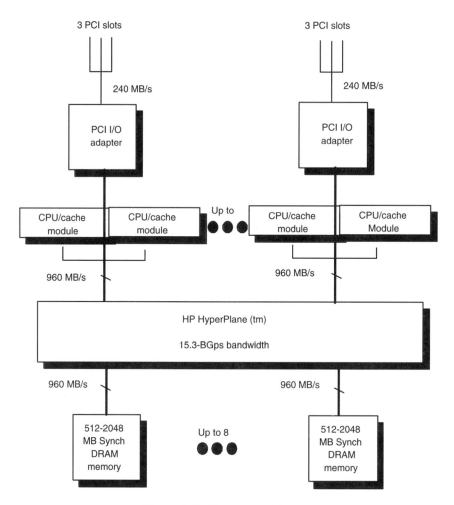

Figure 4-7   V-class architecture
The HP V-class system architecture has a generous 15.3-GBps backplane that multi-
plexes 960-MBps buses among synchronous memory, PCI I/O, and the CPUs.

exact same PC hardware? At this point in the chapter, the reader has
probably formulated the following expression:

"CPU clock speed is nothing—system architecture is everything."

Wider buses, larger on-chip level I caches (one for data and one for instructions), backside caches versus those on the system bus, and clean 32- or 64-bit O/S architectures increase performance. Vector operators that can manipulate large arrays of very wide data types can speed up many applications. Even something as simple as a multitasking window manager separate from the graphical user interface of the application can speed up interactive user tasks. An example is the X-Windows Motif window manager (*mwm*).

The higher the clock speed, the more heat is dissipated in the integrated circuit of the CPU and support chips. RISC chips tend to produce a lot less heat because there is much less real estate on the chip. CISC CPU chips can generate around 60 watts, the same as a standard light bulb, and special cooling enclosures are needed, including a fan mounted right over the CPU. Thinner chip fabrication etching lines and copper-on-silicon technology help reduce the heat produced.

Another limitation to clock speed is the size of the computer mother board. As clock speeds approach the 1000-MHz range, the printed circuit board layouts must be treated as radio-frequency design problems. The 1/4 wavelength is about 3 inches, much smaller than most mother boards and adapter cards. Once again, architecture is more important than raw clock speed.

Scalable HP-UX 11.0 Systems

HP9000 systems running HP-UX 11.0 with 64-bit PA-RISC 8x00 processors enjoy unparalleled scalability. File system sizes can exceed 128 Gb (theoretically up to 1 terabyte), as can file sizes. The 64-bit journal file system (JFS) is supported. This is critical for fast recovery after a crash, since a traditional *fsck* would take unacceptably long to repair the file system. Fibre channel support offers 100-MBps connections to 127 devices. Data can be backed up at rates of 1 TB/hour.

Physical RAM exceeding 16 GB is possible with a theoretical limit of 4 TB. Two billion unique user IDs are possible. Symmetric Multiprocessing (SMP) for up to 16 CPUs is available. The Distributed File System is supported, as is NFSv3 with its 64-bit file size support, and NIS+, with its improved security, performance, and scalability.

Kernel threads based on the POSIX 1003.1c standard give developers the means to have fine-grained control over process control. Applications based on a single thread of execution don't scale well, while threaded applications scale very well.

IP aliasing allows a system to have multiple IP addresses, which helps support high-availability solutions such as MC/ServiceGuard. IP multicasting supports efficient "broadcasting" of data, such a multimedia streams.

DNS 4.9.6 support gives round-robin load balancing and BIND 4.0 improves response time. Both features support the operation of efficient loosely clustered systems.

Miscellaneous features such as IPv6 (with its 132-bit IP addresses) and reservation protocol (RSVP) were in pilot at the time of this writing.

References

Blommers, John, *Practical Planning for Network Growth*. Upper Saddle River, NJ: Hewlett-Packard Professional Books, Prentice Hall, 1996, ISBN: 0-13-206111-2.

Menasce, Daniel A., *Capacity Planning and Performance Modeling, From Mainframes to Client-Server Systems*. Upper Saddle River, NJ: Prentice Hall, 1994, ISBN: 0-13-035494-5.

Newzow, Martin, *Enterprise Network Performance Optimization*. New York: McGraw-Hill, Inc., 1995, ISBN: 0-07-911889-5.

Stuck, B.W., *A Computer & Communications Network Performance Analysis Primer*. Upper Saddle River, NJ: Prentice Hall Inc., 1985, ISBN: 0-13-163981-1.

CHAPTER 5

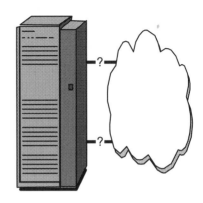

*Network Adapters
for UNIX Systems*

Introduction

Designing a UNIX networked solution requires a clear knowledge of the various types of network adapters generally available. This ensures that the right medium is selected to meet the performance demands of the application. Selection criteria may include the following:

> Media speed
> Latency
> Response time
> Cost
> Distance
> Preexisting LAN environment
> Dedicated versus switched
> Performance under load
> Contention
> Guaranteed bandwidth

Since many of the networking technologies have widely different characteristics, it will be useful here to review the most common ones and understand how they may interoperate by reviewing the OSI layer's 1 and 2 functionality of the following:

> 10-BASE-5, 10-BASE-2, 10-BASE-T, 100-BASE-T, 1000BaseSX
> FDDI
> ATM
> PPP/Serial
> ISDN
> Token ring
> Fibre Channel
> HIPPI
> Wireless

All these network technologies have physical (OSI layer 1) and logical (OSI layer 2) standardized attributes. Each technology has specific design rules for building a LAN with it. We'll review them in this chapter.

Often a UNIX networking solution will have requirements that force us to install several different network adapters in a single system. This is called *multihoming.* By default, the IP code in HP-UX systems will automatically route across multiple interfaces. This tempts the designer to take advantage of this routing feature and design it right into the total solution. The cost of a router is avoided, IP datagram fragmentation and reassembly are done right at no charge, and HP-UX even supports the major routing protocols like RIP and OSPF. This temptation should be resisted on the following grounds:

A router is more reliable than a computer system.
Routers have more useful features.
Routers support security features.
Routers perform better.
A router will reboot in under a minute, faster than a computer system.
Small routers are commodity items and don't cost that much.
A spare router is cheaper than a spare computer system.
A spare router can be installed very quickly.

But see Figure 5-1.

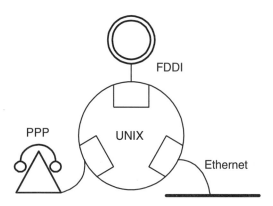

Figure 5-1   UNIX system as a media converter and a router
This is a UNIX system with three different network adapters. FDDI provides a 100-Mbps connection to the campus LAN. The Ethernet provides 10-Mbps general-purpose connectivity to the building LAN. The PPP connection comes in via a telephone and gives remote users 33.6 Kbps uncompressed throughput. The text warns about using a UNIX system as an IP router, but in this instance the remote PPP user would no doubt appreciate the ability to reach the rest of the network.

Designing in the Right LAN Medium

Traffic characteristics may be grouped into three categories. An appropriate LAN medium can be chosen by referring to Table 5-1:

Table 5-1   Using traffic characteristics to choose the right LAN medium

Type of Traffic	Appropriate LAN Medium
Light data rate	Any network medium will do provided it exceeds the sustained throughput requirements of the application
Very bursty, high-volume data rate	Token ring, FDDI, 100VG-AnyLAN, 100-BASE-T, ATM, Gigabit Ethernet
Fixed bit rate, such as voice and video	Dedicated 10-BASE-T, lightly shared 100-BASE-T, 100VG-AnyLAN, FDDI, Token ring, ISDN circuit, very low bit rate PPP with V.34 and compression, ATM

SAP/R3 application servers and their database servers traditionally require a dedicated FDDI ring to adhere to the SAP company's guidelines. This is because multiple application servers sharing multiple database servers is a very bursty, high-volume data rate scenario.

Switched LAN media provide an easy way to eliminate the side effects of LAN contention. Configuring in VLANs provides isolation and control. Even ATM, a cell-switched technology, can handle high data rates provided it's not too bursty and the many-to-many source–destination pattern holds. Additional design features for each network media include

The number of physical connections and devices allowed
Reliability
Noise immunity
Distance covered
Flexibility and expansion

OSI View of Network Adapters

The Open Systems Interconnect (OSI) model of networked systems and applications should be viewed as an architecture. Specific functionality is built into each layer. Some readers may recall an unfortunate experience in taking a datacom class and sitting through a fairly dull, almost disconnected, very theoretical treatment of the OSI model. But the OSI model can be very useful in many practical situations. By understanding the functions that each layer provides and where in the system these are implemented, troubleshooting a network problem can be a very directed and systematic activity with predictable success. The same can be said for architecture and design.

The physical layer is OSI layer 1. It specifies the physical and electrical properties of the network medium. The number and names and functions of each pin (data, handshaking, timing), the voltages, currents, and impedances, the clock frequencies and waveforms, the timing relationships between these waveforms, the shielding of the cables, the number of twists per meter, the amount of shielding, the characteristic impedance, and the maximum distance that the signal can travel are all physical layer specifications. The physical layer moves bits or bytes in sequence, either in half duplex (HDX) or full duplex (FDX), but it's imperfect, so the data may be corrupted by induced electrical noise, intermittent failure, or poor electrical or mechanical contacts. Layer 1 is assumed to be unreliable. Therefore data are encapsulated to ensure transmission accuracy, as shown in Figure 5-2.

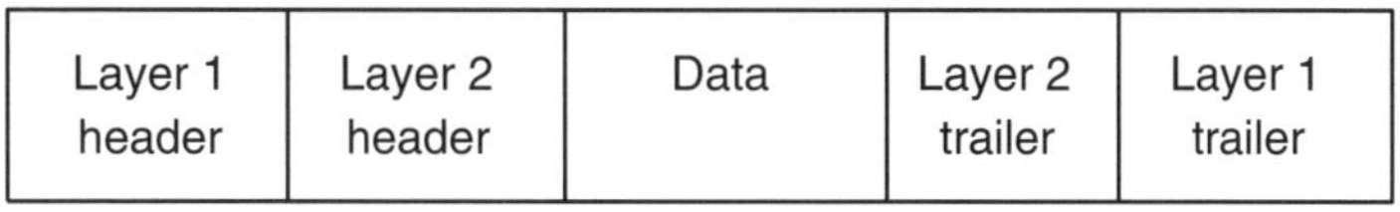

Layer 1 header	Layer 2 header	Data	Layer 2 trailer	Layer 1 trailer

Figure 5-2   OSI protocol encapsulation

Encapsulating data inside OSI layers 1 and 2 protects the data during transmission and ensures that if they arrive safely, they are not corrupted. The layer 2 firmware in the network adapter calculates a CRC for each outbound frame and checks the CRC for each frame received. If this code works correctly for all frame lengths, then layer 2 will perform as advertised.

The link layer is OSI layer 2. It specifies the logical link control (LLC) protocol. Because the physical layer cannot be trusted to move bits and bytes reliably, the link layer creates frames and encapsulates them with headers and trailers. The headers contain the source and destination link layer addresses and a few other flag fields. The trailers always contain a 16- or 32- bit error-correcting code such as a cyclic redundancy check (CRC) or a frame check sequence (FCS). Layer 2 verifies that the data received in a frame match the error-correcting code. If so, the layer 2 header is stripped off and the contents are passed on to the upper layers. If not, depending on the standard, the link layer may choose to ignore the frame (Ethernet does this) or signal the transmitter to resend it (HDLC does this).

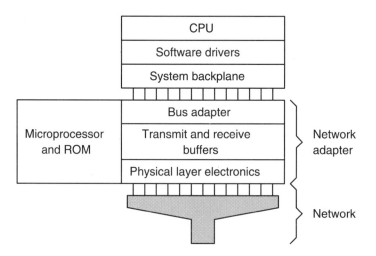

Figure 5-3   OSI model for a network adapter
The functions of OSI layers 1 and 2 are typically implemented in the network adapter. The microprocessor executes code from ROM (often flashable EAROM) and implements the link layer protocols, controls the physical layer signaling, manages the buffer space, and moves data to and from the system backplane.

In most cases, network adapters perform the layer 1 and layer 2 functions, doing the really hard work themselves and off-loading the main CPUs. See Figure 5-3. The computer's interrupt system and software drivers are responsible for moving data in and out of the network adapter. A notable exception is the PPP protocol. This standard encapsulates network packets for transmission over the system's asynchronous RS-232-C lines, so the link layer control has to be implemented in the system software.

The Ethernet Family

The Ethernet family includes the old 10-BASE-5 and 10-BASE-2 coax standard, the 10-BASE-T standard, the 100-BASE-T fast Ethernet, and finally Gigabit Ethernet. Ethernet 10-Mbps LAN adapters are built into the personality card of most systems. Additional adapters are available for the PCI, HP-PB, or HSC I/O cages for expansion and possibly to add 100BASE-T to the system.

Some basic Ethernet topology rules must be observed to ensure that we don't design a solution that won't work properly. Not more than 1024 devices may be attached to one collision domain or the collision detection and avoidance mechanism will fail. Since performance problems will crop up long before 1024 devices are added to a LAN, this problem is the least of our worries. Distances are more important, and each of the Ethernets has it's own unique set of topology and connection rules.

There is a mental crutch for 10-Mbps Ethernet worth repeating here, which is "5-4-3-2-1"; that is, 5 segments, 4 linking repeaters, 3 populated segments, 2 unpopulated segments, and 1 collision domain.

For completeness, we note that the 10-BASE-5 Ethernet standard allows for 500-meter coaxial segments with up to 100 transceiver taps attached at multiples of 2.5 meters apart (see Figure 5-4). Five segments may be connected in series, where the first, third, and fifth segments may have devices attached and the second and forth may not, and are typically fiber-optic cable. Two-port repeaters connect the segments. The transceiver provides the standard 15-pin AUI connector, which accepts an AUI cable that terminates at the LAN adapter or repeater port.

It is interesting to note that the Petronas Towers in Kuala Lumpur, Malaysia, which were completed in 1996, are only 450 meters tall, measured from the sidewalk to the structural top of the building. Masts and antennas are not included. These are the tallest buildings in the world!

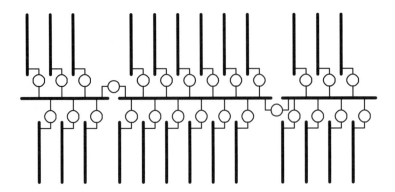

Figure 5-4 Maximum ThickLAN topology
10-BASE-5 LAN segments connected with repeaters showing the maximum extent
of the topology without the fiber links. There are not more than four repeaters between any two LAN segments. With 500-meter segments this LAN covers 1000
meters by 1500 meters. Each repeater counts as one device toward the maximum of
100 devices per segment.

10-BASE-2 topology rules call for 185-meter maximum segment lengths,
with devices not closer that 1/2 meter and not more than 30 devices per
segment. With 10-BASE-2 came the multiport repeater, or hub, to connect
these thinLAN segments together. The "four hubs in a row" rule still applies.
To extend the range of the LAN use fiber-optic links.

10-BASE-T topology rules (Figure 5-5) call for 100-meter maximum
segments, unless special cable is used to extend it. Hubs are required for
more than two devices; otherwise a crossover cable will suffice. Depending
on the vendor, hubs may support 8, 12, 16, 48, or even 96 devices. Again,
"four hubs in a row" applies.

100-BASE-T supports two types of repeaters and three physical media
standards. See Table 5-2. The type I repeater stands alone while the type II
repeater can be connected to additional repeaters with up to 5 meters of
cable. Here the rule is "two repeaters in a row." With stackable hub
technology and fiber links, this is not a limiting factor. See Figure 5-6.

The topology rules are complex. Metallic segments are limited to 100 meters
like 10-BASE-T is. The transceiver has a common media independent
interface (MII), a 40-pin cable limited to 1 meter connected to the compute

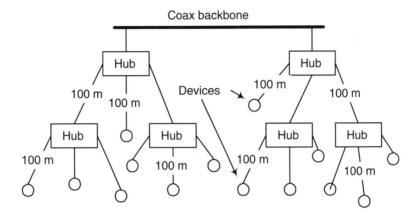

Figure 5-5   Topology rules for standard Ethernet
A 10-BASE-T LAN may use a coaxial Ethernet backbone to distribute the first-tier hubs across the building. A 10-BASE-5 backbone will cover 500 meters, a 10-BASE-2 backbone will cover 185 meters, and if there are just two hubs then up to 100 meters of 10-BASE-2 twisted pair cable will suffice. This balanced structure correctly limits the number of hubs between any two devices to four.

device. This provides flexibility in choosing the physical medium since all three transceiver types have the exact same pin-outs and connector. Three physical media and two repeater types can be connected in a variety of ways. Three cases will be covered: zero, one, and two repeaters. Zero repeaters just mean that two devices are connected, which makes sense if just two DTEs need to communicate or if we're connecting switches, bridges, and routers

Table 5-2   100-BASE-T physical media

Medium	Description
100-BASE-T4	4-pair UTP, category 3, 4, or 5, half duplex, RJ45
100-BASE-TX	2-pair category 5 UTP or type 1 STP, full duplex, RJ-45
100-BASE-FX	2 strands 62.5/125 micron multimode fiber SC/ST/MIC connectors

together. One repeater forms a simple work group, but since a single repeater might be the stackable kind, there is no serious limitation to expansion.

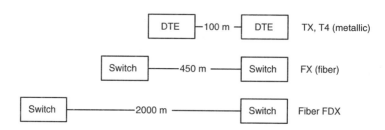

Figure 5-6   100-BASE-T distance rules

100-BASE-T topology rules for two DTE devices using either metallic medium is 100 meters. The fiber optic medium will let switches (and bridges and routers) extend to 450 meters, enough for even the world's tallest buildings, The full-duplex (FDX) fiber supports a two kilometer range - suitable for a small campus

Type I repeaters (Figure 5-7) can't be cascaded. There are four interesting ways of mixing type I repeaters with the three media types The maximum distances allowed for each combination can be calculated using a fairly detailed timing budget. 100-BASE-T LANs have one-tenth the diameter of 10-BASE-T, so the calculations will produce rather odd numbers with a lot less forgiveness in the physics when the distance is exceeded. Due to the 100-BASE-T timing budget, the distances are again seemingly off the wall.

Type II repeaters (Figure 5-8 and Table 5-9) are designed to be connected back-to-back to increase the number of ports, but we lose some of our distance advantages. Even with the fiber FX medium, we're hard pressed to exceed 100-meter segment lengths.

Applications of Gigabit Ethernet at the time of this writing (1998) include the following:

High-speed file server LAN interface (1000BaseSX for HP9000s)
High-speed interconnect between 100-BASE-T switches
LAN backbone

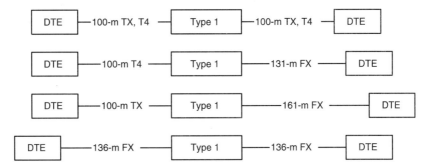

Figure 5-7   Type I fast Ethernet repeater rules

Repeaters provide a common connection point for many devices, though for illustration purposes we show just two devices per repeater. We see that fiber media give us more distance, since their velocity factor is close to 1, while copper media reduce that range, since their velocity factor is about 0.7.

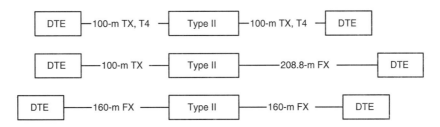

Figure 5-8   Type II fast Ethernet distance rules

The type II repeater is able to support greater distances with the fiber-optic medium than the type I repeater. Note that it is illegal to add a second DTE with 208.8 m FX media in the center drawing. That second FX-connected DTE is limited to 160 m, consistent with the bottom drawing

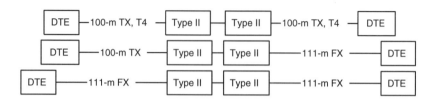

Figure 5-9   Dual type II fast Ethernet repeaters
Topology rules for two type II 100-BASE-T repeaters really tell us that the expense
of fiber media doesn't justify the distance benefit. Fiber's immunity to electrical
noise makes it appropriate for electrically noisy environments.

The IEEE802.z Gigabit Ethernet standard (1000BaseSX) provides the
topology rules for maximum distances allowed given in Table 5-3.

Table 5-3   Gigabit Ethernet topology rules

Distance	Media Type
25–100 m	Category 5 UTP
25–100 m	STP/COAX
500 m	Multimode fiber
2000 m	Single-mode fiber

Token Ring

IEEE802.5 token ring is a twisted-pair technology that operates at either 4 or
16 Mbps and uses a token (as does FDDI) to regulate traffic flow. The token
ring adapter accepts a DB9 connection from the lobe cable, which attaches
to the MAU using a hermaphroditic connector. When an active system is
attached to the MAU, the system electrically and logically connects to the
ring. Up to 260 nodes are supported, and lobe cables may be 100 m long
using IBM type 1 or 2 cable on 16-Mbps rings.

Token ring's major application in the UNIX world appears to be connectivity with legacy SNA hosts. The normal scenario has SNA gateway software residing on the UNIX system with client systems attaching via Ethernet and TCP/IP (see Figure 5-10). The connection often supports a data migration effort for "right sizing" projects. The more complex of these projects can take several years to complete.

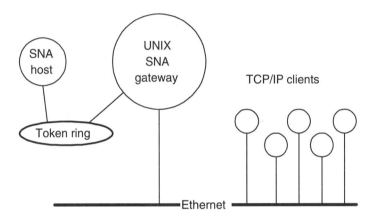

Figure 5-10   An HP-UX token ring SNA gateway
A token ring adapter in an HP-UX system may be used by the SNA/PLUS gateway software to reach an SNA host on behalf of Ethernet-connected TCP/IP clients that have neither an SNA protocol stack nor a token ring adapter.The SNA gateway does seven-layer protocol conversion to allow clients to transfer files, run jobs, receive print output, and run interactive applications supported by terminal emulation. Note that HP-UX is capable of treating the token ring adapter as an IP subnet and communicating with TCP/IP systems located there.

The 16-Mbps speed of the ring, the large MTU, and the token-controlled contention mechanism tend to give token ring greater performance than 10-Mbps Ethernet. Given the huge industry momentum behind the three Ethernet technologies, the complex physical design rules for a token ring implementation, and the perception that it's a proprietary technology, token ring is considered by many to be a dead-end LAN solution.

Regardless, the older nonpowered MAU technology has been supplanted by active hubs and token ring switches. All the major router vendors provide token ring adapters. SNA tunneling technologies are alive and well, so a corporate IP backbone can support the proprietary SNA nonroutable protocol by wrapping the PDUs inside an IP wrapper at each end of the SNA link.

To illustrate a small part of the physical plant design complexity for 16-Mbps token ring, consider a scenario with no repeaters, type 1 or 2 cable, IBM 8228 MAUs and a varying number of wiring closets. The more MAUs or wiring closets, the smaller the ring must be due to electrical signal degradation and induced noise. In Table 5-4, the adjusted ring length is the sum of all the cable lengths between the wiring closets, excluding the shortest one. The lobe cable's length isn't part of the arithmetic.

Table 5-4   Sixteen-Mbps token ring maximum adjusted length in feet

Number of MAUs	Number of Wiring Closets				
	2	3	4	5	6
2	201				
3	179	163			
4	157	141	124		
5	135	119	102	86	
6	113	97	81	64	48
7	92	75	59	42	26
8	70	53	37	20	14
9	48	31	15		
10	26	10			
11	4				

FDDI

Fiber distributed data interface (FDDI) is a very mature, well-understood technology with wide industry support (see Figure 5-11. It's great strengths include the following:

Automatic dual ring wrapping when a link fails
Electrical and RF noise immunity
No collision domains like Ethernet
Performs well under high utilization
Large MTU results in high efficiency
configurable TTRT allows performance tuning
100-Mbps raw data rate
Eight traffic priorities can support priority traffic
2 km between stations (60 km using single-mode fiber)
200-km total ring circumference (100 km for dual ring if it wraps)
500 stations

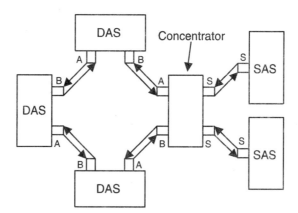

Figure 5-11   Dual attach FDDI topology
This FDDI ring shows three dual attach stations (DAS) and a concentrator. Each arrow depicts a single optical fiber and the direction in which the token rotates around the ring. The concentrator provides two single attach stations (SAS) with access to the ring. The DAS and SAS devices are network devices such as UNIX systems, routers, and switches.

The benefits of fiber optics are that it can be reused. For building to building use, installers traditionally pull more fibers than are needed, say 16 pairs. Spare fibers are a good investment, giving proof against installation defects and providing flexibility to meet future requirements. Fiber can be reused for 100-BASE-T, ATM, and gigabit Ethernet when the need presents itself.

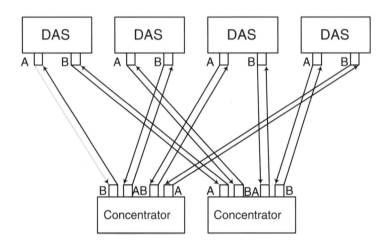

Figure 5-12   Dual concentrator FDDI cabling diagram
A high-availability (HA) FDDI solution takes advantage of a pair of highly reliable concentrators. Each DAS system is connected to each of these concentrators, both of which must fail before total communication is disrupted. Any number of systems can go down without disrupting the other systems' ability to communicate. Note how the A and B ports cross-connect.

FDDI is not as popular as it used to be. Certainly, fewer new FDDI LANs are being installed today (1998) than in the past, mainly because there are now compelling alternatives to FDDI. FDDI still has some strong advantages that make it appropriate for many applications, such as distance and reliability (see Figure 5-12). Reasons for not using FDDI include the following:

> Shared media limit performance.
> High-speed computers need more LAN bandwidth.
> Ethernet switching is all the rage and FDDI is not new technology.
> 100-BASE-T is inexpensive and pervasive.
> FDDI is a complex LAN technology.

FDDI switches are available in the marketplace. Switching technology removes the shared-media contention issues by providing a dedicated connection between two fibers for the duration of a data frame. Latency is reduced because the switch only waits until the destination station address field has entered the port.

The topology rules for designing with FDDI are pleasantly simple compared to those for fast Ethernet technology.

The traditional ring topology is subject to segmentation if two or more failures occur. To eliminate even this possibility, high reliability concentrators can be connected to all DAS devices. This forces the ring topology into a physical star shape, but the logical ring is intact.

ATM

Asynchronous transfer mode (ATM) is a high-speed switching technology based on 53-octet cells. Systems with ATM adapters can use them like any other LAN adapter because of LAN emulation (LANE) support. Advantages of ATM include the following:

High speed
Quality of service support
Video, voice, and data
Many common media interfaces are defined
LAN and WAN capability
VLAN support

There are three kinds of network managers: those who have ATM, those who wish they did, and those who don't know better. Certain features and attitudes about ATM that slow its adoption:

Cell loss probability
Multivendor switch interoperability
The need for a one-legged router
Cost
Lack of familiarity
Need for edge devices

"It's meant for voice"
100-BASE-T and gigabit Ethernet

With that out of the way, let's review the physical interfaces that the ATM standard supports (see Table 5-5). Note the wide range of interfaces available. From RJ-45 for the copper twisted pair interface to SC connectors for single-mode fiber are available.

Table 5-5   ATM physical media speeds

Megabits per second	Interface Description
1.5440	Coax
25	Unshielded twisted pair (UTP)
45	DS3 coax full-duplex (FDX) WAN
51.84	Synchronous Transport Signal-1 (STS-1) FDX OC-1 (optical carrier) over category 3 UTP
100	TAXI MIC interface for FDDI, FDX multimode (MM) fiber
155	STS-3 FDX SONET OC-3, SM fiber ST connector, MM Fiber SC connector, or cat. 5 UTP, max 100 m, RJ-45
622	STS-12 FDX SONET OC-12 on SM (single mode) or MM fiber
1,244	FDX SONET OC-24 on SM fiber
2,488	STS-48 FDX SONET OC-48 on SM fiber
10,000	STS-192

ATM technology supports both WAN and LAN, so a very large switched network can be built. ATM vendors are fond of labeling non-ATM network technology as "legacy." ATM networks scale extremely well. The physical dimensions of Ethernet LANs, by contrast, are limited to the slot time intrinsic to the collision-detection mechanism. 10-BASE-T has a 51.2-microsecond (64-byte) slot time, while 100-BASE-T has a 5.12-microsecond slot time. Gigabit Ethernet fudges this parameter. ATM has no such intrinsic limits. ATM's physical distance rules are given in Table 5-6.

Table 5-6   ATM distance rules

Distance	Interface Type
15 km	OC-3c ATM single-mode Fiber
40 km	Single-mode fiber 155-Mbps SONET STS-3c/SDH STM-1
30 km	Mixed-mode fiber 155-Mbps SONET STS-3c/SDH STM-1
100 m	100-ohm, copper, unshielded twisted-pair Category 5 (UTP-5) cable, 155-Mbps SONET STS-3c/SDH STM-1 RJ-45
500 m	Multimode fiber 622-Mbps SONET, Synchronous Transport Signal level 12, connected (STS-12c)/SDH Synchronous Transport Module level 4 (STM-4) SC-type connector
2 km	OC-3 Multimode Fiber
15 km	Single-mode fiber 622-Mbps SONET STS-12c/SDH STM-4 SC-type connector
40 km	Single-mode fiber 622-Mbps SONET STS-12c/SDH STM-4 SC connector

ISDN

Integrated Services Data Network (ISDN) adapters give UNIX systems native access to the ISDN network. ISDN uses signaling system seven (SS7) to place "calls" into the digital network. Calls use telephone numbers with the same format as the public telephone user is accustomed to, but call setup is accomplished typically in about 1 second since the calling, called, and network are digital. ISDN provides data rates from 64 to 1544 Kbps. Quality of service is available to support voice and low-bit-rate video. ISDN can be deployed as a backup network link, which remains unused until the need arises and which can be brought online within a second. ISDN is a secure service because the called system is able to accept or reject an incoming call attempt based on the caller's number. This automatic number identification (ANI) is a standard part of SS7. The American public knows it as Caller ID.

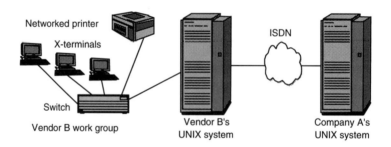

Figure 5-13   ISDN support for remote consulting
Consultants with vendor B work at X-terminals (of course) to develop code, write scripts, create documentation, and set up procedures for their remote client A. Periodically, this requires secure TCP/IP access to company A's UNIX system, which the ISDN line provides. The consultants can take advantage of the XDMCP feature of X-Windows to log into company A's UNIX system and take full advantage of that environment to do testing and validation of their work. Clients at company A can collaborate with the vendor B consultants via HP SharedX to share applications and a whiteboard.

A very interesting application for ISDN is support for remote developers. See Figure 5-13. Suppose that company A hires consultants from vendor B.

The nature of the work requires access to the company's UNIX systems, but not a physical presence. To keep costs down, vendor B consultants provision an ISDN connection, as does client A. The ISDN connection remains unused until either side decides that a network connection is needed. The UNIX machines treat their ISDN adapter an IP network across which standard routing takes place.

A very contemporary (1998) example of ISDN at work is the internet service provider (ISP), which offers ISDN service at 64 or 128 Kbps to their customers. The ISP in turn provisions from its local exchange carrier (LEC) a number of primary rate (1544 Kbps) circuits that terminate on as many ISDN ports on the ISP router. Given the bursty nature of data traffic, the ISP will accept more inbound connections from customers than the raw number of 64- or 128-Kbps inbound channels would suggest. See Figure .

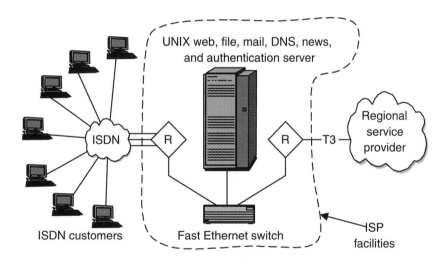

Figure 5-14   ISP ISDN service

An Internet Service Provider offers ISDN service to its customers via the ISDN network. Here we show three primary rate (1544 Kbps) circuits terminating on the router, which appears as a single ISDN number. Many ISPs provide a UNIX server with a shell account, home page support, Email, news, and additional services. The connection to the Internet is typically via one or more Regional Service Providers.

PPP over RS-232

There is no such thing as a PPP network adapter per se. PPP is a protocol for encapsulating network layer 3 packets over serial circuits. It was first used by router vendors to provide a standard interoperable means to interconnect their products at customer sites. PPP also provides dial-up, authentication, multiprotocol, link parameter negotiation, and IP address assignment for the client. Most people recognize PPP as the protocol used by their desktop computers to connect to the Internet with their modems.

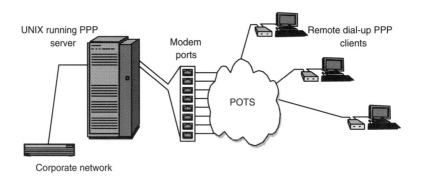

Figure 5-15   UNIX PPP remote access service

Remote clients with a modem and a TCP/IP stack configure their "PPP control panel" or "dial-up connections" control panel with one telephone number, authentication information, link configuration settings, and modem "init" strings. After a successful login and parameter negotiation dialog, the PPP client becomes a node on the corporate network. The UNIX system acts as an IP router to the clients and advertises remote network reachability information via RIP, perhaps.

In a UNIX environment, PPP is used over modem-connected RS-232 serial ports to encapsulate IP packets. When a remote client dials in, PPP authenticates the user, assigns an IP address to each end of the link, sets up a routing table entry for the newly created network connection, and even provides a name for DNS to use with this IP (it's preallocated of course). If Van Jacobson IP header compression is negotiated, the UNIX CPU must do the arithmetic.

PPP can be used to allow remote-client access as a network node, regardless of the type of platform that the user might possess. See Figure 5-15. PPP may also be used to establish a low-speed backup WAN link if the primary one fails. Even ISDN "modems" use PPP. The number of RS-232 ports normally available on a UNIX system is fairly limited. Dedicated remote-access servers or communications servers built into racks that contain built-in modems and an Ethernet adapter are used to economically support a large user base.

Fibre Channel

Fibre Channel is a high-speed, full-duplex fabric operating at 133, 266, 531, and 1062.5 Mbps per link. A major application is high-speed, high-availability connections to high-capacity disk arrays for large Enterprise Parallel Servers (EPS). A fibre-channel adapter may also be a full-fledged network adapter capable of very high performance.

Fiber cable distances of 2 km are typical. The fabric is implemented as a switch with up to 16 ports. Fiber-optic, coax, and UTP media are supported. It is managed from an RS-232 port or an Ethernet connection. To support high-availability environments, the switch will have an additional RS-232 for the UPS.

A major high-availability feature of fiber-channel switches is support for meshing of multiple switches into a redundant larger fabric. Rings, stars, and meshes are typical configurations. These can also be used to increase the number of ports available over what one switch can provide. Consider six 16-port fibre-channel switches in a fully meshed topology (Figure 5-16). Each switch uses 5 ports to connect to each of the other five switches, leaving 11 ports free. A total of 66 ports remain free. The full meshing increases the bandwidth across this virtual switch. Up to 126 addresses are supported on a fibre channel fabric.

Three types of connectivity are provided. Class 1 creates a dedicated connection between ports, and all frames move only between them, guaranteeing data delivery and the frame order. Class 2 service acts like a frame switch, buffering as necessary to ensure delivery, but unable to

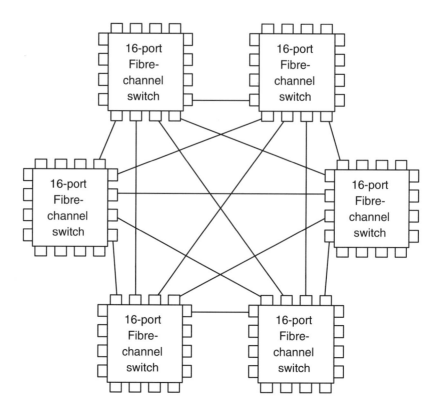

Figure 5-16   Aggregation of fibre channel switches
A 66-port fibre channel fabric is built by cross-connecting six fibre channel switches.
A 10 km diameter is possible using the 9-micrometer single mode fiber. Each full du-
plex-connection into the fabric can move 100 MBps in and out concurrently. This
configuration allows each switch to move 500 MBps into and out of the fabric.

guarantee that frames arrive in the order that they were transmitted. A
connection between ports is made only for the duration of the frame. Class 3
is like class 2 with only a best-effort, nonguaranteed datagram delivery
service.

Table 5-7 Fibre channel topology rules and data rates

Medium	Data Rate, MBps	Maximum Distance	Data rate in Mbaud
Single mode fiber 9 micrometers	100	10 km	1062.50
	50	10 km	531.25
	25	10 km	265.60
60-micrometer multimode fiber	25	2 km	265.60
	50	1 km	531.25
Video coax	100	25 m	1062.50
	50	50 m	531.25
	25	75 m	265.60
	12.50	100 m	132.80
Miniature coax (75 ohms)	100	10 m	1062.50
	50	20 m	531.25
	25	30 m	265.60
	12.50	40 m	132.80
STP 105-ohm type1	25	50 m	265.60
	12.50	100 m	132.80

While we think of data in terms of bytes per second, fibre channel serializes the data for transmission. To ensure data integrity every 8 bits is padded with two more (8B/10B encoding), and there is an additional 6.2% framing overhead. Therefore, a 100-MBps data rate becomes 1062.6 Mbaud, where a baud is a signaling element or symbol. Each frame may carry zero to 2112 bytes of data in addition to 36 bytes of framing. Like ATM, devices must do a "login/logout" to establish a circuit through the fabric. See Figure 5-7.

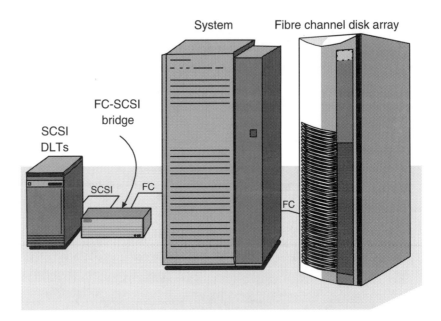

Figure 5-17   SCSI bridge migration strategy
Migration to fibre channel disk arrays can be done while preserving the investment in current SCSI devices such as DLT loaders and disk drives. Fibre channel is a fairly novel network adapter - what other standard lets you do TCP/IP networking and disk I/O? Expensive I/O adapter slots may be used for fibre channel instead of SCSI adapters by taking advantage of a fibre channel to SCSI bridge.

System-to-system network communication and system-to-disk array I/O are popular uses of fibre channel. Typically, disk I/O and network communications don't share the same adapter. SCSI devices like digital linear tape (DLT) and disk drives may still be used in the fibre channel environment with the addition of an FC-SCSI bridge device (Figure 5-17). A UNIX system may use fibre channel exclusively to communicate with FC disks, SCSI disks, and tapes. This not only helps leverage existing hardware, but it may also be the only way to get certain non-FC devices working on the fibre channel. The fibre channel standard actually supports a variety of interfaces and protocols. See Figure 5-7. Not only can the physical medium be coaxial cable, fiber optics, and shielded twisted pair, but the protocols can also transmit SCSI commands. We need the fibre channel-to-SCSI bridge to handle the speed and physical interface differences.

TIA/EIA Standards

The Telecommunications Industry Association (TIA) and the EIA define a set of building infrastructure standards under section 568 that cover fiber optics, 10-BASE-T, 100-BASE-T, and categories 5, 6, and 7 wiring standards. Designers of the physical LAN media will be familiar with these standards.

References

Black, Uyless, *Frame Relay Networks, Specifications and Implementations*, 2nd ed. New York: McGraw-Hill Book Co., 1996, ISBN: 0-07-005590-4.

Breyer, Robert, *Switched and Fast Ethernet: How It Works and How to Use It*. Emeryville, CA: Ziff-Davis Press, 1995, ISBN: 1-56276-338-5.

Jain, Raj, *FDDI Handbook, High-speed Networking Using Fiber and Other Media*. Reading, MA: Addison-Wesley Publishing Co., 1994, ISBN: 0-201-56376-2.

Pitts, J. M., *Introduction to ATM Design and Performance*. New York: John Wiley & Sons, Inc., 1996, ISBN: 0-471-96340-2.

Tittel, Ed, *ISDN Networking Essentials*. New York: AP Professional, 1996, ISBN: 0-12-691392-7.

CHAPTER 6

UNIX Network Configuration Principles

Introduction

Architecting, designing, and implementing networks and UNIX systems requires a healthy appreciation for details. As any architect will tell you, there are three kinds of systems people: those who have all the details, those who wish they did, and those who don't know any better. This chapter will review the many common configuration details that can break a solution if they're overlooked.

Open systems are scary. You have built a solution using open products from vendors A, B, C, and D and "it doesn't work." Each vendor can tell you about its product configuration, but assembled into a complex solution, they can't recommend how their box should be configured to work in your solution. Parameters such as the FDDI MTU size, Ethernet versus IEEE encapsulation, and IP subnet masks are basic and critical to proper operation under all conditions. Too high an MTU and large frames may disappear as they cross a bridge. Ethernet frames are not the same as IEEE frames. Subnet masks are critical for proper routing.

Other IP-related parameters that are important include DHCP, BOOTP, and the BOOTP relay agent. For multihomed systems, DNS configuration is affected. For performance reasons, the UNIX local loopback has to be set "just so/" And whether or not Proxy ARP is enabled by default on a router can make all the difference between a site that works and one that doesn't.

The importance of planning the IP addressing configuration of a UNIX networking solution is critical for reliable operations during errors, outages, changes, upgrades, and expansion.

To sum up, for any networked solution, consider the unique and special aspects of the routers, switches, client and server systems, networked scanners and printers, and the supporting protocols such as DHCP, DNS, and routing protocols.

Why Open Systems Are Scary

Integration by using standards is the foundation of open systems. Anyone building a solution based on open systems therefore has to become an integrator. There are a large number of combinations of standard parameter values and configuration profiles. A highly trained staff is needed to design, implement, and support these solutions, because you really can't call one of the box vendors and expect them to know how to configure their box to work with another vendor's box. Put in ten different boxes such that the nine communicate only with the tenth, and you have only nine combinations to configure and test. But if all ten boxes communicate among themselves, the number of combinations is $10\times9=90$ unique client–server pairs; each of the ten boxes makes one client connection to the other nine boxes. This arithmetic assumes that none of the boxes makes a client-server connection to itself, and a single service is assumed.

Open systems are not just scary because of the potential number of combinations that must be tested. Vendors have historically preferred a closed architecture to protect their market share or simply to provide functionality that is not available using standards. But there is fear of becoming a commodity vendor, with the reduced profit margins of such a marketplace. How can a vendor differentiate itself? Quite a few differentiators come to mind:

Completeness of the implementation
Price
Quality
Support
Documentation
Performance
Ease of installation and use
Added value and features
Availability
Marketing

The historical road to open systems has taken us over rocky terrain. Previously, computer vendors sold proprietary market architectures ("marketectures") with more or less open access to them. In the early 1980s,

IBM sold boxes with SNA, Digital sold boxes with DECNet, and HP sold boxes with AdvanceNet. See Table 6-1. As the open systems movement gathered momentum, TCP/IP became the standard for intersystem communications.

Table 6-1   Proprietary and open architectures

Proprietary Architecture	How It Became Open
SNA	Originally strong on Token Ring, third parties produced TCP/IP gateway products in hardware and software. Later IBM sold a TCP/IP stack and Ethernet adapters.
VMS	VAXen always had Ethernet, then came TCP/IP from third parties like Wollongong and HP, then came OpenVMS.
NetWare	Novell always had Ethernet, then third parties like HP added TCP/IP clients called ARPA services, Novell added NFS services. The NetWare and TCP/IP protocol stacks integrated using ODI and NDIS.
Mac OS Rhapsody	Ethernet is built into the Macintosh, and System 7 made MacTCP integral. Open Transport is the current incarnation of TCP/IP on the Macintosh.
Wintel	PCs required third-party support for TCP/IP and the WINSOCK.DLL set of APIs gave the platform standard TCP/IP access.
HP3000	Ethernet and TCP/IP came early to the HP3000, initially from Wollongong support, and later because HP is an early adopter of open systems and TCP/IP.

Terms like "open system" and "standard" are frequently twisted by marketing hype into unrecognizable shapes. There are several types of standards. Committee standards such as EIA, IEEE, CCITT, and IETF create documented standards by committees of industry and academic experts. EIA gave us RS-232-C, IEEE gave us 802.3, CCITT gave us V.34, and IETF gave us RFC 791. These standards are cast in stone and may not be trifled with by vendors except through the standards body. Defacto standards are just accepted by everybody, like Sun's NFS, MIT's X-Windows, Bell Labs UNIX, and PGP.

Products based on committee standards and defacto standards are generally available from multiple vendors, giving the customer choices. Hence, open systems are good. Hence, there are many vendors that sell UNIX operating systems, X-Windows, Ethernet, TCP/IP, Berkeley services, and DNS for most hardware platforms like HP-PA, Alpha, 80X86, SGI, SPARC, PPC, and MIPS. The variety of hardware to which UNIX has been ported is grand testimony of its portability, scalability, hardware independence, robustness, quality, and architecture. UNIX works on the desktop and it works on multiprocessors supporting thousands of users.

The final aspect of standards is standardizing. Standardizing usually means creating a short list of products from which people pick their systems. It has very little to do with committee standards or defacto standards, and the standardization list may have proprietary products on it. This is because of practical matters. Support costs are a great issue, and one way to reduce them is to limit the amount of choice. For example, if people could choose from five versions of UNIX on ten platforms, the number of permutations is large and the training, support, and spares costs go right through the roof. UNIX is UNIX, but the different hardware and peripheral support does make system administration unique for each combination. SGI, Solaris, Linux, and HP-UX have unique differences in their system administration due to hardware, features, products, and value added.

FDDI and Other Media MTU

LAN and WAN media maximum transmission unit (MTU) vary and can cause serious interoperability problems unless they're considered in the architecture of a networked solution. Let's begin with a list of common media and their standard MTU values (Table 6-2). We say "standard MTU" because the MTU can usually be lowered or adjusted in the implementation.

Table 6-2   Standard LAN and WAN MTU sizes

Medium	MTU in Bytes
PPP/RS-232	1500
Ethernet	1500
FDDI	4500
WAN serial	1500
Token ring	4096
ATM	8192
Fibre Channel	2112

Note that there is a difference between MTU and maximum frame size. The MTU is the data payload and includes network layer protocols and above. Add in the framing characters and you get the maximum frame size. For example, Ethernet's MTU is 1500 bytes, but if you add the 18 bytes of header and trailer, you get the maximum frame size of 1518.

The reason the MTU is important is when packets are bridged or switched across media with different MTU sizes. There is no standard at the link layer for fragmenting and reassembling frames, so, in the absence of this, switches and bridges have no choice but to discard a frame that's too big for the forwarding medium's MTU. Consider several work-group LANs built up with Ethernet switches. Each work group has a server and a group of clients. To facilitate collaboration among the work groups, an FDDI loop joins the switches. Everything will work fine because all systems originate traffic on the Ethernet at the lower MTU. Suppose that we now add a router or another system to the FDDI ring. These won't know their targets are on Ethernet and may create large frames that won't pass through the switch. The solution is to configure all systems in this environment to an MTU of 1500 bytes. Token ring-to-Ethernet bridges have historically had this problem, too.

But even if the configuration specifications call for an MTU of 1500 bytes, when systems are upgraded, the OS is rebuilt, or a new systems is installed, human error can easily insert itself into the equation. How do we ensure that the MTU size remains correct? Network configuration management is the answer. HP OpenView Network Node Manager (NNMGR) can be used to monitor the MTU of all network adapters. If the MTU changes, then a configuration event will occur, so review these for MTU changes. If a new system is installed, a new node event will occur, and again the MTU size should be checked.

There are some functions at the network layer that deal with differences in MTU size. They are fragmentation and reassembly. When an IP stack in a system or router has to forward a packet larger than the MTU, it will automatically fragment that packet and mark each IP header accordingly. These packets will make their way one by one to their final destination, remaining apart and possibly being reordered along their journey. The destination device will reassemble the IP datagram.

Several downsides to fragmentation and reassembly are worth noting here. The task of fragmentation is often left in the lap of the local router, and some network managers don't like to see this load placed on their router CPUs. The fragmentation process tends to produce a packet train of very closely spaced frames on the medium, which can lead to packet loss. Since IP is not connection oriented, there is no mechanism to discover and retransmit the lost packet. The target system's IP stack will hold onto the other IP fragments until it eventually times out and discards all the packets still on the reassembly buffer. TCP will eventually time out and retransmit the entire packet again. Any packet loss will seriously reduce TCP throughput.

On the bright side, a feature called MTU discovery, if it's available, is designed to discover the smallest MTU between the originator and destination and adjust its packet size accordingly. For each new TCP connection, the originator will take advantage of the "don't fragment" bit in the IP header and send a large packet to the destination. If any intervening router has to fragment this packet, upon seeing the "don't fragment" bit set, it will return a packet to the originator indicating the problem. The sender takes this cue and tries a smaller packet, reducing it as necessary until the path MTU is found. MTU discovery only has to be implemented on the client end, which originates the TCP connection.

Ethernet and IEEE Frames

Robert Metcalf invented the Ethernet as a 3-Mbps medium. It soon became a
10 Mbps standard in the Blue Book from Xerox, Digital, and Intel. The Blue
Book defined the frame format, media access protocol (CSMA/CD), and the
physical and electrical specifications for the coaxial medium and gave
names to various components like the transceiver. Some small but useful
changes were added to create Ethernet 2. Then the IEEE standardizes the
Ethernet and in the process enhanced it. The end result was that the Ethernet
and IEEE 802.3 frame formats became slightly different (see Figure 6-1).

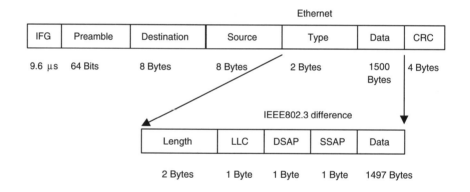

Figure 6-1   Ethernet versus IEEE frame formats
Ethernet and IEEE802.3 frame formats differ only in the type/length field. The structure of the data field naturally differs, but this is not visible at the frame level. The
interframe gap (IFG) is an interval without any clock signals, and it's a minimum
time.

The frame wrapper remained the same. The preamble, source address,
destination address, CRC field, and interframe gaps remained identical, as
did the CSMA/CD specification. This means that these frames can coexist
on the same cable. Early on, Hewlett–Packard supported both IEEE and
Ethernet frame formats on the HP9000 LAN adapters. The LAN drivers are
configured with the "*lanconfig*" command at boot time. The command
"*lanconfig +ieee +ethernet*" enables both formats.

But if system A only understands Ethernet frames and system B only understands IEEE frames, these systems cannot communicate on the same cable. The solution is to have these systems communicate via an intermediate system that understands both frame formats, such as an HP9000 or an IP router. The intermediate system's IP stack will very happily remove the IP packet from the Ethernet frame and rewrap it in an IEEE frame. Keeping IEEE-only systems on one subnet and Ethernet-only systems on a second subnet is a simple solution.

Alternatively, both logical subnets may exist on the same physical LAN. The downside here is that packets sent between these systems are transmitted twice on the same LAN segment. The configuration should be tested to make sure that it works properly.

Table 6-3   Several IEEE 802 standards

Number	Description
802.1	Bridging, spanning tree, virtual LAN (VLAN)
802.2	Link layer (LLC)
802.3	Ethernet physical layer
802.4	Broadband (the older CATV technology)
802.5	Token ring (IBM)
802.11	Wireless

The IEEE standards (Figure 6-3) provide numerous physical layer standards, a link layer standard, plus an interoperability layer that provides the means for moving data between the link layers. Ethernet does have a place in this set of standards, suggesting that IEEE protocols are preferred for interoperability's sake. At any rate, the fact that Ethernet and IEEE are quite different at the link layer (not to mention physical layer differences) will make you question a claim that vendor X has an Ethernet/IEEE802.3 product. Still, you will note that the fast Ethernet (802.3t) and gigabit Ethernet (802.3z) standard physical layers are defined under the IEEE802.3 standard.

IP Subnet Masks and Routing Tables

An implementation plan for a UNIX networked solution is incomplete without the IP numbering plan. This plan reflects considerations about the total number of subnets and the maximum number of devices per subnet that the solution is required to support. An architecture is useless if it is limited to 16 subnets or 32 nodes per subnet, so these considerations are critical and must look to future worst-case requirements. Note that there are cases where careful subnetting is important, as where a given number of class B or class C network addresses must be worked with. Since most companies connect to the Internet via a firewall, they are free to pick a class A address for private use, so there is not much reason to run out of network numbers these days.

When developing the network numbering plan, here is a short list of important considerations:

> Each network adapter has an IP address and subnet mask.
> Each system has a local loopback adapter, such as *lo0*.
> I/O to each adapter's IP address should be via local loopback.
> Each adapter is on its own IP subnet.
> At HP-UX11.0, an adapter may have multiple IP addresses.
> HP-UX routes by default with two or more network cards.
> A default route should be provided.

Routing tables may be established in different ways. One or more static routes may be added at boot time. When routes are not set up correctly, routers will usually generate ICMP redirects to sending nodes that apparently don't have properly set up routing tables. If the system is able to run a routing protocol such as RIP or OSPF (by executing the *gated* daemon process), it can both advertise routes and learn them from its neighbors. When a PPP connection is established, it is common to have a new route to the connection established. Note that there is always a route to the locally attached networks via the adapters themselves.

A quick refresher about how routing works will complete this section. Consider the IP entity in a system. It has an IP packet to forward. First it uses the subnet mask for each of its directly connected network adapters to see if the network portion of the target IP matches the network number of the adapters. If so, then the packet is transmitted on the appropriate adapter. If the target IP address matches the adapter, then the local loopback adapter should be configured and the packet is sent to the local machine itself via the local loopback adapter.

If none of the attached adapters match, then the routing table is again consulted to find an appropriate gateway configured to pass packets to the destination network. This gateway must be attached to one of the network adapters that our IP entity is also connected to. If a suitable gateway is found, then the packet is forwarded to the MAC address of the gateway. If no gateways are found, then the default route is used. If no default gateway is defined, the packet is not deliverable.

Note that a favorite default route for single LAN systems is itself. The syntax is

   /etc/route add default 'hostname' 0

where *'hostname'* returns the name of the local system and 0 is the hop count. This means that the local system will send all packets not meant for itself out on the local LAN adapter regardless of the target network. This works when the local IP router supports Proxy ARP.

Note, too, that the local loopback adapter is intended as an efficiency measure so that, when a client and a server are located on the same system (such as a workstation running an X-client on its directly connected console), the packet does not have to travel up and down the seven-layer OSI stack.

Local Loopback and Shared Memory

Local loopback is a special network adapter typically called */dev/lo0* (ell-oh-zero) that's used to keep packets out of the LAN adapter environment for local network I/O. This is an optimization measure that keeps the packet from being transmitted on the network only to be read right back in again. It avoids fragmentation and reassembly code. The adapter is known by the hostname *localhost* and always has 127.0.0.1 for the IP address. This adapter has an MTU of about 4500 bytes, but the value is unrelated to any physical frame size.

Another important use of the local loopback adapter is for high-speed LAN adapters such as FDDI. The HP FDDI adapter does TCP checksumming to off-load the host and improve throughput, so it's important to configure the route for the IP address of the FDDI adapter to be *lo0*. The command syntax for this is

/etc/route add FDDI_CARD_IP_ADDRESS 127.0.0.1 0

Correct configuration and use of the local loopback adapter are therefore critical in the design and implementation of a UNIX network solution. For very high volume data rates, however, this mechanism for moving data isn't as efficient as a shared memory paradigm is.

Consider the problem of backing up 50 gigabytes of data from disk drives to digital linear tape (DLT) drives. A remote HP OmniBack cell controller has the enviable task of coordinating the backup process from the disk agents to the DLT media agents. The disk and media agents normally use TCP/IP to communicate when the agents reside on different HP-UX systems. That is usually called a network backup. But with 50 gigabytes to back up, we've put the DLTs on the same system with the disks. This will increase performance by avoiding the network.

But the disk and media agents determine that they are running on the same system, so they elect to use a shared memory area to transfer data. This turns out to be much faster than local loopback, since it uses much less code and can move very large chunks of data with one call.

In summary, local loopback is appropriate for local network I/O, but for very high data volumes, a shared memory metaphor is much more efficient.

DHCP, BOOTP, and Relay Agents

One of the messy things about using IP is that, traditionally, every device's parameters had to be manually configured. This is error prone, inconvenient, and time consuming, especially in a dynamic environment with frequent moves, adds, and changes. There isn't any way to administer the configuration of devices from a central point without some automation. Enter BOOTP and DHCP.

The boot protocol BOOTP is a client–server protocol. An uninitialized client system will power up, initialize, and issue at BOOTP request. This takes the form of an all-ones MAC (FF-FF-FF-FF-FF-FF) and IP (255.255.255.255) broadcast. All devices on the local subnet hear this broadcast, and a BOOTP server is able to process it; the other systems ignore it or log an event. The BOOTP server looks at the MAC address of the client and consults a little database. a flat file called *bootptab* in HP-UX. If a match is found, the file will contain a list of parameters such as the IP address, the subnet mask, the default route, and other parameters appropriate to the device. The BOOTP daemon returns this information to the client, which then configures its IP stack. The BOOTP protocol depends on advance knowledge of exactly which MAC addresses need to be assigned to which IP addresses.

BOOTP uses an all-ones IP broadcast, so clients won't be heard across subnet boundaries. Enter the BOOTP relay agent on the router. A special feature on the router can forward a BOOTP request to a given BOOTP server IP address, and forward the BOOTP reply back to the client. BOOTP is used for networked printers, X-terminals, and scanners.

To overcome the limitations of BOOTP, dynamic host configuration protocol (DHCP) was developed. Its major features include the ability to pool IP addresses, extend fixed-duration leases of IP addresses to clients, and lock down fixed IP addresses (necessary for fixed IP addresses for routers, DNS, and WINS). There is nearly universal support for DHCP in the Wintel, Macintosh, and UNIX world. Networked printers, X-terminals, and scanners all support it. With BOOTP relay agents, it's practical to deploy DHCP across the enterprise network. Because BOOTP and DHCP servers are single points of failure (no database replication or backup features), they should be configured and supported in a high-availability environment. An architecture that takes advantage of DHCP will be very easy to install and maintain.

Note that a wide range of IP services uses a broadcast mechanism. Address resolution protocol (ARP) uses a MAC layer broadcast to locate the system with a desired IP address. ORBIX uses a broadcast to find an object request broker. An NFS client uses a broadcast to find an NIS server in its domain. All broadcast-based services are limited to the subnet they're located on, since IP routers are designed not to forward them.

The lesson here is that any architecture that depends on a broadcast mechanism alone will have to include additional mechanisms to scale beyond the limits of a single subnet. Likewise, if two or more versions of some service must coexist on the same IP subnet, their broadcasts must not interfere with each other. For example, NFS can support multiple domains on the same subnet by using multiple domain names. Clients belonging to a given domain will bind to NIS services that service that domain.

Multihoming

The term multihoming has traditionally meant multiple LAN adapters in one system. In the IP world, this implies that the adapters are configured to be on different IP subnets, an essential requirement for proper routing to occur. But times are changing, and terminology changes with it. Broadband used to refer to networking built with CATV technology. Now (1998) it just means high-speed networking. Likewise, the term multihoming has additional meaning.

Netscape pioneered and developed the commercial applications of web technology. A small web hosting service may have to support several customers, each with its own universal resource locator (URL). Thus, one web server may have to pretend that it is all of www.company_A.com, www.company_B.com, and www.company_C.com and not make any mistakes about it. This is also called multihoming. Multiple names for the same computer are not always supported, so care must be taken in developing an architecture that assumes that this feature is supported by the UNIX or application vendor.

Routers are multihomed, of course, and each network adapter has a unique IP address (plus additional helper addresses if it has to support multiple logical subnets on the same physical LAN). Large UNIX systems often have multiple LAN adapters as well, such as SAP application servers. Traditionally, DNS supports this by lumping together all the IP addresses of the multihomed device under the same name. A DNS-aware client like *telnet* and *ftp* will actually take advantage of the list of IP addresses that the name request returns. A reverse lookup on any of the IP addresses will return the same name. DNS administrators make a point to correctly configure the name-server database for multihomed devices.

Multihoming is not to be confused with the ability to have multiple IP addresses associated with a single LAN adapter.

Domain Name System

A networked UNIX solution will doubtless take advantage of the domain name system (DNS) to allow clients to address servers using names instead of IP addresses. The advantages include ease of use and flexibility in administering IP addresses. For example, if Email clients always refer to their POP3 server as emailserver.company.com, then if it becomes necessary to migrate to a replacement server with a different IP address, the change can be loaded into DNS and the Email clients will never notice the change.

A quick discussion about how DNS works is appropriate here. DNS is a client–server architecture. There is a DNS client and a DNS server. The client looks up records, such as domain names, IP addresses, and mail exchange (MX) records. If the DNS server is authoritative for the information (i.e., it has the original data on hard disk), then it replies directly to the client with the information. Otherwise, it refers the request to an authoritative DNS server (if known) or just refers it to the root name sever which knows the location of all authoritative DNS servers. Information received is cached by the DNS servers in RAM.

A generic client uses a resolver to look up names. On HP-UX, the resolver can take advantage of */etc/hosts*, DNS, and NIS. The DNS configuration file */etc/resolv.conf* is configured with the IP addresses of up to three DNS servers, the client's subdomain, plus a list of SEARCH subdomains that may be searched. The resolver will try the IP addresses until if finds a DNS server that responds. If the DNS server does not return the IP address for some name, the resolver may prune off subdomains until only a basic domain name remains. For example, if the lookup for *mybox.bellevue.nsr.hp.com* failed, the resolver can try *mybox.nsr.hp.com* and *mybox.hp.com* also. A lookup for just *mybox* first appends the local domain name *bellevue.nsr.hp.com* to form *mybox.bellevue.hp.com,* and if this lookup fails, the SEARCH domains are appended one at a time to *mybox* until a match is found.

DNS-aware applications like *telnet* and *ftp* take note when they get a list of IP addresses from DNS for multihomed devices. The first IP address of the list is "closest" to the client, and if the client can't reach its server at that IP address, it will try the others in succession. This makes for a very robust client design and is the recommended model for all client–server architectures.

DNS servers may be

> caching only (no authoritative database),
> authoritative for one or more domains (local database records),
> secondary (copies records from authoritative DNS to local disk), or
> pointing to root name servers to resolve other names

This design allows the DNS service to be distributed. Local sites can administer their own IP addresses and domain names autonomously, DNS servers can be located in reliable places and administered remotely, and the hierarchical nature of the domain name space supports a massive number of names. The proof is the Internet with its millions of hosts. Lookups are fast and accurate when humans don't place errors in the data. A scalable architecture will take advantage of DNS.

The ARP Hack

For some years my colleagues and I found that, by simply using the following statement into the */etc/netlinkrc* file, most HP-UX boxes would work just about anywhere regardless of their IP address and domain name:

> */etc/route add default 'hostname' 0*

This tells the local HP-UX system (hop count 0) to handle the *default* route (when no other routing entry matches) and to ARP anyway on the adapter *'hostname'* even though the remote system wouldn't hear the ARP. This resulted in fairly large ARP caches, as shown by the command *arp -a,* but everything worked like a champ. We did not need to know the IP address of the local router, and the command didn't have to mention the system name either. Even if the subnet mask was left at the default of 255.0.0.0, the systems continued to work. Truly, this was an accomplishment in system network administration.

The reason this works is that the local router hears the ARP request (it's a broadcast) and notes that the target IP address isn't local. Taking pity on the poor ignorant sender, the router returns an ARP reply containing the router's MAC address. The client system thinks it's made contact and starts sending data to the router, which dutifully forwards the IP packets along to the intended recipient.

Why do this? In the absence of DHCP and in the interests of simplicity and high availability, the ARP hack makes sense. What if there are several routers available to the local site? If one goes down (which is why there are several), the ARP hack will switch systems over to the remaining router (possibly after the arp cache ages out in about 20 minutes). If the routers don't supply a RIP feed to the local LAN, UNIX systems can't figure out the best route during an outage.

The final word is that tricks like the ARP hack (a.k.a. ARP proxy) can improve the robustness of systems and networks. Seek them out and use them often.

References

Comer, Douglas, *Internetworking with TCP/IP, Principles, Protocols, and Architecture*. Upper Saddle River, NJ: Prentice Hall, 1988, ISBN: 0-13-470154-2.

Huitema, Christian, *Routing on the Internet*. Upper Saddle River, NJ: Prentice Hall, 1995, ISBN: 0-13-132192-7.

Hunt, Craig, *TCP/IP Network Administration*. Sebastopol, CA: O'Reilly & Associates, Inc., 1994, ISBN: 0-937175-82-X.

Liu, Cricket, *DNS and BIND in a Nutshell*. Sebastopol, CA: O'Reilly & Associates, Inc., 1993, ISBN 1-56592-010-4

UNIX Compute
Cluster Designs

Introduction

We cluster UNIX systems physically to improve their manageability and performance, and we cluster them logically to improve their functionality. DCE and NCS may be used to increase performance at the discrete function level. HP's Network Connection Policy Manager helps load balance clusters. An example is a build farm of Atria ClearCase servers.

By clustering systems we can raise the compute power beyond that of a single multiprocessor or uniprocessor system. The overhead of intercluster communications (protocols and latencies) is ideally less than 10% by design and optimization. Clustering adds a dimension of scalability to an architecture. It takes load balancing and software tools to make it work. And the systems must be interconnected in some way.

Why We Cluster UNIX Systems

Clustering gives us a product able to handle huge compute jobs that a single system wouldn't be able to handle. Even the biggest, fastest, largest, and baddest systems have limits to the number of CPUs, amount of RAM, disk performance, network bandwidth, and bus speed.

As a bonus, the physical diversity of the cluster increases its overall reliability. Indeed, it is often the case that high availability is the sole reason for creating a cluster. Assuming that the proper redundancies are in place and that any interdependencies are eliminated, then the nines after the decimal point can be appended. If one system can provide 0.99 uptime, then a two-way cluster can theoretically provide 0.9999 uptime, and three can provide 0.999999 uptime.

The physical clustering is preferably standards based using LAN or WAN technology. Historically, clustering has been based on proprietary hardware interconnects. Low-bandwidth links are acceptable provided that compute time is at least ten times the data transfer rate. Ethernet, FDDI, fibre channel, and ATM make excellent clustering media. Disk drives connected to the cluster will be multiported, mirrored, and heavily buffered.

Diskless computers are also a clustering technology. The boot server is called the cluster server, a single point of administration. Diskless nodes use the cluster server's file system for swap, program access, and file storage. With this arrangement the RAM and CPU of the diskless nodes become compute resources. NFS diskless technology works this way. The latest such technology is the network computer (NC) and the NetPC.

Logical clustering also increases performance. Here systems are loosely linked via Email or a lightweight protocol. This has applications for such academic tasks as breaking cryptographic keys via the Internet. During late 1997 there was an exercise to find the cryptographic key for RC-64. Multiplatform clients contact a central server for a range of keys to search. The clients return the results to the server whenever a connection to the Internet is available and the client has results to report. Participation is totally voluntary.

Protocols that can be used for clustering include UDP, TCP, and DCE RPC. Products that support clustering include the HP Network Connection Policy Manager for load balancing and the DCE RPC toolkit.

MC/ServiceGuard

Last, but not least, by clustering systems you create high-availability (HA) solutions. Consider HP's MC/ServiceGuard and two HP-UX systems. Everything is redundant. There are at least two computers, two LAN cards in each, dual disk controllers and mirrored disks, two LAN hubs, two routers, and so on. There is no single point of failure.

Of three LAN adapters in each system, one is used exclusively for a heartbeat between the systems, one is the active adapter, and the third is unconfigured. When a failure condition occurs, the unconfigured LAN adapter may take over for the formerly active one, taking on its IP and MAC addresses. When the heartbeat is not detected from the primary cluster machine, the backup can take over completely.

Packages of applications participate and run under the MC/ServiceGuard high-availability rules. Applications not inside packages may use the cluster's resources, but are not able to take advantage of the fail-over features. Packages define application services that MC/ServiceGuard monitors, which can cause a restart or fail-over to an adoptive node in the event of an error on the primary node. The package thus moves from one system to another. To ensure that remote clients can still connect to the package, an IP address is assigned to it, regardless of which node it runs on. This works because the active LAN adapter may have multiple IP addresses assigned to it.

For a wonderful well-presented book on MC/ServiceGuard, see *Clusters for High Availability, A Primer of HP-UX Solutions* by Peter S. Weygant, Prentice Hall, Upper Saddle River, Jew Jersey, 1996, ISBN 0-13-494758-4.

DCE (NCS) RPC Principles

Consider a single application written in C. It has the usual *main()* function which governs the entire application execution. Assuming that it's written in a fairly modular fashion, all the work is done by auxiliary functions. The main program simply passes parameters to the functions and receives the return values. This overhead is probably less than a few percent maximum. Such a program cannot take advantage of a second CPU. Only a faster system will increase its performance.

The DCE RPC, based on the network compute system (NCS) from Apollo Computers, includes a tool that lets you break the functions out of the main program, replace them with stubs, and move the code to server systems. The main program is unaware that the stubs are packing up the calling parameters and sending them across the network to one of many server systems. The functions in turn don't realize they're getting their parameters from remote server code. Admittedly, this program won't be able to take advantage of the multiprocessing available to it unless its coding is slightly modified to allow some parallelism. The main program needs to coordinate the remote functions.

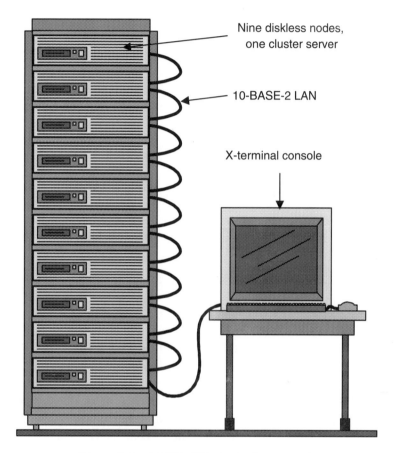

Nine diskless nodes,
one cluster server

10-BASE-2 LAN

X-terminal console

Figure 7-1   A 2000-MIP cluster in one rack
A simple compute cluster consists of 10 HP-UX workstations. The one "diskful"
cluster server is the single point of administration and holds all the O/S images and
application files for the cluster. The X-terminal logs the user into the cluster server,
which is used to coordinate the nine diskless compute nodes. With 200 MIPS and 128
MB of RAM per system, we have a 2000-MIP cluster with 1.28 gigabytes of RAM
to support it. This is a supercomputer built from scratch, and it's very scalable.

Consider a Snake farm, a cluster of HP-UX 700 series HP9000 diskless
workstations assembled into a single 19-inch rack and connected with small
thinLAN segments (see Figure 7-1). Only the cluster server has disks, and an

X-terminal is the user interface. Rack up ten 200-MIP systems and you have a 2000-MIP compute cluster.

Now take our parallelized application and load up each diskless system with a server process containing all the functions. The main program puts out a bid for each function call, and the server with the most available resources wins the bidding and gets to process the function call. This tends to load balance the cluster. Assuming that each function call takes 1000 milliseconds to execute and there is a 10-ms overhead for the calling sequence, this is 90% efficient. Therefore, ten diskless nodes in the cluster will perform as nine. Computer applications that can be parallelized include 3D rendering, ray tracing, computing fractal images, and searching for cryptographic keys.

With the general availability of DCE user threads, creating code to take advantage of compute clusters has never been easier.

Atria ClearCase Build Farms

ClearCase is a modern and sophisticated software development environment well suited for large teams of developers. It offers full source code control and supports distributed builds across multiple systems by taking advantage of custom *make* files. The source code resides on a single repository and NFS is used for file sharing. Builds tend to monopolize a system for the duration, so a load-balancing mechanism is needed to prevent too many builds from running on one system. An entire build farm lets the distributed *make* be spread across multiple systems via the *clearmake* command. See Figure 7-2.

Developers sitting at X-terminals (or desktop systems running X-terminal emulators) do their editing, scripting, documenting, and preliminary testing on development servers. A farm of development servers is required to support large teams, and load balancing plays a major part in assigning the best development server to a developer logging into the cluster. HP NCPM can be used to automate this.

A typical scenario will clarify all this. Suppose that our developer decides to work on some code and logs in at the X-terminal. NCPM assigns the best

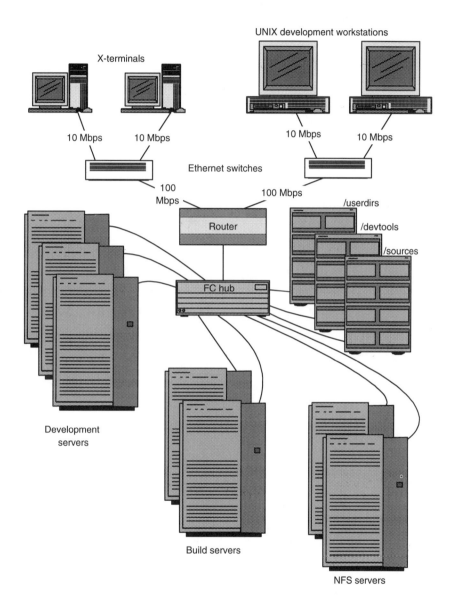

Figure 7-2   A ClearCase development architecture
This ClearCase software development environment shows both X-terminal and
UNIX workstation developments stations. All the UNIX server systems share a fibre
channel hub for NFS, intersystem communication, and disk access.

development system at that moment. The developer checks out some source code for modification, and the ClearCase NFS file server makes it available via an NFS mount to the development server. The developer works on this code for some time and then checks the code back in. At some point in time, sufficient code has been updated and it's time to do a build. The *clearmake* command constructs a dependency tree and writes a distributed *makefile* to take advantage of as much parallelism as possible. The development server executes the *makefile* and uses the resources of the build farm for the actual compiling and linking of the code.

This architecture is extremely scalable, because the number of development servers and build servers can be increased as necessary to accommodate the workload. If the source code NFS file server becomes too busy, it can be scaled or replicated, with an appropriate redistribution of source code. For large projects, a separate NFS file server is appropriate to contain the tools and home directories of the developers. Suffice to say, a LAN with adequate bandwidth is necessary to support the fairly serious NFS traffic generated by large development projects.

Note that we've talked about users with X-terminals gaining access to UNIX development servers. "But why not put UNIX workstations on each developers desk and avoid the need for development servers altogether?" you cry. In an all-UNIX environment this is quite common. But in other office environments, the desktop standard is an X-terminal, a Wintel box, or a Macintosh. Running X-window emulators on these desktops and using a development server farm makes sense in these environments because it reduces the cost of administering individual UNIX workstations, a few large development servers can be shared by many, it keeps the desktop system standard and general purpose, and office politics is followed.

Server Consolidation

Traditional distributed computing architectures place servers close to the user communities. A company with 200 offices worldwide would locate at least one server at each site. The servers host most of the local application binaries on network drives which users "share" or "mount" before using them. Hence the curious term "application server", when the term "file server" fits better. The network infrastructure capacity needed to support the traffic patterns of this configuration is modest.

Economies of system administration are a curious thing. The more remote the systems are, the greater the cost of administering them at the remote sites. It turns out that by consolidating servers into data centers, upgrading local desktop computers (especially their hard drive capacity), standardizing on productivity applications, and storing them on each desktop, serious money can be saved. This is so despite the expense of upgrading the network infrastructure to support the centralized approach.

UNIX servers are a natural choice in server consolidation projects. They scale very well, come with high-availability configurations, are remotely manageable via OpenView solutions and good old *telnet*, and come with industrial strength-applications.

References

Open Software Foundation, *Introduction to OSF DCE*. Upper Saddle River, NJ: Prentice Hall, 1995, ISBN: 0-13-185810-6.

Weygant, Peter S., *Clusters for High Availability, A Primer of HP-UX Solutions*. Upper Saddle River, NJ: Hewlett-Packard Professional Books, Prentice Hall, 1996, ISBN 0-13-494758-4.

CHAPTER   8

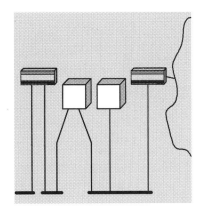

Network and UNIX Security

Introduction

UNIX network solutions are subject to security concerns because of real and perceived threats against the business that the solution supports. It's easy to list security features that are needed. Password protection, encryption, locked computer rooms, network firewalls, and virus protection are all popular security products and practices. This chapter will attempt to describe the more commonsense practices in UNIX system and network security.

The following is a list of technologies, tools, and products. Having them does not mean that you are secure.

SSL, C2, PGP
Password aging
Switched backbone
Smart card
Encryption
Cipher locks
SNMPv2
Kerberos, CHAP
Virus protection
Certificates
Screen covers
Firewalls
Badge reader

What is important is that security is more than buying and installing products. A very comprehensive threat analysis should be conducted to identify what is at risk, from whom, how the threat can be mitigated, and how to learn from security events. Thus the installation of a firewall against the potential threats posed by the unruly Internet does not itself provide protection.

In this chapter we'll see that security means different things to different organizations, so a methodology is needed to structure our analysis. We will present a few examples of security products such as DCE (distributed communications environment) and B-Level Security (BLS). And no UNIX security treatment is complete without discussing UNIX O/S and network application security measures, including auditing tools. Finally, we examine two contemporary service-denial attacks: the ping of death and the SYN attack.

Defining What Security Means in a Networked Environment

One definition of security is the prevention of loss by whatever means, such as the theft of equipment, illicit use or theft of resources, alteration of data, deletion of the data, theft or disclosure or ransom scenarios of data, and other threats to the business.

Simply having auditing tools, virus checkers on the Email gateway servers and desktop computers, locks on equipment rooms, and a staffed help desk does not mean that there is effective security. These are merely the trappings thereof.

The needs for security are best defined in the context of the business itself. Commercial banks need to control access to their business systems because they contain sensitive and confidential customer and banking data that must not fall into the wrong hands. Software developers need to guard access to their source code, trade secrets, and marketing plans lest a competitor acquire their most valuable secrets or delete their work efforts. An engineering company has to keep its technical plans safe to prevent disclosing sensitive information to clients that are also competitors. A manufacturer's product schedules and marketing plans are competitive information to be guarded at all cost. The White House is also very interested in maintaining the necessary secrecy to protect the contents of confidential and secret discussions. Even countries have their own definitions of national security. In general, security should be a part of all business continuity planning, even if that business is running a country.

Structured Security Requirements Analysis

Consider a security "event," break-in, or theft as a sequence of six subevents (Figure 8-1). The event that happens first is that somebody becomes aware that there is something they can do to your business. They find out where your offices are located, learn the nature of your business, observe the coming and goings, check the Internet for public information, and even make contact with employees. The purpose of this activity is clear - to find a way to steal something. Therefore the first step in establishing security is to limit your visibility and make it hard to monitor your activities. For example, locking up datacom gear limits "sniffing" opportunities.

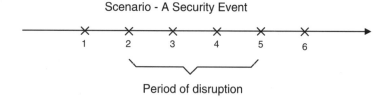

Scenario - A Security Event

Period of disruption

1 You are being cased   4 Correction

2 An attack occurs and succeeds   5 Normal operations resume

3 Detection   6 Ask "What did we learn?"

Figure 8-1   Phases of a security event

Each of the six phases of a security event should be analyzed to devise the means to limit exposure and mitigate risk (avoid, deter, prevent, shorten, minimize). Take advantage of asking six basic questions at each point: "who, what, when, where, why, and how."

The second event is the actual attack, whereby access to equipment or people is gained and stolen or information is altered or deleted. Given that a break-in will occur, the appropriate countermeasure is to limit the amount or degree of the theft. For example, by insisting that users have different passwords on different systems, a break-in of one system limits the damage to one system because the same password is not used anywhere else.

The third event occurs when the attack is detected. Detection may occur almost immediately in the case of a service-denial attack. But if information is merely copied, it may take a private detective of the caliber of Sir Arthur Conan Doyle to figure out exactly when and how the attack occurred, and it may be months to years before it is apparent at all. Swift detection is obviously a critical requirement, and the frequent review of audit logs is one way to ensure this.

The fourth event is correction. Given that a successful or unsuccessful attack occurred, what can now be done to avoid a repeat performance? Was something overlooked? Was someone careless? Is there a heretofore unknown bug or loophole in the firewall? What can be done to repair the damage? A backup tape with a known good version of the deleted or altered information should be available on short notice. A bug fix from the firewall vendor will close the loophole.

The fifth event is the resumption of normal service. Ideally, this happens as soon as possible after the correction phase, and the staff and customers are advised that the coffee break is over.

The sixth and last event is a "what did we learn?" exercise, a meeting with affected parties to share all information related to the break-in. Table 8-1 provides some additional details.

Table 8-1   Risk mitigation

Security Event Phase	Steps to Minimize Exposure
1. You are being cased.	**[privacy]** Limit information available and hide it: encryption, limited DNS, paper shredders, switches, secure hubs, security policy, training, screen covers, nonstandard SNMP community name, limit server SAP packets, no RIP, digital signatures.
2. An attack occurs.	**[opportunity]** Minimize access opportunities and limit exposure: strong authentication such as a password policy (password aging, system assigned passwords, delete users who leave the project), access controls, locks on equipment rooms, virus checkers active, periodic audit, all the usual security products are in place and checked out, limit dynamic configurations (no RIP, ARP), router filters, firewalls, RAS.
3. You detect the attack.	**[detection]** Event logs, monitoring, event correlation, system audit logs, error messages, complaints, crashes (other than the usual), loss of data, unimaginable horrors, cameras, audit tool (SATAN, COPS, O/S), sniffer tools, virus checker, 5 PM news.
4. You fix the mess.	**[correction]** Planning, support, backup tapes, written procedures, help desk, security force, CERT, vendor patch, tools, disaster recovery plan, incident response team gets to work, fix the damage, restore files, close loophole.
5. Service is restored.	**[communication]** Relay the security facts to the users.
6. What did you learn?	**[analysis]** Post-mortem, review logs, interview affected users, modify tools and procedures, plug the hole, update security policy.

For each of the six phases of a security event, it is critical to devise the means to avoid, deter, detect, prevent, shorten, minimize, and document all aspects. A simple methodology to assist in this activity is to ask six simple questions: who, what, when, where, why, and how?

Table 8-2 gives an example of using this methodology.

Table 8-2   Risk analysis: Who, what, where, when, why, and how

Category	Examples
What is the asset at risk (any resource - information, hardware, market share, credibility)?	Data, hardware, reputation, trade secrets, methods, timely information, servers, workstations, print-outs, backup tapes, ATM machine, reports, competitive information, trust, market share, mind share, credibility, loyal customers
How is the risk realized (method of attack)?	Destruction, fire, deletion, duplication, interception, modification, deny access, Email spam, virus, protocol attack, *.rhosts*, configuration errors, bug in O/S, special feature of the program, public disclosure, Email message, laser microphones, physical theft, sniffers, RF scanners, EMP guns, ESP
Who is the risk due to (persons, organizations)?	Competitors, customers, visitors, governments, Internet users, insiders, family members, spies, aliens
When does the risk take place (time of day, an event)?	Lunchtime, midnight, shift change, an employee is fired, the weekend, long weekend, during backup time
Why does this risk exist (motivation)?	Profit, competitive advantage, embarrassment, revenge, sensationalism, win a bet, rather steal than buy, accident
Where does the risk exist (physically, logically, conceptually?	Computer room, remote office, datacom closet, foreign country, sales office, copy room, the minds of the public

Internet Firewall Design

Businesses often need direct connections to the Internet, but don't want their business systems exposed. Security inside the corporate network is generally inadequate to withstand the rigors of Internet exposure, so a firewall is inserted between the ISP and the corporate network (Figure 8-2). The firewall acts as a filter to allow specific services to pass traffic into the network, to allow specific services to pass out, and to block the rest. Table 8-3 lists the major components of a firewall.

Table 8-3   Major features of a firewall

Feature	Why Is It There?
Proxy server	Application gateway passes local client packets to *sockd* circuit relay
Sockd	Circuit relay passes client-initiated connections to the Internet
Bastion	Provides packet filtering, limited services, and event logging
Public DNS	Offers only required Address, Name, and MX records to the Internet
Router R1 and R2	R1 filters allow incoming protocols to specific network destinations
DMZ	Insecure LAN segment known to the Internet
SSN	Secure server network, reachable at bastion's discretion
Remote access	Authenticates remote dial-up PPP users and connects them to the little i

A general rule for configuring the elements of a firewall is to hard wire all configurable parameters. This means static routing tables instead of RIP protocol, */etc/hosts* files instead of DNS, and fixed arp tables. Another rule,

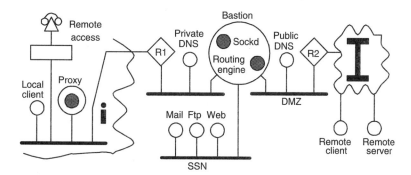

Figure 8-2   Internet firewall architecture
This firewall design connects the Internet (the big I) with the private corporate network (the little i). The demilitarized zone (DMZ) is usually a small class C subnet,
which may host a public name server and optionally mail, web, and FTP servers. The
DMZ is directly accessible from the Internet, and all systems connected directly to it
may be attacked and cracked. The bastion host polices access to systems on the secure server network (SSN). The bastion also runs the *sockd* daemon to support circuit
relay connections initiated from the private network destined for the internet.

adopted from satellite payload designers, is that the components should be
simple. Bent pipes are very reliable. All exposed servers should run just a
single service to keep them simple.

DCE Security Model and HP Praesidium

The DCE security model uses Kerberos to provide authentication services between client systems and servers. Because a client cannot be trusted to authenticate itself, DCE provides the Kerberos authentication server, which is trusted by both clients and servers alike. This way the server can be sure that the client is who it says it is, and the client can be sure it's connecting to a legitimate server.

The trusted Kerberos database contains information about clients, including their ID, password, and session key. When a user logs in with its ID, its client system encrypts it and sends that to Kerberos, Kerberos creates a new session key and stores it and then encrypts the key along with the user password and returns it to the client. The client system then asks for the user password and checks it against that given by the ticket. If this is successful, the client system now has the necessary credentials in this ticket to access the necessary servers.

Kerberos is secure because it uses DES encryption, an industry standard, to protect all data transmissions. It is reliable because slave servers may be added to the network to protect against the failure of the primary server.

HP's Praesidium product is a Kerberos product that allows application developers to use APIs in their client and server code to provide a standards-based security model supportable by a Kerberos ticket granting server. To integrate legacy applications, gateways and surrogates are provided.

B-level Security

For completeness, Table 8-4 lists features of the official B-level security definition. Commercial products implement these additional security features.

Table 8-4   BLS features

Requirement	Meaning
Accountability: I&A	Individuals must identify themselves to the system, and the system must be able to authenticate user identities.
Accountability: Audit	Users must be accountable for their actions. The system records in an audit trail each security-related event and the user who caused that event to occur.
Object reuse	When an object is initially assigned, allocated, or reallocated to a subject, that object must not contain any data that the subject is not authorized to access.
Discretionary access control (DAC)	An owner of an object containing data must be able to allow or deny access to that object based on a need-to-know basis.
Labels	The system must maintain a sensitivity label associated with each subject and object.
Mandatory access control (MAC)	The system must determine whether a particular subject has authorization to access a particular object based on the sensitivity labels of the subject and the object.
Privilege mechanism	Capabilities necessary to perform its assigned operation, and should keep those capabilities only for the duration of the operation. *Note*: This is an extended security function that is not a requirement for B1 rating.

UNIX System Security

The security of a running UNIX O/S is maintained by running the auditing and reporting tools provided with it. Account management ensures that user passwords are hard to guess and easy to remember, user IDs are unique and uncompromised, and access to files, scripts, client software, and applications is thus protected using session controls. This includes remote-system access via UUCP (UNIX to UNIX copy), RAS (remote-access server), or PPP (point-to-point protocol). Duplicate user IDs and correct membership in group IDs is also checked periodically. Passwords are checked to ensure they're not easy to guess or found in */usr/dict/words*. Password aging may be enabled to force users to pick a new password periodically and to prevent them from changing them too soon after.

Account management also includes a backup and recovery strategy. The system itself may be converted to a "trusted system," which, among other things, removes the encrypted passwords from the world-readable */etc/passwd* file and saves them in an unreadable shadow password file.

Product files are those files that are installed when a product is loaded onto the system. The integrity of these product description files (PDF) can be checked using the *pdfck* command to see if executable files have permissions altered, file sizes changed, and configuration files removed. For example, the following command checks the integrity of the EDITORS file set:

pdfck /system/EDITORS/pdf

System auditing is done using commands such as *last* and *lastb*, which allow the system manager to check the recent login history as well as the failed login attempts. These logs can also be checked automatically by HP's IT Operations (ITO) daemons to report suspicious user activity. The system's auditing subsystem is capable of monitoring and logging system calls and file accesses. A partial list of audit events is given in Table 8-5.

Table 8-5   HP-UX audit events

Event	Description
create	File and directory creation
delete	File and directory removal
moddac	Modification of discretionary access controls
open	Open files or directories
close	Close files or directories
removable	Media actions like mount and umount
login	Logins and logouts
ipccreate	Interprocess communication socket creation
ipcopen	IPC open
ipcclose	IPC close

Additional routing system checks are also made to verify the correctness, existence, and proper file permissions of

> Disk special files for I/O in */dev/rdsk* and */dev/dsk*
> Kernel files, such as */hp-ux, /dev/mem,* and */dev/kmem*
> Setuid and getuid bits on executable files
> Permissions on system directories, such as */dev, /etc/, /bin*, and */usr*
> Command files, such as *sh, csh,* and *ksh*

One threat to the security of a UNIX system is insufficient care in administering the superuser *root* account. Therefore, *root*'s password should be difficult to guess and changed often. Cloning *root* entries in */etc/passwd* will allow multiple users to login as *root*-capable to ensure *root* is never locked out of the system. Also ensure that *root* does not login directly as *root*, but uses *su* to change login IDs only when *root* capabilities are needed.

Only allow *root* to login directly at the system console, not through the network, by configuring */etc/securetty*. Ensure that the *$PATH* variable does not contain a period to prevent a *PATH* attack, and ensure that the default *umask* in not all zeros to prevent *root* from inadvertently creating world writable files by default.

UNIX Network Application Security

Application security begins with the HP-UX */usr/adm/inetd.sec* file. It lists the permitted services by TCP and UDP port numbers and permitted client systems by IP address (or name) via an allow or deny paradigm. Access to all services started by *inetd* as given in */etc/inetd.conf* can be so governed. Specific network services have specific security features that may be used, as given in Table 8-6.

Table 8-6   Securing network services

Service	Security Files and Other Notes
NFS	*/etc/exports* limits access to listed clients. */etc/netgroups* limits access to those listed in the group. Export files read-only wherever possible. Deny *root* access (even though it may be useful at times).
telnet	Comment out the */etc/telnetd* line in */etc/inetd.conf* to prevent users from logging into the system. Configure *telnetd* to issue a "permitted use" message.
FTP	*/etc/ftpusers* denies listed users access. Ensure that anonymous FTP users are rooted at */users/ftp*.
TFTP	Limit access to the home directory listed in */etc/passwd*.
SMTP	Audit sendmail.cf for wizard or decode entries.
r-commands	Avoid "++" entry in */etc/hosts.equiv*.

Table 8-6   Securing network services (Continued)

Service	Security Files and Other Notes
SNMP	Don't run it on firewall bastions. Configure community names.
finger	Turn it off.
routed/gated	Configure in trusted sources of RIP.
rwhod	Turn it off.
bootp	Use DHCP instead if you can.
printer/lpr	Ensure that client systems are in the DNS.

UNIX Tools for Auditing

COPS, CRACK, and SATAN are public domain tools for checking UNIX
system and network security. COPS checks the system's network services
configuration, CRACK checks for easily guessed passwords, and SATAN
checks UNIX network service integrity via the network itself.

UNIX Remote Access Checklist

Modems allow remote terminal users to dial up a UNIX system, log in, do
useful work using text-based tools, and log out. Since a modem makes it
easier for crackers to attack the system, special files should be configured to
limit access and reduce the risk of penetration:

/etc/dialups
/etc/d_passwd
/etc/securetty

These files allow the system manager to establish an additional dial-up password that users must know in addition to their personal account ID and password. It is interesting to note that the UNIX system will give no clue as to which of these three strings are incorrect.

Modem access requires the system manager to address these datacom cases:

The user logs off normally from the remote terminal. The system modem should hang up and reset to allow a new call and a new login sequence.

The user's remote terminal is powered off during a session. The system modem should hang up when it detects the loss of data carrier. The user session and all its programs should be terminated by the system.

The telephone connection is broken during a session. The system modem should hang up when it detects the loss of data carrier. The user session and all programs should be terminated by the system

The modem detects a loss of data carrier during a session. The system should terminate the session and all the user programs.

The login program terminates for any reason during a session. This causes all child processes to terminate and the modem to hang up.

A long period of session keyboard inactivity is noted. This should invoke the terminal timeout feature and automatically log out the user.

Wiretapping threats exist whenever a leased or switched line is accessible. Data encryption can protect the data.

Callback modem support. The user dials in, enters an ID, and hangs up. The system consults its database and calls the user back at a fixed telephone number. The user logs in as usual and terminates the session as before.

Modems pick up in originate mode (no carrier on answer). This prevents a modem detection program from randomly dialing the system and discovering the modem via its answer tone. The calling modem is in answer mode and the system modem is in originate mode. This is reversed from what is normally done.

PPP authentication. The PPP protocol provides connection setup, authentication, and network services between the remote computer and the system.

Credit card challenge–response system. The user logs in and the system challenges with a one-time sequence of digits. The user enters these into a credit-card-sized device to calculate the response. It's valid for 1e minute. The user enters this response as a password and is authenticated.

HP9000 RS-232-C ports connected to modems should be configured to require the user to type in a dial-up password. This is controlled from the file */etc/dialups*. All ports listed here (by their UNIX device file name) cause the

UNIX login program to request a dial-up password as well as the usual login and account password. This applies to SLIP, UUCP, and interactive logins.

A sample */etc/dialups* file might be

```
/dev/culd0p1
/dev/culd0p2
/dev/culd0p3
/dev/culd0p4
/dev/ttyd0p1
/dev/ttyd0p2
/dev/ttyd0p3
/dev/ttyd0p4
```

Incoming modem callers on these lines are prompted for a dial-up password found in the file */etc/d_passwd*, which might look like this:

```
/etc/ppllogin::
/usr/bin/ppl::
/etc/tz_uucico::
/bin/sh:sH43RZykWIvjE::
```

The first three entries (ppllogin, ppl and tz_uucico) are SLIP and UUCP protocols. The entry for sh applies to all interactive users running the C, Bourne, or Korn shells.

Note that SLIP is a protocol to allow IP datagrams to be transmitted over RS-232 connections. Where MODEMS are used to extend RS-232 lines, SLIP may be used as well, creating a simple wide-area network (WAN) point-to-point link.

Also note that, in general, the analog data transmitted by a modem onto a telephone circuit are subject to the usual wire tapping attack associated with voice callers. Here the line is tapped and the signals are recorded on ordinary analog tape. The tape is played back later into a modem connected to a printer, CRT, or computer. The ASCII data stream may be examined at leisure for sensitive information.

HP Support Watch, which uses many of the same modules as Remote Watch, is usually configured by the HP account CE. It uses *cron* to time schedule checks of log files such as disk and memory error logs, examines configurable thresholds, and calculates some predictive statistics. It can be configured to use the support modem to dial the HP Response Center to upload the summary of a problem. A Response Center engineer will review the log and arrange to dial into the system to examine the detailed logs.

There is no security risk with the system autodialing the HP Response Center computer and delivering its summary report, since no capability to reverse-log in exists during this connection.

The Ping-of-Death Attack

The ping command is used to send an ICMP loopback packet to a remote system, which loops it back to the sender. It verifies IP connectivity. The user can vary the size of the packet. The command invocation parameters are

> ping [-rvo] host [packet size] [npackets]

where

> -r: bypass normal routing tables
> -v: verbose, shows ICMP traffic other than the echo response
> -o record the route of all packets sent
> Host is the name/IP of the target system
> Packet size number of bytes from 8 to 4096
> Count is the number of packets to receive before quitting

ICMP (internet control message protocol) is defined in RFC 792. It is used by network management stations like HP OpenView Network Node Manager as a keep-alive check on all managed devices. Systems that support multiple default routes use it to check the state of these routes. Turning it off limits the manageability of a system.

The ping-of-death attack takes advantage of any */etc/ping* program that allows the user to send ICMP loopback packets of arbitrary size. Some IP stacks will crash their O/S when they receive an ICMP request larger than 65,535 bytes, making this a service-denial attack.

The O/S or IP stack vendor needs to patch its code to prevent this attack, but in many situations a network manager can simply filter out ICMP loopback request packets entering via a router.

The SYN Attack

A TCP connection is established between an originating client and a target server according to Table 8-7.

Table 8-7   TCP connection establishment sequence

Step	Packet	Description
1	SYN	Client sends SYN to server; server allocates TCP buffer pool and table space, which may be from 2 to 128 Kbytes.
2	SYN-ACK	Server sends client a SYN-ACK to acknowledge the connection request and provide its byte sequence number.
3	SYN-ACK	Client sends server a SYN-ACK to acknowledge server's byte sequence number and provide client's own.

A SYN attack is mounted by an application that transmits a fast stream of SYN packets to a server, with the intent of forcing the server to allocate all available memory resources in a very short space of time. This service denial attack will not crash the server, but it prevents new legitimate TCP connections from being accepted until the hanging connections are timed out. A vendor patch is needed to prevent SYN attacks from succeeding.

A Security Tale

Suppose you found out that a certain system administrator created new accounts and assigned a temporary password equal to the account name. Suppose you also know that many users granted such accounts don't use them for several months. So one day you find (or legitimately obtain) such an account, log in, and copy the *etc/passwd* file to your desktop computer over the network. *etc/passwd* lists all the account names, so you write a small script that tries each account in turn, using the account name as the password. You change the account password for all those cracked. Next day you sell these accounts to paying customers, who may not know better. Free enterprise is alive and well.

Why tell such a tale, you cry? Because it exemplifies the potential consequences of disregarding well-established network and system security practice. Passwords should not be easily guessed, idle accounts should be deactivated, and better authentication schemes should be used.

References

Contemporary references on almost any subject, including security, are available on the Internet by visiting one's favorite search engine, such as that located at

http://altavista.digital.com

and using the search terms such as

+"white paper" +"unix security"

where the plus signs indicate mandatory fields and the quotations define an exact string to be matched. The string "white paper" can help produce a relatively short list of high-quality hits.

UNIX systems are extremely robust and virtually immune to virus attacks due to their remarkably robust architecture and design. Because UNIX file and Email servers may be the repository of Wintel or Macintosh viruses, it is useful to remain current by visiting antiviral vendor web sites such as those of MacAfee, DataWatch, Dr. Solomon, and Symantec.

Firewalls and Internet Security, Repelling the Wily Hacker by William R. Cheswick and Steven M. Bellovin (Reading, MA: Addison Wesley, 1994, ISBN: 0-201-63357-4) is a good reference. It has a good UNIX flavor that you'll enjoy.

CHAPTER 9

Electronic Messaging

Introduction

This is a chapter about Email. The parts that comprise a messaging system include gateways to translate messages between various proprietary and standards-based mail systems, user agents (mailers), a protocol to transfer messages between mail hubs, a protocol to let users read their mail, and a protocol to send complex messages that include exotic data like documents and multimedia content.

We will review why we have difficulties even today sending and receiving even simple messages, never mind messages with attachments between different platforms. A discussion about messaging architectures will precede a review of HP OpenMail and its gateway features that make it such a great Email hub.

Sending messages is made easier when we have a directory service to look up somebody's Email address, beyond using a carefully cultivated personal electronic address book or resorting to an Internet search engine such as *www.four11.com* or *www.switchboard.com*.

Email on the Internet is basically the simple mail transfer protocol (SMTP) implemented using the UNIX *sendmail* daemon, a simple ASCII-based protocol. The addition of multipurpose Internet messaging extensions (MIME) allows SMTP to pass multiple ASCII or binary attachments via MIME headers and ASCII encoding.

And no discussion of Email systems is complete without a review of the post office protocol (POP3), which gives Internet users access to their Email servers.

Why Can't We Just Send Email?

Let's list what we need to send Email:

> A user agent (Email program) for manipulating messages
> A distribution list (directory service) for looking up Email addresses
> A mail hub (where user mailboxes sit and other functions live)

A connection to the mail hub (such as dial-up PPP or LAN)
Store and forward messages (get messages to their destination)
A valid POP to store messages
A user whose agent retrieves the messages

To support all this functionality, additional support is required:

DNS MX records stored in DNS servers
SMTP relay systems, perhaps the mail hubs themselves
TCP/IP network links for end-to-end transport of the messages
Disk space to store messages

So what can possibly go wrong? At each point along its journey an Email message is subject to grief. Problems with the user and system ID, the network, the intermediate mail systems, the DNS servers, and the user's configurations can all prevent delivery of Email messages. Let's explore these problems in a little more detail.

The message user ID may be wrong (it's misspelled, become inactive, or the user account is deleted) and can't be delivered into a mailbox. The domain name attached to the ID may be incorrect (a forgotten period, a missing subdomain, or a misspelling). *Firstname_Lastname@company.com* is an example of very common convention for Email addresses. But the user may actually be known internally as *firstname@mailer1.eng.company.com* to the corporate Email system. This is called address mapping. The chances are that both address forms will be used to send messages, so the company's Email system must be well administered to avoid bouncing back messages.

What else can go wrong? Intermediate SMTP remailers may be congested, unresponsive, or misconfigured. The user's PPP connection may be noisy, preventing transmission of the messages. The message may be so large that some mail systems refuse to process it. The SMTP/POP server may be down, so messages can't be sent or received by the user. The client system has incorrect DNS entries that prevent successful lookups. Variations in the MIME encoding support can trash an attachment (UUDECODE, BinHex, and Base-64). Some mailers break up large messages into smaller chunks, and this may destroy the attachment unless the user is very skilled in the reconstruction process. Filters at SMTP remailers may block messages because they are mistaken for spam. Even the user agent may have filters set that give the appearance that a message wasn't delivered.

Messaging Architectures

In this diagram-rich section we'll review the flow of messages and the relationships among the various components that comprise a messaging architecture. One point of view will be of the physical connections among the components (Figure 9-1), and another will be the open systems interconnect (OSI) view (Figure 9-2). Both are very useful representations to help understand electronic messaging.

The OSI viewpoint looks at the seven functional layers of our messaging system. Two systems communicate via a client–server paradigm. Recall that the OSI model requires that information physically move up and down the layers. Logically, each layer communicates with its peer on the corresponding system. Each layer has an address that it uses to identify itself and its peer. For example, the IP address of the source and destination systems is always present in the packet header at layer 3.

The structure of the messages is very simple. All the data are 7-bit ASCII as defined by the SMTP standard. This includes the simple ASCII headers that SMTP uses to determine message source, destination, and routing information. SMTP supports just one simple text message. When the mail client program supports attached text and binary files, it will add additional MIME headers to mark such attachments. Binary attachments will be encoded to convert them to 7-bit ASCII using UNIX-style *uuencode*, Macintosh-style *binhex*, or general-purpose *base-64* standards. MIME will mark the start and end of these attachments with special character strings to let the recipient's mailer find their boundaries. MIME headers and data look like ordinary ASCII text to SMTP and not processed at all, just treated like text.

Note that the Email system described can work perfectly, but if the message recipient should suddenly switch to an email program that does not understand one of the MIME encodings, then the message received will be a "garbled mess." This is a technical term for what the user will report when trying to read the ASCII encoding of the attached file. The name of the attached file is usually visible in the headers.

A good hacker will have no trouble passing the message through one of the freeware encode–decode programs like the UNIX *uudecode*, the Macintosh

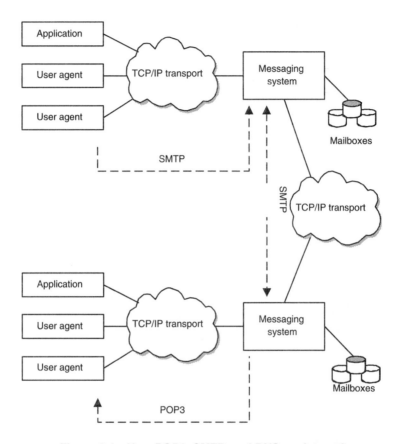

Figure 9-1   How POP3, SMTP, and DNS work together
Physical connectivity among the Email components begins with a user agent such as
Netscape Messenger or an MAPI-enable application sending a message, possibly
with MIME-attached components, to the designated SMTP mail server. From there
the *sendmail* daemon uses SMTP to move the message toward the destination messaging system. The destination system name is found by looking up the mail exchange (MX) record for the destination system using DNS. The destination
messaging system will deposit the message into the user mailbox, where it languishes
until the user agent or application retrieves it and (optionally) deletes it from the mailbox using POP3.

StuffIt Expander, and the general-purpose *Ya-Base64*. For particularly
challenging messages, some manual editing of the message may be
necessary, a good application for the *vi* text editor. There are three kinds of

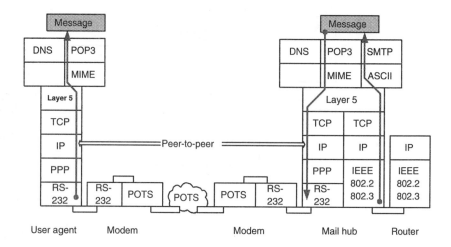

Figure 9-2   The OSI view of messaging
This OSI view of Email begins with the SMTP mail server accepting a message for
a recipient with a local mailbox. When the user agent connects via their PPP connection and authenticates with the POP3 daemon (layer 5 session functionality at work),
the message is copied to the user hard drive and deleted from the server mailbox.

users: those who use *vi*, those who wish they could, and those who don't
know any better.

From the user point of view, a messaging backbone supports their Email. A
messaging architecture may consist simply of a backbone of interconnected
SMTP machines supported by DNS. The POP3 servers reside on the outer
systems where the users are located.

Such an architecture (Figure 9-3) has three tiers: the client, the POP3 server,
and the SMTP backbone systems. The backbone may be configured to be
highly reliable and capable of surviving outages. The means to this end
require serious administrations over the *sendmail* configuration files. Should
a POP3/SMTP server goes down, the user is in trouble, because its mailbox
isn't accessible. But by replicating user accounts on these servers, the user is
able to reconfigure its Emailer to use an alternative POP3 server. The
backbone SMTP servers need to be configured to take advantage of the
alternative local mail server.

Back in the good old days, everybody had a trusty UNIX workstation on their desktop or an account on a shared UNIX system and used an X-terminal to take advantage of the excellent multitasking X-window system. The text-based mailer *elm* or the *Zmail* X-window mailer gave users direct access to their mailboxes. Each UNIX system would run *sendmail* with a suitable *sendmail.cf* configuration file. The workstations were powered up and connected to the network at all times. Under these conditions, there was no need for POP3.

Enter desktop computers that don't have a reliable multitasking operating system, that are not always turned on, and that might even be taken home in the case of laptop computers. There is no stable mailbox for reliable Email delivery. Then came the Internet with users dialing in at random to read their Email. Clearly, another Email protocol is needed to collect Email messages from the point of presence (the stable UNIX mail server at the ISP) and copy them over the dial-up PPP connection to the home computer. That is the reason that the POP3 protocol is needed today. It is build right into the popular web browsers, and many fine stand-alone POP3 Emailers such as Qualcomm's Eudora are available, too.

Directory Services

To call someone on the telephone you don't just pick up the phone and say "call The Shadow". We are not in the 23rd century and Communicators haven't been invented yet. You have to dial a number not found in any telephone directory in this case. If someone doesn't want you to know their number, they pay the telephone company good money for an unpublished number. If you want to find someone's published phone number, you can look it up in a directory yourself or call 555-1212 for this information. But you know all this.

To send Email to someone, you need to know their Email address. But you may not know it, so you can look it up in your personal Email address book or go through some old Email messages in the hope that a message from this person is still saved. You may have to call them on the telephone to get their email address. The Email address firstname_lastname@company.com will work on a good day. Otherwise, you can try the Internet and visit

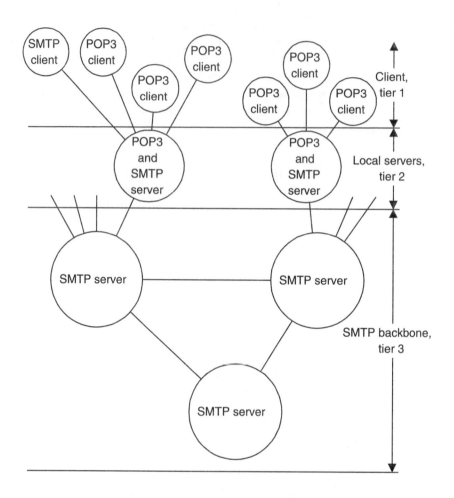

Figure 9-3   Three tiers and the messaging backbone

A three-tier messaging architecture looks like a messaging backbone to the user community. The backbone is redundant from a messaging perspective, and the network itself must be redundant, else all this is for naught. Tier 2 POP3/SMTP servers should be configured to allow users to switch in the event that a local server goes down. Indeed, this may turn out to be an excellent application for the HP Network Connection Policy Manager. At the upper-left corner of the diagram sits a rebellious UNIX workstation running *sendmail*. This user has placed an entry in the *.forward* file in the *$HOME* directory, so *sendmail* forwards mail to the UNIX workstation. This workstation is still able to use Netscape Communicator and POP3.

www.switchboard.com or *www.four11.com*. What we're sorely missing is a directory service for looking up the Email addresses of people. We also need a directory repository, of course, with its privacy implications.

Proprietary Email systems such as HPDesk have no problem with this. HPDesk users just type in the name of the intended recipient, and the system automagically finds their location and fills it in for you. cc:Mail works the same way, as does IBM's PROFFS program. These systems are used by private companies, so the community of users is well known, and the maintenance of these directories is standard operating procedure. As employees join and leave the company or if they change locations, there are procedures in place that touch corporate Email system configuration.

The X.500 distributed directory service provides a standard way to build Email directory services, but it's not been adopted widely. Programs like Qualcomm's Eudora provide directory lookups via *finger* and *ph servers*. Lightweight Directory Access Protocol (LDAP) is a contemporary (1998) standard that shows some promise, but the matter of building the directory itself remains.

HP OpenMail and Email Gateways

Email gateways accept messages over a variety of formats, protocols, and networks, convert them as necessary, and forward them toward their destination. The HP OpenMail product is capable of accepting messages from HP Desk, SMTP, cc:Mail, X.400, and UUCP. The administrator defines a set of forwarding rules that the gateway executes for each message received (Figure 9-4). These rules deal with transforming user names, attachments, urgency and acknowledgment flags, and the "cc" and "bcc" fields. Note that the *sendmail* daemon itself is able to act as a gateway among SMTP, UUCP, X.400, and user agents like *mail*, *mailx*, *elm*, *advmail*, *pine*, and *Zmail*.

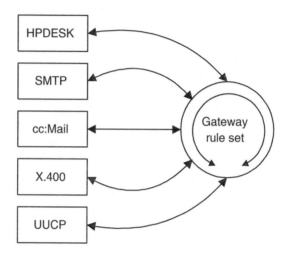

Figure 9-4   The Email gateway rule set
This is an overview of an Email gateway that moves messages between five nonin-
teroperable systems: HPDesk, SMTP, cc:Mail, X.400, and UUCP. HPDesk, SMTP,
and cc:Mail all use TCP/IP, but X.400 uses the OSI protocols, while UUCP uses dial-
up modem connections and the UNIX's own UUCP protocol. This means the gateway has to support multiple protocol stacks and network interfaces in addition to the
messaging protocols unique to each Email system.

SMTP

Simple mail transfer protocol (SMTP) is designed to be simple. It provides
simple ASCII commands and single-part 7-bit ASCII messages. SMTP is so
simple that with just a little effort a knowledgeable user can use the
command *telnet hostname 25* to engage *sendmail*, which listens on TCP port
25, in a conversation and send a message to a user. Even a help command is
available. SMTP uses specially formatted ASCII headers to process
messages. The *sendmail* daemon implements SMTP. It also understands
UUCP and X.400 messaging when properly configured. The file *sendmail.cf*
drives *sendmail*.

The *sendmail* daemon deposits messages into user mailboxes. If the user has a file called *.forward* in its home directory, then *sendmail* will use the forwarding address it finds there and transmit the message to that system.

The sendmail daemon is able to deliver mail even to unreachable systems, such as those behind corporate firewalls. For example, if *dick@dickssystem.dickscompany.com* and *jane@janessystem.janescompany.com* want to exchange Email, and both *dickscompany* and *janesscompany* use firewalls, then their systems cannot send messages directly back and forth.

Enter the domain name system (DNS). Each company places a mail hub on the Internet side (DMZ) of their firewalls. See Figure 9-5. Each company's DNS server, also on their respective DMZs, serves up not just IP addresses but also mail exchange (MX) records. The internal DNS systems at each company supply MX addresses for internal use. Thus, when dick's system wants to sent a message to jane, *sendmail* will look up the MX record for *janessystem.janescompany.com* and DNS will return the name of the system to which the message should be forwarded. This will be *mailgateway.dickscompany.com,* and a name request to DNS will return the IP address for it. So *sendmail* passes the massage to the corporate gateway.

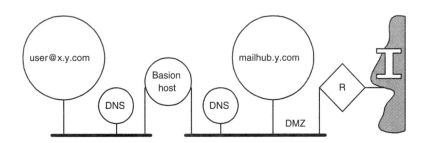

Figure 9-5   SMTP and the Internet firewall
SMTP messaging between a private network and the Internet (the big I) takes advantage of the domain name system (DNS) to locate the mail exchange (MX) record of the forwarding system. Thus, mail from *user@x.y.com* to *user2@a.z.com* (not shown) will be forwarded to *mailhub.y.com*, then to *mailhub.z.com* (not shown), and finally to *user2*'s mailbox on *a.z.com*. Note that this is a simplified example, since the network topology will be more complex, there are likely more intermediate SMTP systems than shown, and the effects of the bastion host and router are ignored.

Now the mail hub *mailgateway.dickscompany.com* has to forward the message to *janessystem.janescompany.com* and so *sendmail* there looks up the MX record, gets the name *mailgateway.janescompany.com*, looks up its IP address, and forwards the message. Now *sendmail* at *janessystem.janescompany.com* looks up the MX record for *janessystem.janescompany.com* and gets back (as a hush falls over the audience) *janessystem.janescompany.com*. A name request to DNS returns the IP address and sendmail delivers the message to the *sendmail* at *janessystem.janescompany.com,* which delivers the message into jane's mailbox. Each store and forward adds a header to the message to mark its passing through that point.

To overcome the single-part ASCII message limitation, we have multipurpose Internet mail extensions (MIME) for encoding attachment files into ASCII format. The MIME ASCII headers are transparent to *sendmail,* which sees just one possibly very long ASCII message. It is up to dick and jane's Email programs to parse the MIME headers, decode each attachment, and create a properly named file for each.

POP3

Post office protocol version 3 (POP3) provides Email access to users whose systems are not permanently connected to a network, not always powered on, or otherwise unable to reliably receive Email. Given that SMTP mailers will eventually give up trying to deliver messages, some means is needed to deliver the mail into the user mailbox even when that user's system isn't available.

Enter POP3. See Figure 9-6. Users are given accounts on a system with a POP3 server, and their computers run a POP3-capable client like Eudora or Netscape Messager. The POP3 client connects to the POP3 server, identifies the user by name, and offers a password for authentication. The POP3 client can then discover what messages are waiting, copy them to the user's local hard drive, and delete them from the server. Suppose that a user (for some reason) is having problems with the POP3 mailer. The user can simply *telnet* to the UNIX POP3 server, log in as itself, and use the ASCII-only *elm* mailer to read the mail in its mailbox, even reply to it or delete it. Internet service providers offer this capability as a standard service to their customers.

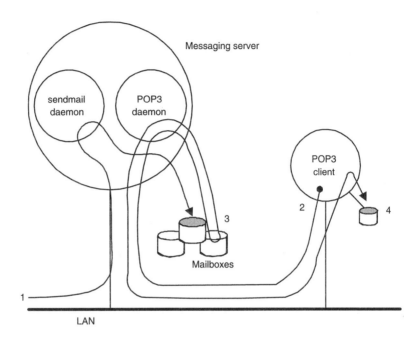

Figure 9-6   POP3 message flow
Mail arrives (1) at the mail server via SMTP and sendmail deposits it into the user mailbox. Later the user (2) logs into the POP3 server and downloads the message from the mailbox (3) onto its local hard drive (4).

POP3 clients are minimally configured with the following information:

       Domain name of the SMTP mail server to send mail to
       Domain name of the POP3 mail server to read mail from
       User name and password
       User email address and a reply-to email address
       Name of a signature file

Miscellaneous Email Issues

Sending large attachments is still a problem today (1998) because mail server administrators have to limit the total disk usage to avoid filling it and rendering the server useless. Store-and-forward systems only save messages for retransmission, but again disk space issues may force their administrators to limit maximum message size. The user has no recourse but to compress the data, break up the file into smaller pieces, and try again.

Since the commercialization of the Internet, spam Email has increased the total message flow considerably, because of the large distribution lists. Server capacity issues such as limited disk space for users are a constant headache. How many users can a server support? ISPs solve this problem by allowing each user a maximum amount of disk space, including web pages, email, and other files owned by the user. If users go over the limit, they are billed.

There are privacy issues. Post to a news group and your Email address is now in the public domain. Messages may be intercepted, so some users are taking advantage of freeware versions of pretty good privacy (PGP) software to encrypt their messages. A private secret key is retained by the sender and the other half of the key is made public. You encrypt a message to the recipient using their public key, and only the intended recipient can decrypt it. PGP key servers on the Internet have sprung up in support, even though a simple plain text message can be used to send your public key to anyone who needs to send you a secure message.

A common problem in Email systems relates to large distribution lists. Users can reply to a message directly to the sender or to everyone on the distribution list. One sure way to bog down an Email system is to send a message of no interest to a large list of recipients. Many will write back to ask to be taken off the list, and a few of these will reply to the entire list. This in turn will cause additional users to complain, and again some will reply to the entire distribution list.

A common problem with attachments sent among heterogeneous system users on UNIX, Wintel, and Macintosh systems is file system differences (see Table 9-1). Sending attachments among these platforms requires users to adopt conventions. Uniformly administered MIME types help map file types and extensions.

Table 9-1   Heterogeneous file system differences

Platform	Attachment File Name Issues
UNIX	File names may be 255 characters long, except forward slashes, and spaces are allowed but discouraged. No file name extensions exist.
Wintel	Older applications and versions of the OS allow only 8.3-style file names. The extension is critical for determining the type of file. Newer versions allow 255 character names, with some disallowed characters, and the extension may be four characters.
Macintosh	File names are limited to 31 characters, with some forbidden characters. But files have TYPE and CREATOR codes to indicate content.

References

For a complementary point of view on electronic messaging, try one of the Lotus Notes books, such as this one:

Tamura, Randall A., *Lotus Notes 4 UNLEASHED*. Indianapolis, IN: Sams Publishing, 1996, ISBN: 0-672-30906-8.

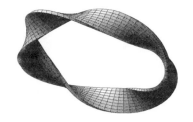

Desktop Integration
Principles

Introduction

Multiple computer platforms are used for some very different reasons. All of them have to do with requirements, and one computer simply does not fit all jobs, no matter what the salesperson says. Some of these differentiators include the following

Purchase cost
Ease of use
Special features
Compute power
Graphics performance
Multimedia features
Low administration
Low total cost of ownership
Networking capabilities

Once in place, these systems may be integrated at some level, preferably using standards-based technologies, to allow collaboration and the sharing of resources such as files, networked printers, networked scanners, and applications. Application sharing is a little harder, requiring protocols such as *telnet*, client–server, and X-Windows.

In this chapter we discuss the benefits of integrating multivendor desktops with UNIX. Multiple protocol stacks will be encountered as we attempt to integrate Netware™, IntraNetWare™, Wintel, Macintosh™, OpenStep™, and Rhapsody™. Integration of UNIX and UNIX-like desktops will prove much simpler. For the Wintel clients, we'll review LAN Manager products such as HP's Advanced Server/9000. However, a preference for NFS will be argued.

Indeed, much will be argued on the basis of open systems, draft standards, freedom of choice, and the benefits to the organizations that go this route. Open systems is more than "integration using standards." Ideally, it gives the customer vendor independence in a commodities marketplace. The vendors have to differentiate their products on the basis of tangibles like reliability, low cost, support, and consulting services to grow their company and gain market share.

Finally, we'll look at integrating the newer (but not so new) network computer (NC), thin client, diskless computer, X-terminal, and NetPC. And a word about authentication models is given.

Benefits of Integrating Multivendor Desktops with UNIX

UNIX is the preferred operating system for integrating disparate desktops, because UNIX is the most open operating system in the world. You can actually choose which vendor you buy your UNIX from, making that choice based on your own requirements. UNIX easily handles multiprotocol stacks and various network adapters because of its open architecture, linear memory model, and flexible I/O subsystem. UNIX hardware platforms are among the most scalable in the industry, in terms of memory, I/O channels, disk storage, number of users, number of CPUs, and reliability.

Creating a common file repository can streamline work flow via file sharing using standard file formats. UNIX supports 255-character file names, so any desktop system can create, read, write, delete, change permissions, and navigate the shared file system located on the UNIX file server. Because different desktop operating systems have some conflicting file naming conventions, the file server software will map characters as necessary. For example, a Macintosh client may try to create a file with forward and backward slashes in it, which Wintel machines don't care for. And a Wintel machine may create a file with a colon in it, which Macintoshes don't accept. UNIX machines may be able to create 255-character files, but Macintoshes can only read 31 of them. Wintel machines depend on file name extension like ".book" and ".txt" to denote content, while UNIX systems associate no such meaning (although HP VUE and CDE can, in fact, associate file extensions with file types, even though the OS itself cares naught), and Macintoshes use file type and creator codes stored in the resource forks of its files, a concept no other operating system understands.

Peripherals controlled by or connected directly to a UNIX system can be shared by the desktop systems. PostScript printers, pen plotters, wide-format printers, FAX machines, and modems can be shared. As a bonus, the UNIX system can perform all the functions of an Email hub, since SMTP is a standard part of UNIX.

Note that we aren't talking about really tight, seamless integration. File and print sharing is fairly easy, but differences in computer instruction sets, the operating systems, the APIs, and the windowing system don't generally allow us to move an application from a desktop system onto a UNIX system and actually execute the code there. We can place Wintel code on a UNIX file system and share that executable code with a shared network drive. The Wintel clients can attach to this drive and actually load and execute the .EXE files from the network drive. Note that many applications can be installed onto a file server as one of the fully supported installation options. Such applications understand this mode of execution and are written to account for the consequential multiple instantiations of the code. They don't modify their own code or data, don't do disk I/O directly to the hardware, do create unique scratch files for each user, are careful to properly locate supporting library and configuration files, and may even check out a user license for the duration of their instantiations.

So while we can't run a Macintosh or Wintel application directly on a UNIX file server, we can take advantage of desktop emulation environments like the HP-UX version of SUN's WABI or Apple's (now mature) MAE. These emulate the Intel and Motorola CPUs, interface to the X-window system, allow access to CD-ROM, floppy, and fixed disks, and provide a fairly complete environment for executing the common desktop productivity suites. The emulation environment taxes the UNIX CPUs more heavily. Multiple users at their X-terminals will tax the system that much more, so scalability of these emulation technologies is limited. It's interesting to see a UNIX workstation with WABI, MAE, and UNIX applications all running on the same screen.

A UNIX file and print server desktop integration solution lets users share network resources and provides a central repository for executable productivity tools (See Figure 10-1). These are fairly trivial tasks for a UNIX system. Given UNIX's legendary reliability, any downtime will almost always be due to scheduled upgrades to hardware and software. But once a UNIX system is in place, additional uses will be found for it.

We covered HP OpenMail in Chapter 9. There is every reason to implement an Email system on our UNIX system. This can integrate Email arriving

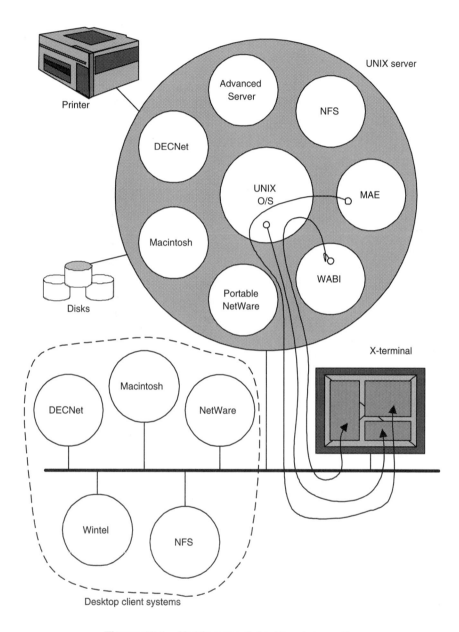

Figure 10-1 Multiprotocol desktop integration
Desktops running UNIX NFS, Wintel, NetWare, DECNet, and Mac OS may access
a UNIX file and print server either natively or with NFS and TCP/IP protocol stacks
loaded. The UNIX server can also be an Email hub and an X-client application server.

from the Internet and from work-at-home users who use the POP server on the Email server to collaborate. In fact, users will line up outside the office asking to have their printers attached to the UNIX file server. This makes it available to others and relieves their owners of their own desktop system administration blues.

Another benefit of desktop integration is file format conversion. From time to time, a 3½-inch or even a 5¼-inch floppy disk needs to be read in. If just one machine has these floppy disk drives attached, then the file server can be used to move it to the machine that needs the data.

Many desktop users are now using high-capacity removable media such as Iomega's 100-Mbyte ZIP drive to back up their own data or to share their "stuff" with other users. The shared UNIX network drives make this expense unnecessary. Indeed, because the UNIX server is backed up on a nightly basis, the need for users to back up their personal data disappears. This, in turn, reduces the need for large disk drives on the desktop systems. Taking this a step further, if all applications and data reside on the network drives, then why have any disks on the desktop? Disk drives are still the least reliable mechanical component, even though disk mechanism vendors boast of MTBF figures in the hundreds of thousands of hours.

"Capt'n, thur be multiple stacks here!"[1]

To integrate the various desktop operating systems with UNIX, we depend on its excellent ability to handle multiple protocol stacks (Figure 10-2) without after-the-fact band-aids like NDIS or ODI. These stacks are independent due to the UNIX protected memory model. Given the linear memory model that it was born with, UNIX can scale to accommodate many protocol stacks. Thanks to scalable hardware and fast system buses, UNIX machines can accommodate a wide variety and a large number of high-speed network adapters. This extends the functionality of UNIX solutions.

---

1. A liberal adaptation of Engineer Scott's exclamation after he beamed George and Gracy aboard the Klingon Bird of Prey. From <u>Star Trek IV—The Voyage Home</u>.

NFS	SMB	NCP	AFP	DECNet	SNA	Daemons
UDP	TCP	SPX	Apple Talk	DECNet protocols	SNA protocols	Kernel drivers
IP		IPX				
Ethernet and/or IEEE 802.2/802.3					802.5	LANIC

Figure 10-2   An OSI view of multiprotocol network adapters
A simplified view of the multiple protocol stacks and network adapters that a typical
UNIX system can support. The top layer is the application layer, typically implemented as one or more daemon processes. The server-side daemon uses the services
of its native transport and network protocol stack to communicate over a (possibly)
shared network adapter to its desktop client systems. In this diagram we see all protocols sharing a single 10-BASE-T adapter, with the SNA stack using its own token
ring adapter to communicate with the SNA host.

Each protocol is subject to its own special requirements. For example, a
NetWare server makes use of its server advertisement protocol, typically
announcing its resources on all network adapters once a minute. This allows
NetWare clients to discover which servers and what resources are available
to them, in true plug-and-play fashion. AppleTalk (Figure 10-3) works in
like fashion, as does LAN Manager. SNA and NFS are preconfigured. Each
protocol requires some support from the network routers, lest the client
systems become blind to the server presences or unable to connect to them at
all. This is because routers prevent broadcasts from passing to other subnets,
except for special support like that provided by AppleTalk and NetWare.

When multiple protocols are present on the same physical LAN, their
broadcasts will be heard by all systems. A UNIX desktop system with just a
TCP/IP stack may receive IPX, DECNet, and AppleTalk broadcasts sent to
MAC address FF-FF-FF-FF-FF-FF. But the Ethernet type field (or the IEEE
DSAP field) will contain a protocol code (other than that of IP) not known to
the kernel, so the LAN driver counts this as an "unknown protocol" and
discards the packet. The output from a diagnostic tool like *landiag* lists this
statistic for a given LAN adapter.

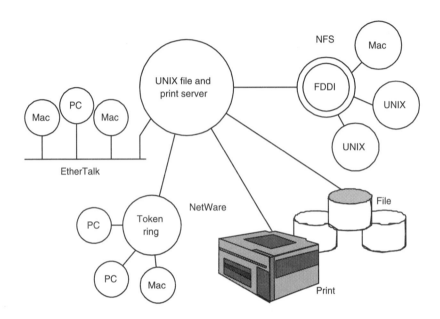

Figure 10-3   UNIX as a server for Macintosh
This UNIX file and print server is providing support for Macintosh desktops using
EtherTalk, PC and Macintosh desktops using Novel NetWare over IEEE 802.5 token
ring, and UNIX and Macintosh desktops using NFS over TCP/IP over FDDI. The
UNIX print spooler accepts all print jobs from each desktop print environment.

Portable NetWare

HP's Portable Netware solution is called NetWare 4.1 Services/9000. It
allows NetWare clients to take advantage of a UNIX system to extend the
capabilities of the environment. This product is based on Novell's C-code,
intended to allow third parties to extend NetWare support to their hardware
platform. Portable NetWare puts the server and protocol software stack on
the HP-UX system. User administration services, volume sharing, print
spooling, and server advertisements are provided (see Figure 10-4). A Guide
to NetWare for UNIX is an HP Professional Book written by Cathy Gunn. It
is recommended reading on this subject.

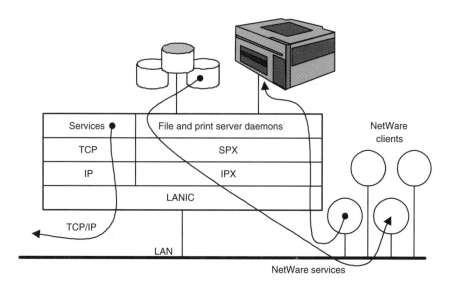

Figure 10-4　Portable Netware server
Portable Netware on HP-UX supports native file and print sharing for a group of Net-
Ware clients, while providing the usual TCP/IP support over the same LAN interface
card (LANIC). Both NetWare print services and TCP/IP services use the same UNIX
spooler, so the printer sharing is transparent to users.

NetWare assigns addresses to devices by concatenating a 32-bit network
address and the 48-bit MAC address of the LANIC. The local router
broadcasts the network address onto each network adapter. A NetWare
device simply listens for its network address at start-up time and adds its
own MAC address to complete the network address. It is up to the IPX
routers to assign unique IPX network numbers to all LANs, and LANIC
vendors guarantee that their LAN adapters have unique MAC addresses. See
Figure 10-5).

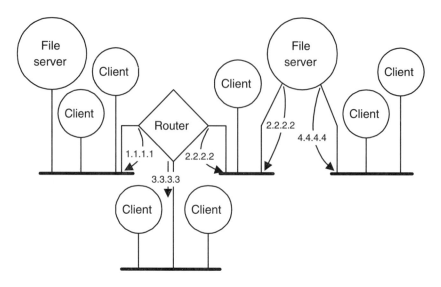

Figure 10-5   Routing with Netware servers
Routing in a NetWare network depends on routers advertising the correct subnet on each LAN that they are attached to. When a NetWare file server is pressed to support two LANs, then it must participate in the routing. In addition, each router must be configured to pass the service advertisement protocol (SAP) for each file and print server, if in fact that is a desired feature.

Macintosh, OpenStep, and Rhapsody

These three Apple platforms are a unique breed of desktop and server-capable systems. All of them incorporate leading-edge technologies and incomparable ease of use. The Macintosh is found where demanding multimedia, print, and graphics work is done. The OpenStep platform is an advanced UNIX derivative and is found in rapid prototyping application development environments. Rhapsody is a modernized melding of Mac OS, OpenStep, UNIX, and Wintel capabilities.

The contemporary Macintosh desktop computer uses Open Transport for its TCP/IP and an Internet connectivity suite consisting of two popular browsers, POP3 mailers, telnet, ftp, and miscellaneous utilities. The

LaserWriter 8.5.1 software supports networked TCP/IP access to printers attached to systems that support *lpr*, which means any UNIX system. NFS client products for Macintosh come from several third parties, such as Attachmate's Pathway NFS. X-window client software in the form of Mac-X from Apple and also from third parties lets Macintosh clients participate fully in a UNIX network.

Products such as Pacer Software are also available for HP-UX systems that run Macintosh services such as file and print sharing and Email over an AppleTalk protocol stack. Even Apple's (now mature) Macintosh Application Environment (MAE) supports AppleTalk, although TCP/IP is preferred over it. Note that Apple refers to AppleTalk over Ethernet as EtherTalk. Certainly, among Macintoshes in a closed group, it's so simple to enable AppleTalk and share files and printer among them that AppleTalk just isn't going away—it's a wonderful plug-and-play technology that's just not accepted in large networks because of its proprietary moniker and its so-called "chattiness." Regardless of whether NFS or Apple File Protocol (AFP) is used, the Macintosh user works with the Chooser to select a file server (see Figure 10-6).

UNIX servers are capable of supporting the classic Macintosh networking environment in much the same way as for PCs running NetWare—by putting the appropriate protocol stack and services on the UNIX machine and letting clients access the printers and disk drives attached. Indeed, Netware for Macintosh is also quite common. Given the long lifetime of the Macintosh desktop computer, using UNIX servers to support the classic AppleTalk networking is appropriate. It is therefore possible to have older and newer Macintoshes using the same UNIX file and print server, with the older ones using AppleTalk and the newer ones using TCP/IP, *lpr*, *telnet*, POP3, WWW, and NFS (see Figure 10-7).

Wintel Clients and AdvancedServer/ Advanced Server/9000

History reveals that 3COM developed LAN Manager and HP worked on the HP-UX server version and provided server and client TCP/IP support for it,

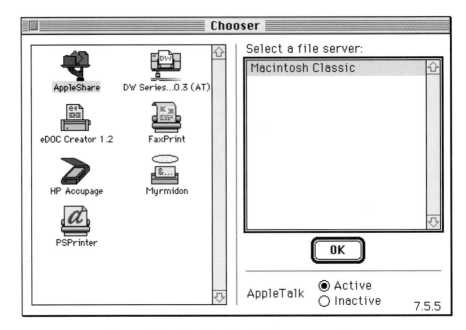

Figure 10-6   The Macintosh Chooser paradigm
The Macintosh Chooser is a single GUI that lets the user pick a file server or a printer
to connect to. The AppleShare icon is shown as selected, so the system locates file
servers in this zone. In this case a Macintosh Classic is found. Note that the user could
have selected the *DW Series 6.03 (AT)* printer, which is an HP 560C DeskWriter on
the same LocalTalk port, to locate a printer in the zone. In business environments using contemporary equipment, all this networking will be done over Ethernet LANs.

and it is now the standard Wintel file and print sharing system. The HP-UX
server product name for LAN Manager has changed over time, staring with
LM/X and changing to LM/U, and now it's called Advanced Server/9000.
LAN Manager servers offer file and print shares to their clients via a list of
share names. See Figure 10-8.

LM/X was very careful about file names and enforced the FAT file system
8.3 naming convention. Shares with client-created files always complied, but
in the spirit of UNIX-to-PC file sharing, files and directories that violate the
8.3 convention are invisible to the clients. This was in the spirit of the day
when all PCs had 8.3-style file names. Today, AdvancedServer/9000
supports long file names.

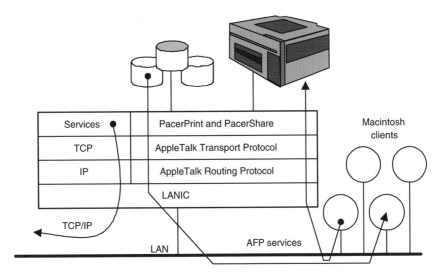

Figure 10-7 Macintosh file and print sharing

UNIX file and print server support for Macintosh clients may use the "legacy" AppleTalk file and print protocols using the Pacer Company's products as an example. Contemporary Macintosh users will probably prefer to use TCP/IP and NFS services. Transport protocols are AppleTalk Data Stream Protocol (ADSP) and Datagram Delivery Protocol (DDP). Network protocols are Routing Table Maintenance Protocol (RTMP), Zone Information Protocol (ZIP) and AppleTalk Address Resolution Protocol (AARP).

Despite issues of resolving share names across IP subnets, once a client is connected to the share, normal TCP/IP communication occurs. Note, too, that WINS and DNS may be integrated; so if a NetBIOS lookup for *hpbvjpb* should fail, a DNS request for *hpbvjpb.nsr.hp.com* may produce the sought-after IP address. A final note about Wintel clients is that it's desirable to have them request their IP configuration from a local DHCP server. This is proper for client systems, but not for server systems, and especially not for WINS and DNS servers, which are contacted only using their fixed IP addresses.

There is a UNIX freeware implementation of LAN Manager called Samba available on the Internet, which supports file and print sharing. Samba runs on HP-UX, Solaris, and several versions of Linux, the freeware UNIX O/S.

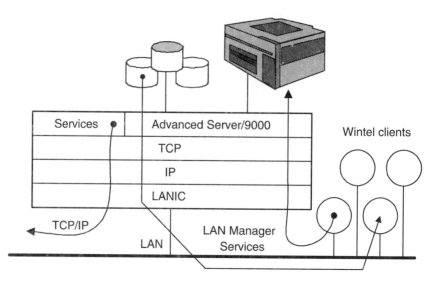

Figure 10-8   Advance Server/9000

An HP-UX server running Advanced Server/9000 supports the Server Message Block (SMB) protocol running on top of NetBIOS over TCP/IP. Wintel clients on the same subnet (as shown) take advantage of NetBIOS name requests to locate the server. For example, when a user tries to attach to a printer share called *hpbvjpb\\laserjet*, a NetBIOS name request is broadcast to the local IP subnet. The server *hpbvjpb* will respond appropriately when it hears the broadcast. For LAN Manager servers located on remote subnets, the Wintel client must take advantage of the Wintel name service (WINS) running on a WINS server anywhere on the network, or depend on a local *LMHOSTS* file to resolve the server name into an IP address.

NCs, Thin Clients, NetPCs, and Diskless Computers

Network computers (NC), thin clients, netPCs, and diskless computers are all attempts at reducing the total cost of ownership (TCO) of networked desktop computers in the enterprise. The TCO includes the following

> Original cost of purchasing the computer hardware
> Original cost of purchasing the software

Installation of the computer and connecting it to the network
Configuration of the computer hardware and software
Updates to software, firmware, and possibly hardware (technology refresh)
Maintaining the computer configuration
Troubleshooting problems
User lost time spent "futzing" with it to keep the computer running
User self-learning
Formal learning
Lost user and business productivity
Cost of the help desk and on-site IT staff

TCO figures between $10,000 and $15,000 annually are commonly cited for Wintel computers. Competitive pressures to reduce this TCO have resulted in various solutions to reduce the cost of desktop hardware, configuration management, and support. Significantly, the very architecture of the desktop systems has been called into question as a likely cause, and systems based on the cross-platform Java language have even been produced. Apple computer cites ease of use, reliable hardware, and superior under-the-hood technology as a way to reduce TCO. Competition is alive and well.

There is a common thread to these diskless computers. They all depend on a server to download their configuration, operating system, fonts, and application software. The OS and applications execute on the diskless computer CPU. They share files and use printers courtesy of network servers, just as before. UNIX NFS diskless workstations operate much like this. Even X-terminals operate this way, except that the user applications are X-clients executing on the UNIX application server, and the X-terminal is the networked application interface to the user. These arrangements simplify configuration management because there is almost nothing at the computer to configure; everything comes from the server, the central point of administration. Admittedly there are reduced features, such as no floppy disk drive, no hard disk, and reduced ability to attach peripherals, so this is not a solution for all situations.

Just after powering up, a ROM code in a diskless computer will broadcast or multicast a download request on the LAN. The address 09-00-09-00-00-04 is used by an HP-UX diskless computer to locate a cluster server. Only servers whose LAN adapters are configured with this multicast address will hear the boot request. The server will reply to the request and download basic configuration parameters, perhaps an interim loader program, and finally the operating system, which in turn will take over the machine, initialize, and configure itself on the network. Depending on the implementation, swap space may still be local (such as with HP-UX diskless computers), or it may be remote (again like HP-UX diskless computers). Network swap is deemed slower than local swap.

An X-terminal is a diskless computer too. When an HP X-terminal powers up, it will issue a broadcast for either BOOTP or DHCP to configure its IP stack. This returns the name/IP of the boot server, the IP address of the name server, the name/IP of the login server, and the name/IP of the font server. Then it will use either trivial file transfer protocol (TFTP) or the network file system (NFS) to download the X-window operating system. The OS boots, grays out the screen, and issues an XDMCP request to the login server. The *xdm, dtlogin,* or *vuelogin* daemon will project an X-window log in to the display and lock it. After authenticating, the user's start-up script typically "loads the user environment" by launching X-clients for desktop and window management. These X-clients all run on the UNIX system and let the user browse the file system, launch tasks, perform printing, and switch work spaces.

No discussion of diskless computers is complete without addressing server reliability and performance and network bandwidth concerns. If there is a single highly available server cluster, then all the eggs are in one basket, and the basket should be watched closely. If the cluster fails, the entire user community is offline. Since software failures are more common than hardware failures, MTBF and MMTR data should not be taken at face value. See Chapter 2 for the necessary reliability mathematics.

Instead of a single boot server, an alternative would be work group boot servers. Theoretically, it isn't necessary that the boot server also be the only boot server that a client can boot from, nor is it theoretically necessary that the boot server also be the file server for applications. The only sticky point is the location of the user's personal data. If the data are not mirrored and not accessible from another computer, then users will be able to boot from another boot server, and they can run standard applications, but they'll have to wait for their "home" directory server reboot to access their nonmirrored data.

Servers clearly must be sized in accordance with the projected group workloads. Acceptable user performance metrics are needed. This is a job for the system capacity planners, who must not just size the server, but also understand how it performs under load. A well-balanced system will behave predictably as the offered load increases by leveling off its throughput and increasing response time in a linear manner (see Figure 10-9). The leveling

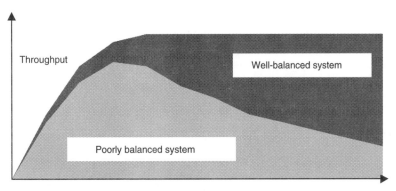

Number of active users

Figure 10-9   Server performance characteristics
This is the performance two hypothetical boot servers for a group of users with disk-less computers. For the well-balanced server, throughput levels off in a graceful man-ner, but remains fairly steady well past the sensible operating point. The poorly balanced system reaches its performance peak but reduces its throughput as the offered load increases. This type of ungraceful degradation bodes poorly for the work group.

off of througput simply means that a server resource is reaching 100% utilization. At 100% utilization the server is said to be in saturation. As the offered load increases, the server cannot, in fact, produce more output. The four classical resources are CPU, memory, disk I/O, and LAN. Saturate any one of these and the system througput will level off. A poorly tuned system will reduce its throughput as more load is offered. This may happen because a second resource becomes saturated, because of blocking effects, or because the cache hit ratio for the file system starts to deteriorate. How do you know what the behavior of a UNIX server will be? Look at the vendor's benchmark data or at a well-respected publication's server evaluation article. Skilled system capacity planners will be able to recommend configurations that are well behaved.

The response time of any lightly loaded server will be constant. As the server's first resource approaches saturation, the response time will increase linearly as the offered load increases. Realize that this is the average response time. At low loads the response time is fairly consistent and has little variation for similar file downloads. As response time goes up, so does the variation. Near the right hand side of the response time curve, the variation can be quite large. See Figure 10-10.

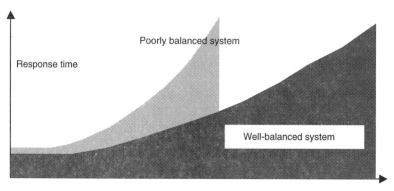

Figure 10-10   Response time and the well-balanced system
A pair of hypothetical servers for diskless computers shows how the average response time of the well-balanced system is better than its poorly balanced counterpart. Initial response time may be better, too, as shown here, but that's not necessarily always the case.

As for network congestion issues with diskless computers, the concern is that with all the booting, application file loading, shared library loading, and document I/O going across the LAN to the server, it will bog down the LAN and the server, too. The present LAN design may not be adequate, so the cost of designing, installing, and testing a new LAN has to be factored into the TCO for the diskless computers. Given the low cost of 10-BASE-T switches, bringing a dedicated 10-Mbps line to each desktop computer is fast becoming the new defacto wiring design in larger corporations. See Figure 10-11.

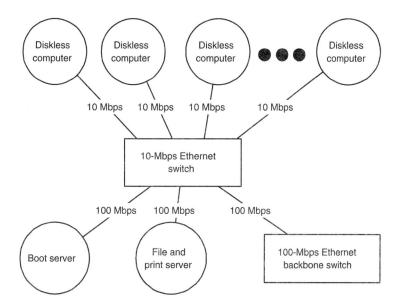

Figure 10-11 Scalable LAN design for diskless computers

A scalable LAN design provides a dedicated 10-Mbps connection to each diskless computer. A boot server and a file and print server support this work group. A 100-Mbps uplink to a 100-Mbps backbone Ethernet switch connects this group to the site backbone. Note that 100-BASE-T supports full-duplex operation, so a maximum of 200 Mbps is available at the server connections. But, depending on the application, there may be a 80–20 read–write ratio or a 60–40 ratio, so numbers like 200 Mbps are rather optimistic.

Even without the diskless computer traffic concerns, the increased use of collaboration technologies (like shared whiteboard, video conferencing, and Email with large attachments) and web technology may eventually lead IT departments to retool the LAN for 10 Mbps to the desktop.

While it's fairly easy to draw these logical LAN designs, validating that they in fact deliver the desired level of performance to the user still requires some engineering work to ensure that the performance is obtained economically. For example, a design may allocate one 100-Mbps-connected server per 10 10-Mbps users. But perhaps the same server can support 20 or 30 clients, or a faster one might support 50 clients on a 100-Mbps server connection. Benchmarking may shed light on the correct design choices, or discrete event simulation tools such as the BONes Designer from the Alta Group or OpNet from Mil3 may be used to evaluate many engineering designs without endless benchmarking.

NFS for Open Multiplatform Integration

The Network File System (NFS) provides multiplatform file and print sharing. Client and server software are available in the marketplace from a wide variety of vendors for UNIX, Macintosh, and Wintel platforms. NFS was originally developed by Sun Microsystems. To provide cross-platform functionality, NFS is built using an external data representation (XDR) that takes care of annoying details like byte order and file system semantics. For example, a Macintosh user and a Wintel user may both access files on a UNIX NFS server using the semantics and syntax of their native operating systems. The Wintel user will use the familiar backward slash as a path name separator, and the Macintosh user will use the colon character. Because both user types are most likely using their native file managers, even this layer of abstraction is concealed from them.

Note that this XDR feature does not alter the contents of the data in the files in any way. Multiplatform clients may store data and executable files safely on NFS file servers with the sure knowledge that the data will be read back in exactly the same byte order as they were written. Executable files physically stored on the NFS file server may be launched directly from the desktop of an NFS client, and it will load into the client's memory and execute there without trouble. ASCII files are not "tweaked" to take care of differences in the special characters used to denote the end of line.

Even better, suppose that a graphics shop has UNIX, Wintel, and Macintosh users that all use Adobe Photoshop and store their image files on a common NFS server. These users can share images since photoshop file formats are constant across platforms. Likewise, common file formats like GIF, JPG, TIF, and PNG can also be shared across platforms, regardless of which image processing package is used.

NFS servers are intrinsically stateless, the idea being that a server crash should not allow the client to believe that a write has occurred when in fact it has not. Thus, standard NFS servers force the client to wait until the data have been written to disk. NFS uses the connectionless user datagram protocol (UDP), so all packet sequencing, time-outs, and retransmissions are done directly between NFS client and server. But, in practice, most NFS implementations allow the server to "spoof" the write operation. HP-UX does this by allowing the file system to be exported with the *-async* option in the */etc/exports* file. Write performance increases dramatically.

NFS includes the network information server (NIS) feature to synchronize the */etc/passwd* and */etc/group* files, plus others such as */etc/hosts* and */etc/services*. This ensures that the file system access rights are consistent across all UNIX file systems. The NFS client supports file server login support, so the single-user, non-UNIX client platform user can authenticate with the file server. Without such a log in, NFS clients have only "world" access to the file system that they mount.

Print sharing and spooling are also provided by NFS via an auxiliary daemon called *pcnfsd*. The NFS client sends the data to the server via *pcnfsd*, where the data are inspooled onto the appropriate UNIX printer queue. This lets Wintel, UNIX workstation, and Macintosh users share expensive color laser postscript printers with ease.

The Distributed File System

The Andrew File System (AFS) from the Open Software Foundation (OSF) is now called the Distributed File System (DFS). This technology, introduced in 1991, improves over NFS, SMB, and proprietary file systems by possessing some very desirable properties: openness, high availability, high performance, excellent scalability, superior security, and remote administration.

DFS is open because it is a standard not tied to one particular vendor. It enjoys platform independence, has multivendor support, and works in heterogeneous environments. Client implementations are available for OS/2, UNIX, Wintel, Macintosh, and IBM. Server implementations are available for UNIX, IBM, Cray, and Wintel. The domain controller can be any of these server types.

DFS has inherent high availability in its design. There is no single point of failure in the architecture. Redundancy is due to replica servers, replication of read-only file systems, and on-line backup and restore. Automatic fail-over and fault tolerance ensure that a client can always reach a DFS server. On-line load balancing between servers and clients capitalizes on all running server hardware. This works because the clients use logical file names instead of physical names and locations. Log-based recovery at the server using the Local File System (LFS) ensures that files can be restored after a failure occurs.

DFS is designed to give maximum performance. Files can be moved around to a more optimum server without advising the client systems. Yet clients can set their server preferences. On-line load balancing lets a client take maximum advantage of replicated files on multiple servers. File and directory caching on the client disk further increases performance. The working set and cache size can be adjusted to ensure a high cache hit rate.

DFS is highly (some say boundlessly) scalable because of the distributed design. It can handle millions of files and tens of thousands of users. It is designed for the LAN and the WAN environment and will adjust packet size to adapt to bandwidth and congestion. There is high tolerance for latency and low bandwidth. Only file changes are written back to the server, so WAN overhead is kept minimal. The DFS protocol is not chatty, so large implementations don't drown in their own overhead.

DFS security supports POSIX ACLs for fine-grained access control and provides for multiple domain controllers. Kerberos can be used for single-user sign on via an ID and a password. Security for authentication and access control is via the DCE registry. Encryption is provided for directory accesses and file I/O is also encrypted on the wire.

DFS is designed to be administered and accessed remotely from any location. This is due to the global name-space concept. End users don't need to know where the data are stored physically by server name, as is the case in most other client–server file-sharing products. Administrators can perform file moves and backups and take servers up and down without effecting the clients at all. There is no need for the administrators to manually track every single file and directory by server.

All these great features of DFS are a great benefit to mobile users. They can now access their data from any location reliably, consistently, and efficiently. Read-only data such as product data sheets, news, web pages, and document repositories can be replicated as needed and updated as necessary to give the mobile worker the most up-to-date data as quickly as possible from any access point available.

The DFS four-layer architecture is deceptively simple to lay down. The (usually) replicated file location database (FLDB) contains the actual (possibly multiple) locations of the file sets, the basic unit of distribution. As usual, the file sets contain directories, which in turn contain files.

To provide a way for its customers to use DFS while leveraging existing NFS and Windows NT servers, Hewlett–Packard, in its Enterprise File System (EFS) strategy, contains an NFS gateway and an Advance Server for UNIX (AS/U) gateway (a.k.a Windows NT workgroup bridge). This gives these "legacy" work groups access to the DFS global name space.

Authentication Models

In order to do their jobs, employees need access to network and system resources. Access controls are needed to ensure the following:

> Sensitive data are not seen by the wrong eyes.
> Important files are not renamed, altered, corrupted, moved, or deleted.
> The number of active users is limited to a reasonable number.

These are usually accomplished by giving employees user names and passwords and possibly associating these with a computer name. The operating system enforces access to resources accordingly.

For example, suppose that 50 UNIX machines need general access to each other. NIS is configured to create a consistent user ID (UID) and group ID (GID) for all users on all systems. NIS is configured with a master NIS server and several NIS slave servers for increased availability. Clients are assigned an NIS domain at start-up and bind to any NIS server for that domain. NIS clients locate NIS servers via a broadcast. If there are no local NIS servers, then clients are configured with the IP address of a remote server. Adding non-UNIX clients to this UNIX assembly is fairly simple: configure the NIS domain name, make it easy for the user to authenticate via a login GUI, and use the client platform's standard method for connecting to servers and printers. Note that this means all the non-UNIX users will have valid accounts on all 50 UNIX machines as well.

There is nothing about NFS that forces the use of NIS. If the system administrators have set up the means to coordinate UID and GID files, NIS isn't necessary. And a small "renegade" group within our 50 can set up a small private NIS domain for local purposes.

References

Stern, Hal, *Managing NFS and NIS*. Sebastopol, CA: O'Reilly & Associates, 1992, ISBN: 0-937175-75-7.

CHAPTER 11

Integration Using
X-Windows

Introduction

X-Windows is one of those rare jewels that comes along and makes life better. It is brought to us free, courtesy of the Massachusetts Institute of Technology (MIT). The source code is freely available on the Internet, and all UNIX vendors incorporate it. The fundamental premise of X-Windows is that a client program executing natively on computer A can run separately from its windowing GUI on computer B across a network. This is pure genius.

In this chapter we see how X-Windows provides vendor and network-independent windowing capabilities to applications. We review the X-Windows architecture, dispel a few myths along the way, and expound on the benefits of platform-independent clients. We see how X-Windows can be integrated with Macintosh, Wintel, and UNIX desktop systems.

HP's collaboration products based on X-Windows can increase productivity by reducing travel, so we review SharedX here. Finally, we look at how the publishing industry uses X-Windows.

Vendor and Network-independent Windowing

X-Windows separates the client application from the display server. This client is often called the X-client, and the display is often called the X-display server or simply X-server, and often the X-terminal. The user works at the X-server, which has all the usual desktop computer parts: display, keyboard, mouse, memory, CPU, and LANIC. The X-client is compiled on the hardware and O/S on which it executes, completely independent of the X-display server hardware implementation.

X-Windows has enjoyed tremendous support from the UNIX community, and has seen many releases. The current version (1998) is X11R6. The users are not only free to choose the best UNIX compute platform for their applications; they can also select the most appropriate desktop X-terminal.

This is the open system at its finest. There is also simplicity and economy to consider. How simpler can it be than to have the application execute on one compute server and to allow the user to be located anywhere on the enterprise network, without downloading the application to the desktop?

The X-client application is optimized to run in its native environment. The data it needs are on the local hard drive (or NFS mounted if not), and so access to the data is very fast. The X-display, too, is optimized to run in its native desktop environment. The display server can be any hardware and any O/S and have any performance rating, any display resolution, and any color depth.

X-Windows is the standard for windowing interoperability and implements the presentation layer 6 of the OSI model. TCP is the standard transport protocol, and IP is the standard networking protocol. The X11/TCP/IP combination is the most popular, although X-Windows implementations have run over DEC's LAT and DECNet protocols.

Normally, X-clients run on the UNIX operating system. HP-UX 700-series workstations have built-in accelerated graphics cards, and HP's X-Windows implementation gives users unparalleled performance. The industry uses the X-stone metric to measure X-Windows performance.

It is interesting to note how generalized the X-Windows architecture is. There is implicit support for multiple X-displays attached to the desktop system. Display number 0 listens on TCP port 6000, display 1 listens on TCP port 6001, and so on. This is not to be confused with HP VUE (visual user environment) or CDE (common desktop environment) which support multiple full-screen work spaces on a single monitor.

Another generalized feature is that a single display can accept windows from any number of X-clients located on different UNIX systems. A user might invoke a Photoshop session on system A by entering

photoshop myfile -display myxterminal:0

and invoke a web browser on system B by entering

netscape -display myxterminal:0

This kind of flexibility is unheard of in other desktop computing architectures.

X-Windows Architecture

The OSI view of the X-Windows architecture is simplicity itself (see Figure 11-1). In this discussion we assume that the TCP/IP transport and network protocols are used. As usual, the X-client application at layer 7 talks to its peer, the X-display server. The client code makes calls to *xlib* APIs to instruct the display server what to draw on the screen. These are drawing instructions being sent to the display, like "draw a line from (x1,y1) to (x2,y2)," and not the actual graphics bitmap pattern that results.

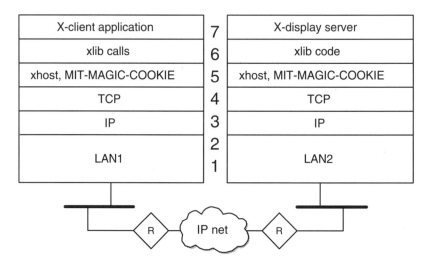

Figure 11-1   X-Windows architecture
The X-terminal architecture as mapped out using the OSI model shows the simple elegance of the design. A lot of the functionality of X-Windows is buried inside the sixth layer - the presentation layer. Calls to the *xlib* APIs are completely open and documented, and provide an unprecedented degree of interoperability between multiple platforms.

Authentication is handled in several ways. First, to launch an X-client, a user has to have an account on the UNIX system. The *xhost +hpbvjpb* command (an X-client) can be used to allow a remote host *hpbvjpb* to connect to the display. Any X-client run by any user on *hpbvjpb* can connect to the display, so this is not totally secure. The MIT-MAGIC-COOKIE feature is an X-Windows security scheme that overcomes this. Each time a user logs into an X-terminal, a window manager (also an X-client) such as *mwm* or *vuewm* generates a "cookie," a long string of random characters, and appends it to a file called *.Xauthority* in the user's home directory. All X-clients that the user starts later during the session are able to read this cookie and present it to the X-display server for authentication. X-clients launched by other users on this or any other computer won't know the correct cookie and won't be allowed to connect to the user's display.

A physical view of the X-Windows standard reveals some very practical aspects of X that the OSI model does not (see Table 11-1). The components of an X-station are the same ones found on most desktop computers. Indeed, the same cases, monitors, keyboards, and mice are used, and you need to look at the sticker on the front of the case to know whether the device is an X-terminal or a UNIX workstation.

Table 11-1   Physical components of an X-terminal

Component	Typical Configuration
Display	1280 × 1024 horizontal × vertical resolution (in pixels)
Memory	8 MB RAM holds downloaded code, backing store, fonts
ROM	4 MB holds start-up code and diagnostics
Mouse	3 Buttons
Keyboard	101 Keys
LANIC	10-BASE-T, 10-BASE-2
CPU	i960 Microprocessor
Serial port	PPP or serial printer support for network printing
Parallel port	Centronics connector for network printing
Parallel port	Parallel printer support for network printing
MPEG card	MPEG-1 decoder and sound card for multimedia support

The X-Windows display manager may run on the X-terminal, or it may be an X-client running on the system that the user logs into. The window manager's role in X-Windows is to

Provide the window decorations
Enable pop-up menus when the user clicks on the desktop
Help move windows around the screen
Raise and lower windows that overlap
Iconify, close, and restore windows
Resize windows
Authenticate new client connections

Window decorations are the rectangular areas that surround the window. The user learns to drag the window around by the title bar, resize the window by dragging its sides or corners, pop up a menu at the upper left, and iconify or maximize the window at the upper right. When the window manager isn't running, these decorations disappear, and the user can't manipulate the windows.

The applications remain active even if the window display manager is dormant. The X-client application is responsible for dealing with keyboard and mouse inputs within the application window area, while the display manager deals with them outside this area.

On HP-UX workstations, the application that implements the X-Windows environment on the graphical display is called simply X and is able to run multiple graphics heads if necessary. On real X-terminals, is a similar process monitors the mouse movement and button clicks and sends these to the X-client as a stream of messages.

For each special screen object that the user can press (called a widget), there is a corresponding call-back function in the X-client. Widgets include radio buttons, ordinary buttons, X-boxes, scroll bars, text boxes, and pop-up menus. Complex X-client applications such as web browsers and simulation packages benefit from threaded code so that the user enjoys immediate feedback. For example, while Netscape Navigator is downloading a lengthy web page, the user may wish to stop it. If the code were single threaded, the user's press of the "stop" button would remain queued until the download function exited. With multiple threads of execution, Netscape can detect the button press almost immediately and signal the download thread to terminate and clean up.

X-terminals with 8-bit color displays use color maps (palettes). The X-client *xcolormap* displays the color map. There is a shared color map and a private color map. X-clients indicate which map they will use. The shared color map can allocate up to 256 unique colors. As sharing clients allocate new colors for their windows, they are added to the color map. When the map is full, clients may choose to request a "close" color or revert to an alternative color that is available. The user benefits when applications share the same color map because the appearance of all windows remain the same as the user moves among them. When an application needs a private color map, it can allocate its own 256 colors while the window is active, but when the window is put in the background, the shared color map is reasserted, garbling the private window colors displayed. Similarly, when the private color map client window comes to the foreground, all the other window colors are garbled. Users can choose between the private and shared color maps by setting a command line option when they execute the X-client. For example, the image viewing utility *xv* can be invoked with the *-private* option so that the application can display color images with maximum fidelity. The window display manager controls the color maps.

Note that for graphics terminals supporting 16-bit true color there is no palette issue. X-Windows emulators on 24-bit color displays (millions of colors) are not subject to palette issues. The X-display server is aware of the color depth of the display and interacts with the X-clients for their color display needs. X-clients may still take advantage of 8-bit palettes on true color displays.

Myths about X-Windows

Many myths surround X-Windows, and in this section we will try to dispel them. The first myth is that X-Windows uses a lot of network bandwidth because it sends a stream of bitmapped graphics across the network from the UNIX machine to the X-terminal. In truth, it is *xlib* commands that are sent across the network. These instructions tell the X-display what to draw in the window. If a 100 by 200 forest green rectangle is needed, a simple brief instruction is sent, and the X-terminal draws this region locally. No 100 by 200 bitmap is manufactured by the client and sent across the network. Of course if the application is a web browser, and a web page contains a GIF image, then this image has to be sent inside the *xlib* parameters across the network. And if the application is an image-editing program like Adobe Photoshop, then cursor-down drawing activities will result in a steady stream of cursor tracking information going to the client and a steady stream of screen update commands will go to the X-terminal. But this is client-specific behavior.

The second myth is that applications are hard to write for X-Windows. HP sells UI/MX for developing X-Windows GUI applications. The tool lets the programmer lay out the structure of the window and generates a C-code template. The developer supplies the actual code for the call-back routines in the template and the glue of the main program. The Java software development kit (JDK) for UNIX implicitly lets you write X-clients because the applets run inside browser windows, and Netscape Navigator is an X-client that supports Java applets. Perl's TK feature provides rapid GUI development, too.

The third myth is that X-Windows is limited to the UNIX environment. Many third parties offer X-terminal emulation software for Wintel and Macintosh desktops. Other vendors provide products that will wrap a proprietary Wintel window inside an X-Windows wrapper for display on X-terminals. HP offers a windows server product that works this way. Third party solutions include Citrix and Ntrigue.

The fourth myth is that X-Windows isn't secure. Yet users must first authenticate with a UNIX login host, and using the MIT-MAGIC-COOKIE scheme, users can't project windows on each others terminals and attempt to copy their displays with an X-Windows dump command. The window manager in HP VUE and CDE even provides screen locks that activate after extended inactivity or when the user clicks the lock. The lock inhibits mouse and keyboard entries and can even cover the display. A password is needed to unlock the X-terminal. When an ordinary desktop computer freezes up or loses power, data may be lost; but an X-terminal has no data, and the client can detect the loss of contact with the X-terminal and either exit gracefully or be safely terminated by the user. Because there is no disk drive on an X-terminal, there is not one line of code that can be stolen by making off with the terminal. X-Windows solutions are thus even more secure than desktop computers are.

Myth number five says that X-terminals can't be used with the Internet. But the history of the Internet is rich with UNIX. There is no reason that systems on the Internet can't allow users to "X in," even though they routinely *telnet* to systems, run their shell accounts, or execute *archie* searches. Perhaps most users don't have X-Windows emulators, perhaps system managers realize that X-Windows users tend to run more programs at once, and perhaps firewalls usually block the X-Windows TCP ports.

Platform-independent Computing

This section will reinforce the benefits for users sitting behind X-Windows emulators. The X-terminal displays are platform independent because the X-Windows display server is available for all major desktop platforms—Macintosh, Wintel, and UNIX variants. The X-Windows *xlib* layer is independent of the CPU used to implement X on the desktop system—HPPA, Alpha, SPARC, PPC, Merced, or x86.

This frees the solution seekers from the desktop environment and lets them choose application execution platforms that are "best" in some sense. An application is supported in the X-Windows environment either because it's a proper X-client, because it's a text-based program that will run in a terminal X-Windows emulator like *hpterm* and *xterm*, or because the application GUI can be wrapped up in an X-Window. See Figure 11-2.

The X-client application is generally independent of the X-display type because the X-client will adapt to the display's number of available colors, the screen dimensions, the available fonts, and even the number of mouse buttons and behave properly. For example, many UNIX X-clients expect three mouse buttons, but some desktop computers have only one or two. The X-terminal emulation software will offer alternative ways to simulate the missing buttons. X-Windows even supports keyboard mapping by abstracting key codes, so common ASCII codes for backspace, such as control-H or DEL, can be addressed.

Some performance-related issues differentiate X-terminals and X-terminal emulators. Raw X-stone performance requirements for some draw-intensive applications like Photoshop and CAD products are sufficiently high that certain X-emulator products just won't perform well enough to make the application run properly. For environments with a great many open, iconified, and overlapping windows, the X-terminal's ability to provide local backing store is critical for performance. Otherwise, instead of the X-terminal redrawing a window's contents locally from backing store, a client will be signaled by the X-terminal to redraw its window. This not only wastes application server machine cycles, but it also incurs unnecessary network traffic and forces the user to wait out the redrawing operation.

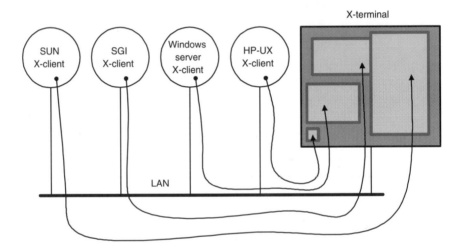

Figure 11-2   Multiplatform computing with X-Windows
Platform-independent computing courtesy of X-Windows. A user with an X-terminal is shown tapping the compute resources of a SUN, SGI, HP Windows Server, and an HP-UX application server at the same time. Each X-client uses the reliable TCP transport protocol to maintain communication with its window. The user can switch between windows to work these applications. Note that a client may continue updating its window constantly even while the user is working in another window in the foreground.

X-Windows Clients for Macintosh, Wintel, and UNIX

We have already established the multiplatform nature of X-Windows display server technology. Given a UNIX or Windows Server environment, any desktop system can access the applications that run there. All flavors of UNIX already provide support for both X-clients and X-display service. Indeed, for UNIX systems, the standard graphical user interface is implemented on top of X. In this section we'll review some of the specifics about Macintosh and Wintel X-Windows products.

Vendors of X-Windows display server emulators for Macintosh include Apple Computer (MacX). Mac OS already has a windowing system and a windows manager. MacX therefore provides two modes of operation: rooted and rootless. The rooted mode creates a single window inside which the entire X-display exists. This allows the entire HP VUE or CDE desktop to appear within a single Mac OS window, and lets the X-Windows window manager take over this one emulated display. The rootless mode opens a separate Mac OS window for each X-client window connection, and the Mac OS window manager is used.

Screen capture in the rooted mode may be done within the X-Windows environment. The command "*xwd -frame > screen1.xwd*" will capture the window that the user selects with the cursor and save it on the UNIX file system. In rootless mode, the same command will let the user capture any window on the screen and save it to the UNIX file system. Any window can also be captured using the native Mac OS window capture keystrokes (CAPSLOCK-command-shift-4), in which case the snapshot file will be saved at the root of the start-up disk.

Vendors of X-Windows display server emulators for the Wintel platform include Walker Richer Quinn (WRQ) Reflection/X and Hummingbird Exceed. These also offer rooted and rootless modes of operation. The *Alt-PrtSc* keystroke sequence captures the forefront window to the local clipboard, and the *PrtSc* keystroke captures the entire visible display to the clipboard.

Another practical matter is how to start the X-client in the first place. Each X-display emulator provides several methods for starting X-clients on remote UNIX servers. XDMCP can be configured to "poke" a UNIX system to project a login window and, after the user authenticates, the environment is configured to start up a few standard X-clients such as *xterm* and *xclock* and *xload*. Other start-up methods use *telnet*, *rsh*, or *rexec*.The user can always manually *telnet* into the UNIX system and start the application manually.

Some Interesting HP X-Solutions

HP's X-terminals provide a parallel and serial printer port. A daemon process listens on TCP port 9001 and accepts print output from the HP-UX print spooler. Local terminal and window manager clients are provided, and the terminal can even boot from a local ROM card. The serial port may be used for a PPP session over a dial-up connection. There are also multimedia extensions such as CD-ROM, an MPEG card for displaying movies, and a local floppy disk. These X-terminals are offered in a range of high-performance configurations. The terminals also support HP's SharedX collaboration environment.

HP SharedX is an extension to X that allows the user to share copies of local windows with remote X-terminal users in either read-only or read–write mode. More in the next section. HP's X-terminals also support an extended MIB (management information base) that provides information about the memory available, how much fragmentation there is, and other details specific to X-Windows. A wide range of monitor sizes and characteristics is supported.

SharedX Collaboration

SharedX allows HP X-terminal users to collaborate with any other X-terminal users by sharing selected windows with them. Any X-window displayed on the screen can be shared with one or more remote X-terminals.

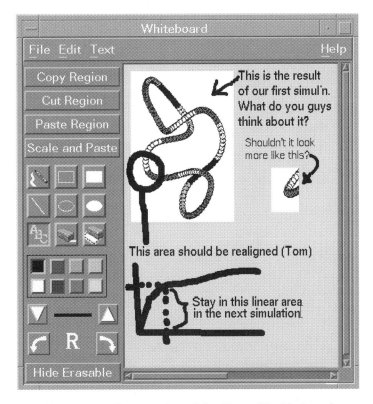

Figure 11-3   Screen shot of the SharedX whiteboard

The SharedX *whiteboard* lets remote collaborating X-terminal users draw pictures with simple drawing tools like lines, squares, and circles. Users can write text in several fonts and point sizes and make annotations with a pencil tool. They can also paste graphics "grabbed" from other windows on the display. There is also an eraser tool to clean up mistakes. There is even a rotation tool that lets the user turn graphics by 90 degrees. Multiple whiteboards can be shared at the same time, and each user can make a screen copy (or printout) of the contents to record the valuable information. The user initiating the *whiteboard* windows can save their contents with the file menu in TIFF, JPEG, or X-PIXMAP formats and Email these to the collaborating participants for their information. Remote users are able to take their own screen shots with a standard CDE or HP VUE utility such as *imageview* or with the standard X-Windows screen shot utilities *xwd* and *xpr*.

This makes SharedX application independent. A whiteboard X-client (Figure 11-3) is provided so that collaborators can draw little pictures, write little notes, and even paste graphics onto it. This is possible because SharedX allows windows to be shared in read–write mode. The default is read only. SharedX is supported on all HP X-terminals and HP UNIX workstations, meaning that users sitting at these terminals can initiate the window sharing using the *SharedX* command. Any remote X-terminal, including desktop computers running X-Windows emulators, can receive these shared windows.

SharedX does not copy the graphics areas of the shared windows to the remote windows. It accurately retransmits the *xlib* calls to the remote X-terminals, where the users there can move, resize, iconify, and close the cloned window. For example, SharedX can share these X-client's windows:

> *hpterm*
> *xclock*
> HP OpenView NNMGR windows (including child windows)
> Netscape Navigator
> *mpegplay*

Read-only sharing is much faster than read–write sharing, and graphically dynamic X-clients like *mpegplay* do not share well in real time.

The value of remote collaboration is very high. An HP consultant in Bellevue, Washington, can share network simulation results with a customer visiting the HP sales office in Paramus, New Jersey, using SharedX. They can talk over the telephone, make notes on the shared whiteboard, review shared images of the application response time graphs, and mark up sample charts for revising. Within an hour, the meeting is over and the expense of traveling 2500 miles is avoided.

The Publishing Industry and X-Windows

Computer platform requirements in the publishing industry include: the following:

> Stable and crash-proof systems
> Ease of use

      Interoperability with UNIX, Macintosh, and Wintel platforms
      High performance
      Large memory and file-size requirements
      PostScript fonts and support
      Color management system (CMS)
      Large monitors and millions of colors
      Multiple monitors per workstation

Applications used in the publishing industry often run on UNIX systems and include X-clients like Adobe FrameMaker and Photoshop. Collaboration via X-Windows is easy here. Taking advantage of NFS mounting increases the ability of users to share large files easily among systems. From an economics standpoint, multiple users can even share the same computer, since UNIX allows multiple concurrent interactive users to log in at the same time. One UNIX workstation with applications and data can be shared by users at their X-terminals.

X-terminal Features Summary

X-terminals support font servers, file servers for downloading code and configuration files via TFTP and NFS, login servers, and BOOTP/DHCP servers for IP configuration data. Authentication with UNIX hosts is via XDMCP direct, indirect, or broadcast modes. A local SNMP agent provides MIB-2 plus special MIB support for X-terminal management. Security of active windows is via *xhost* and the MIT-MAGIC-COOKIE, plus the screen locks and covers supplied with HP VUE and CDE.

Additional features include local clients like *xterm*, *mwm*, and CDE, but also a web browser and a Java Virtual Machine (JVM). Support for multimedia is via an MPEG card, printer daemons can intercept spooler data on TCP port 9001, and the local floppy disk can be NFS mounted by a remote system or accessed as the A-drive from the NTRIGUE Windows Application Server.

CHAPTER 12

Managing UNIX Networks

Introduction

U NIX systems will generally be spread across the enterprise and located near their users, managers, and resources. Remote administration is a must. Tools for administering a UNIX network include local physical control via an RS-232-C access port, the HP-UX system administration manager (SAM) X-client, Software Distributor, IT/O (a.k.a. Operations Center), and Network Information Services (NIS) for user administration. A successful UNIX networking architecture will include such features to support design and implementation.

HP network consultants will tell you that there are three kinds of customers: those who have Network Node Manager, those who wish they did, and those who don't know any better. In this chapter we'll review network management architectures (NMA), including SNMP and the HP OpenView suite. Also covered are basic event storms and event correlation theory. UNIX system administration issues and web-based administration tools will be introduced.

Network Management Architecture

The International Standards Organization (ISO) defines six standard areas of network management. <u>Configuration management</u> defines taking inventory of the existing network, designing and implementing IP address and DNS hierarchies, implementing DHCP and routing servers, monitoring changes, planning for upgrades and expansion, software and firmware updating, and report generation.

<u>Performance management</u> defines collecting operational performance data, setting thresholds for the collections, performing trend analysis, tuning network devices to improve throughput and response time, and network modeling and capacity planning.

<u>Event management</u> involves fault detection, diagnosis, analysis, and recovery. Operational aspects include help desk management, problem

management, escalation procedures, and disaster recovery (a.k.a. business continuity planning).

Security management defines documented company-wide policies and procedures that affect how users may access their systems, how the networks and systems are configured to log, audit, and detect and send alerts for security events, and how firewalls and access controls are designed, implemented, and operated.

Accounting management defines how network resources are utilized. This is perhaps the least practiced of the arts, but includes managing inventory, setting up and working with service level-agreements (SLA), monitoring network license servers, and establishing training for staff.

Systems management encompasses the five areas defined above and extends them to include

> Operational system control
> Storage management
> Printer management
> Database administration
> Application control
> Backup and recovery
> License distribution
> Software distribution

HP's adoption of a standards-based network management architecture (NMA) helped make the OpenView umbrella of products a compelling product line for network managers and developers alike. The underlying architecture can be represented in a fairly straightforward manner using the famous "backward-C" diagram depicted in Figure 12-1.

The backward C models the architecture of a network management station (NMS) by surrounding three sides of management applications (capital ems) with an application programming interface (API) for communicating with the user, the database, and the managed objects (capital ohs) elsewhere on the network. At a higher level, multiple levels of NMS functionality are possible, with a manager of managers (MOM) acting as the top-level administration console and intermediate management systems handling local events and passing along significant information upwards, filtering information that isn't important and dealing with it locally. This filtering involves the notion of an event sieve. In practice, the distributed product features of the NMS covers three tiers: the managed objects or devices, the collection stations (CS), and the management station (MS). The OSF/DME standardized on much of this functionality.

The term managed objects refers not only to real-world devices like hubs, switches, routers, desktop computers, X-terminals, LAN-attached printers and scanners, and server systems. These all have SNMP agents on board. But each network adapter inside a router or a server is also a managed object, and so is each 12-port Ethernet card in a hub. So is an application running on a server. A managed object has a name and a variety of attributes and values. For example, the LAN adapter in a UNIX workstation has the attribute isCard set to TRUE. The SNMP agents executing in smart equipment return some of these attributes, and the rest are provided by the autodiscovery engine *netmon*.

In addition to SNMP agents, managed UNIX systems may run additional agents for specialized tasks, such as

> Configuration management (such as a kernel parameter) via HP-UX SAM
> Software updates (such as a software distributor) via SDU utilities
> Disk backups (with OmniBack)
> Spooler management (such as OpenSpool) via the Palladium Print system
> Router management (such as CiscoWorks) via SNMP
> System monitoring (with the OPCenter agent) via DCE RPC

The suite of HP OpenView bolt-on products for these additional tasks is staggering, but to some degree or other, they integrate into the backward C network management architecture. Tightly integrated (using APIs) applications can create their own OpenView Windows maps and submaps, add customized menu items, use customized icons, store information inside the database, and communicate with the devices that they manage in a truly seamless manner. Loosely integrated applications typically use the menu system to launch component applications that put up their own windows independently of OpenView windows directly to the native windowing system of the platform that they run on.

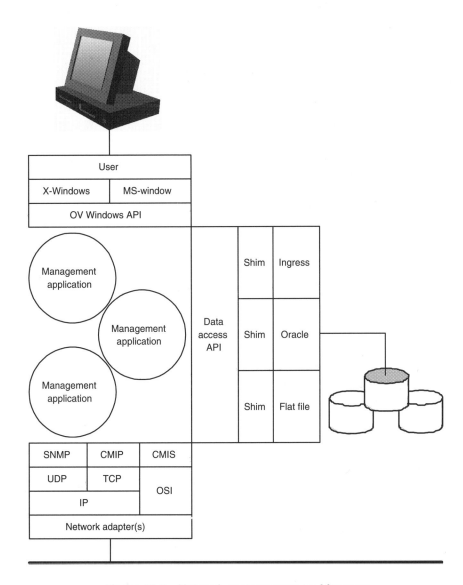

Figure 12-1   Network management architecture

A basic network management architecture (NMA) is a backward letter C, which network management applications access with standard APIs to communicate with managed devices like routers or UNIX systems. A standard database API offers access to a database, and the OpenView Windows API gives the applications transparent access to the user GUI, be that a networked X-Window GUI or the Wintel GUI.

SNMP Architecture

The simple network management protocol (SNMP) follows a two-tier client–server model. It is designed to be simple, and this has contributed to its overwhelming acceptance and success in the marketplace. SNMP is simple because the protocol has very few operations: get, getnext, set, and trap. SNMP has very low overhead because it takes advantage of the user datagram protocol (UDP). The SNMP agent does not have to store information between requests; it is stateless. This reduces the complexity of the code and keeps the agent footprint on the managed device small. See Figure 12-2.

SNMP operations are normally sent on UDP port 161, and SNMP traps are sent on UDP port 162. Since UDP does not guarantee datagram delivery, it's up to the network management application (the M) to manage time-outs, retransmissions, out-of-order replies, duplicate responses, and multiple outstanding requests.

The ability to handle a queue of multiple outstanding requests is an essential aspect of the architecture of a network management application if it is to scale well. Consider an SNMP time-out of 5 seconds with three tries. An unresponsive SNMP agent would stall the management application for a full 15 seconds. Suppose that a 5000-node network is being managed and 5% of them are down at any time. These 250 devices would accumulate 3750 seconds or add over 62 minutes to the polling cycle. Assuming that an active device replies within 1/10 second, the remaining 4750 polls would take 475 seconds or about 8 minutes more, for a total polling time of about 70 minutes average. The average polling rate is only 71 devices per minute.

SNMP is also popular because it's an open standard; it isn't trifled with by the vendors. A vendor may extend the management information base (MIB) in a standard way and distribute the abstract syntax notation one (ASN.1) ASCII code of the MIB so that network managers can compile it on the network management stations. This way the network management application will know the correct way to request information from the managed device from the vendor. The polite term for this is an enterprise-specific MIB, and there is a proper place for it in the MIB tree. For example,

HP's JetDirect printer interfaces provide additional SNMP traps to signal "paper out" and other service-oriented conditions.

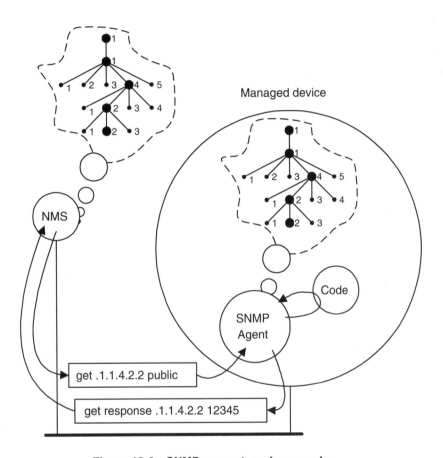

Figure 12-2   SNMP request–reply example
The SNMP architecture may be viewed as data exchanges between the network management station (NMS) and the managed device. The NMS client and the SNMP agent server both understand the same view of the MIB tree, so when the client sends a GET request, the agent will know what code to execute to obtain the necessary value to place in the GET reply.

An extensible SNMP agent is able to compile additions to the MIB tree when it first executes. The codes to support the reading and writing for the new variables defined in this MIB are provided. For UNIX systems, the MIB refers to script or applications by name; thus when the agent receives a request for an extended variable, the agent knows exactly how to get the necessary information. For example, to instrument a domain name server (DNS) so that its status can be determined with SNMP, some scripts can be written to interface with the DNS command line status commands and be called by the extensible SNMP agent.

The standard MIB-2 tree structure is supported by all modern SNMP agent implementations. This means that a considerable amount of configuration information can be discovered about a network of devices merely by interrogating the SNMP agents at the appropriate points of the MIB tree. For example, the NMS can "demand poll" a router's interfaces and IP groups to determine the networks it's connected to and what devices have used the router.

A MIB browser is a GUI supplied by all NMS vendors for navigating an SNMP agent's MIB tree, reading the values at the leaf nodes, or even changing a "settable" value. For example, the MIB browser can be used to navigate the IP configuration branch of a printer to discover what the subnet mask is. If it's wrong, the subnet mask can be corrected with an SNMP set issued in the MIB browser.

As of summer 1998, the nearly complete SNMP version 3 sports two important new features. The enhanced security model (versus the original unencrypted community name paradigm) allows for "safe sets" and 64-bit counters that avoid frequent counter wrap on high-speed circuits.

The Remote Monitoring (RMON-2) SNMP standard instrumentation may be embedded directly in hubs and switches or provided via stand-alone segment monitors for 10-BASE-T, 100-BASE-T, IEEE802.5 Token Ring, FDDI, or WAN serial lines. The RMON-2 standard provides for monitoring from the physical to the application layer of the OSI model. HP's NetMetrix product can display correlated views of network data from multiple HP LanProbes for performance management.

The HP OpenView Suite

HP OpenView is a marketing umbrella term describing system and network management products that run on Wintel, HP-UX, and Sun computers. The UNIX implementation will be the focus here. An OpenView application takes advantage of the OpenView runtime software running underneath it. HP sells a range of OpenView solutions, as do third parties. These products take advantage of core runtime support, such as

> Automatic device discovery (autodiscovery)
> Automatic map creation (autolayout)
> Default flat file database
> Basic event handler
> X-Windows GUI for interacting with the maps
> Multiuser support
> Remote access

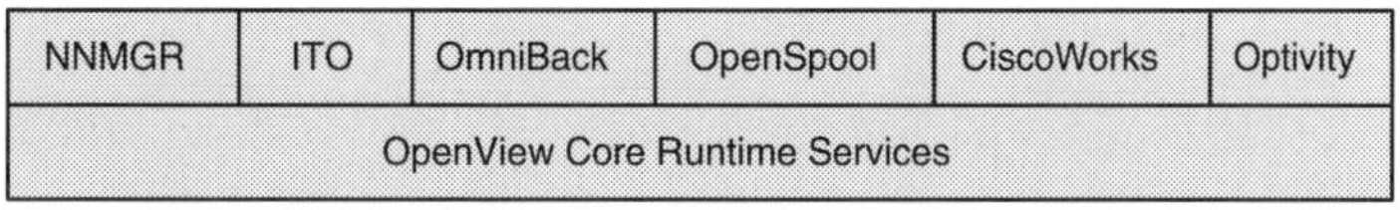

NNMGR	ITO	OmniBack	OpenSpool	CiscoWorks	Optivity
OpenView Core Runtime Services					

Figure 12-3   The OpenView runtime support layer
This simple architecture of OpenView shows how the core runtime services such as SNMP-based autodiscovery and an X-Window GUI for automatically created network maps supports value-added system and network management applications. By taking advantage of these powerful core services, third parties avoid the expense of duplicating them in their own products. Note that HP's Distributed Management (DM) developer kit is an integral tool for creating well-integrated management applications.

OpenView applications add functionality on top of the underlying platform (see Figure 12-3). For example, Network Node Manager (NNM or NNMGR) adds the SNMP data-collection subsystem and a GUI for creating MIB applications. IT/O (IT Operations) provides HP-UX system management functions. Software Configurator provides single-point administration software update services across the network. OpenSpool offers distributed spooling control from a single point of administration, and OmniBack supports single-point administration of distributed backup devices. Third parties such as Cisco and Bay provide element managers to manage their hubs, switches, and routers, which run on top of the core OpenView services.

Figure 12-4 is a slightly customized Network Node manager 5.0 map showing LAN segments and layer two devices such as hubs and switches.

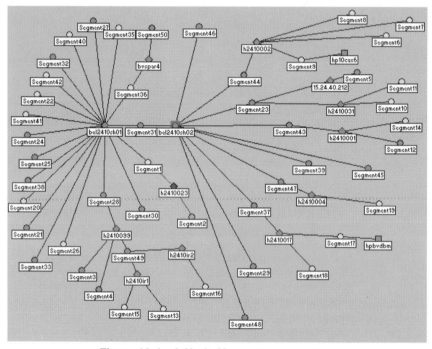

Figure 12-4   A Node Manager screen shot

This is an HP Network Node Manager subnet map showing segments (the circles), hubs, and bridges (the diamonds). All device and segment connections shown are based completely on information obtained via SNMP from network and system devices.

Many OpenView applications communicate with corresponding agents distributed with the product. Network Node Manager depends on SNMP agents to collect performance data. IT/O depends on an intelligent IT/O agent that resides on managed UNIX systems to monitor system events outside the scope of SNMP. OmniBack orchestrates the data flow between the media agents (typically, tape drives such as DAT and DLT arrays) from the disk agents. CiscoWorks depends on the SNMP agent built into the network electronics in order to control, configure, and collect data from Cisco network hardware products.

Events, Storms, and Correlation

Managing UNIX networks involves a paradigm called "management by exception," which means "no news is good news." "News" is delivered in the form of an event, which is received at the network management station in the form of an SNMP trap. What sort of event will generate an SNMP trap?

> A link-up trap is sent by an SNMP agent on a managed device.
> A hub detects a high collision rate and sends a trap to the NMS.
> A hub segments a bad port and sends a trap to the NMS.
> A device powers up.

NNMGR can generate a great variety of traps because of events that it observes via the routing polling it performs. Such traps include the following:

> Configuration event (bad subnet mask, MAC address changes, bad route)
> Status event (node up, node down, segment marginal)
> Threshold event (SNMP data collector arm or rearm)
> Custom event (software not responding)

A large managed network will usually give rise to a great deal of event activity at the NMS. Although it's possible to organize events into categories to avoid visual overload, in truth, there is so much activity here that the root cause of the events is buried in the noise, and the user tends to ignore the event subsystem entirely. In many cases, the network manager determines that it's best to simply take advantage of the status propagation properties of the OpenView hierarchical maps and react on the basis of outages presented on the maps. A green map means the network is healthy.

The solution to restoring the usefulness of network events is to break down the problem into manageable pieces. Except for the smaller networks, trying to manage an entire network from a single console invites information overload. By partitioning the network logically and managing these partitions with smaller collection stations (CS), activities such as polling, autodiscovery, and event handling are kept within the partition. Events and maps can be filtered before being passed to the single management station (MS). These are standard features of OpenView Network Node Manager 5.x.

While partitioning gives some control over event propagation, simple filtering does not give optimum results. A single event such as the failure of a network adapter can, in turn, cause dozens or hundreds of subsequent events—an event storm. Event correlation technology, an evolving field, gives the event management subsystem the intelligence to pass only key events, or even to generate a new event based on its inputs. This intelligence comes in the form of customized filter rules input by the network manager. An event correlation subsystem is a standard component of HP's OpenView Network Node Manager 6.0.

Note that events may be generated from a variety of agents, including the lowly SNMP agent, customized SNMP agents, MeasureWare, the IT/O agent, and third-party agents such as BMC's Patrol. Hooks available for these system-resident agents include APIs, scripts, and log file monitors. These events arrive at the IT/O console and find their way into message groups and event categories. IT/O's event correlation engine can reduce the event stream to a trickle of high-quality events. When a nice, clean, safe automated action is available to correct a problem, IT/O can instruct the remote agent (via the process *ovactiond*) to do so.

UNIX System Administration

A network of distributed UNIX systems may be managed from a central point of administration. A software depot concept can help assure consistent versions of code run on all systems. The HP Software Distributor facilitates this. A depot may consist of a simple CDROM containing software or be a small disk farm available through the network, accessible via the distributor daemon. In addition to software updates, the software configurator can be used to manage configuration files as well.

Even without a centralized approach to system administration, simple existing tools can suffice. It's always possible simply to *telnet* to a remote system, log in as the great and powerful *root*, and perform the necessary administration. HP-UX comes with the system administration manager (SAM), an X-client, which is a more convenient tool than *telnet* and the ASCII version of SAM.

For networks of NFS clients and servers, the network information service (NIS) keeps the "database" files consistent. These include the password and group files, the services file, and any automounter maps. The NIS slave (replica) servers are periodically refreshed from the NIS master server. NIS servers provide NIS clients within their domains with replies to queries for simple information. For example, when a user attempts to log in to a UNIX system, the login and password data are verified with the NIS server. This avoids the need to maintain a full password and group file on each system.

A small practical matter must be addressed with NIS. An NIS client binds with an NIS server by broadcasting a bind request on the local domain name on the local subnet. If no local NIS server exists, then the NIS client must bind directly with a specified remote NIS server by name.

System Performance Tools

In addition to the standard MIB-2 and enterprise extensions to the SNMP agents running on UNIX systems, extensive system performance information can be extracted using the HP MeasureWare agent technology. The MeasureWare agent collects and stores system performance statistics for later download and display by tools such as HP Perf/RX and PerfView. Even Oracle databases may be remotely monitored using MeasureWare agent technology. Application developers may instrument their code using HP's Application Response time Monitor (ARM) API to allow system managers to monitor application performance operationally.

Web-based Administration Tools

Web-based software is compelling because it advances the case for platform independence. The widespread availability of excellent web browsers for all desktop systems makes this technology widely usable. Netscape has done a particularly thorough job, with browsers for Macintosh, various Wintel flavors, and many UNIX platforms. The UNIX Netscape Navigators are X-clients, so you can run a web server on a UNIX machine and use X-Windows on the desktop.

Rather than write a new GUI and client–server software on a proprietary platform, developers can take advantage of the browser GUI for display functions, HTTP for client–server communications, Java for advanced functionality at the browser, and common gateway interface (CGI) scripts for the server-side processing (see Figure 12-5). The open nature of web-based technology makes it truly useful.

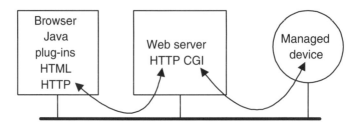

Figure 12-5   Web-based network management architecture
The three-tier model of web-based network and system management offers the user a web browser interface that may take advantage of plug-ins (platform specific) or Java applets (platform independent) to enhance the GUI. Java applets can provide a richer interface, including charting features and sophisticated user interaction. The browser communicates with the web server with standard HTTP. Back-end CGI scripts driven by image maps and web forms can communicate with the managed device using an appropriate protocol such as SNMP.

From the user perspective, a device can be managed by selecting the proper web server URL and navigating the GUI that presents itself in the browser window. Quite a bit of hay is being made about web-based network management. Some hardware vendors are even building HTTP daemons right into their equipment. HP now sells a web back end to NetMetrix 5.0 to let network managers view network performance data. HP Network Node Manager 5.0 now sports a web interface. Even the venerable HP JetAdmin tools for managing HP network-connected printers now has a web front end. Newer HP AdvanceStack hubs now have an embedded web server (Figure 12-6).

Web-based administration tools take advantage of static or dynamic HTML to create a basic GUI. Users enter information with standard web forms, and buttons and image maps can provide additional ways to interact. CGI scripts execute on the web server when users submit forms. This is how the user "reaches into" the real world to control devices and systems.

HP's OpenView Network Node Manager 6.0 offers a Java user interface that allows the user freedom to pick the browser of their choice or, theoretically, use a Java Applet runner instead.

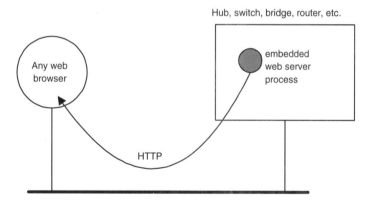

Figure 12-6   Embedded web server
Network element management using an embedded web server frees the user from the tyranny of management platform dependence. Here we see a network device responding to a simple HTTP request from the web browser, which may run on a Wintel, Macintosh, X-terminal, or UNIX box. This approach also frees the manufacturer from a major software development project on multiple platforms and lets it focus on the firmware in its product.

References

For the network management software developer, the following title will complement this chapter nicely:

Caruso, Raymond, *Power Programming in HP OpenView*. Upper Saddle River, NJ: Hewlett–Packard Professional Books, Prentice Hall, 1997, ISBN: 0-13-443011-5.

UNIX-based Video Servers

Introduction

D igitized video is becoming commonplace. It is finding applications in remote monitoring, in collaboration among multiple parties, and for recording and disseminating multimedia content to provide training, entertainment, and information distribution. Information in the form of computer animation and "screen capture" demonstrations for computer products are emerging as new forms of video content.

In this chapter we ask the question "Who needs talking heads to collaborate?" and introduce the technology behind digital video. We distinguish between streaming video servers and broadcast video servers. White Pine CU-SeeMe video conferencing software is discussed. HP's Broadcast Video Server and Starlight Networks products are reviewed.

Who Needs Talking Heads to Collaborate?

This opener smacks of attitude. Video conferencing is not a solution looking for a problem, but it's not necessarily a better way to collaborate just because you can see the speaker. Some real benefits of remote video-assisted collaboration are as follows:

> Reduced travel costs, time, and inconvenience
> People are readily available for a video conference
> Retains one-on-one spontaneity
> Ability to share applications and documents
> The talking head can be turned off

A great deal of job dissatisfaction results when people are required to travel to attend meetings in distant cities. The time overhead of the travel and the cost overhead of airplane tickets, parking fees, hotel room and car rentals, and meals is not trivial. Major corporations are spending hundreds of millions of dollars annually on travel-related expenses. They are also losing employees tired of living out of their briefcases. Proponents of physical meetings cite the high value of interpersonal interaction, and some meetings would be unsuccessful without physical presence. It is also a very interesting phenomenon that people are much more available for a video conference that for an airplane trip.

The interactive use of an electronic whiteboard is a major innovation. Many can follow along, anybody can contribute, and everybody can keep a copy of the proceedings. This beats copying the contents off a conference room wall board and even beats the poor little FAX-quality copy from expensive copy boards.

Additional applications for video conferencing include the following:

> Remote multiparty conferencing
> Two-party calls between software developers
> Operating room surgical assistance by a remote doctor
> Monitoring an assembly line
> Taking a legal disposition
> Remote demonstration of a software product

Digital Video Technology

The flow of video information begins at the moving image. It is sampled and digitized at a fixed frame rate and compressed to reduce the data to a manageable rate. The data may be stored for later transmission. Then the data are accessed for transmission and sent to the receiver. The receiver reconstructs the video and plays it back. Let's go into the details at each point the video data pass.

The moving image has attributes such as detail, color, and movement. The more detail in an image, the more information it contains. This is spatial information. The amount of color in an image also affects the amount of information. This is spectral information. Movement within an image means that it's changing between frames. This is temporal information.

The image is sampled and digitized. This is where the term digital comes in. A temporal sample rate is measured in frames per second (fps). Thirty fps is considered commercial quality. Each image is sampled spatially like a grid of points called picture elements, pixels, or pels. The number of horizontal and vertical samples is called the picture resolution. A typical resolution is 320 by 240. The number of bits per sample is typically 24, with 8 bits for each of the red, green, and blue channels. The typical raw video data rate is therefore a very impressive 30×320×240×24 = 55,296,000 bits/second.

Table 13-1   Video conference standards

Standard	Description
H.320	Defines how H.261, H.221, H.242, and H.230 integrate
H.261	Defines video coding and decoding (codec) algorithms
H.221	Defines the video frame transmission packet format
H.242	Defines data transmission protocol between sites
H.230	Defines control and indication (all setup and operation)
NTSC	525-line, 30-fps, 60-field/second TV video standard
CIF	Common Intermediate Format video, 288 by 300 at 30 fps
G.711	Audio compression of 3-KHz bandwidth at 64 Kbps
G.722	Audio compression of 7-KHz bandwidth at 64 Kbps
G728	Audio compression of 3Khz bandwidth at 16Kbps
Cinepak	Codec with 25:1 compression used for CD-ROM playback
JPEG	Joint Picture Experts Group lossy compressor 5:1 to 50:1 ratio
Intel Video R3.2	Intel Indeo codec
AVI compressor	Codec for Audio Video Interleave (AVI)

Clearly, some serious data compression is needed to reduce our 55,296,000-bit/second data rate for transmission. Even 100-BASE-T (fast Ethernet) can carry just a single video stream. Data-reduction methods include subsampling (sending fewer pixels and a smaller picture) and reducing the number of bits per pixel (to 8 bits per pixel). Compression methods such as LZW are lossless, but can typically achieve only 2:1 compression. Lossy methods such as MPEG and JPEG are capable of very high compression ratios by discarding visually unimportant information. The more advanced compression methods actually track the motion of image areas between frames and send the positional information. Surprisingly good video can be transmitted using the Apple QuickTime Cinepak compressor, which takes advantage of this. As a final twist, National Television Standards Committee (NTSC) television is interlaced for transmission.

Video is often stored on CD-ROM for mass distribution. CD-i formatted CD-ROMs can store about 60 minutes of MPEG-1 encoded video. Video clips can be stored on hard drives and in databases. Nonlinear video editing tools (such as Adobe Premiere 5) are typically based on QuickTime technology because it's cross-platform. During the edits, video sections can be copied and pasted, but pointers to the data are moved instead of copying megabytes of data per operation. Prior to being burned to CD-ROM, the video file is resequenced and then processed to ensure that its average and peak data rates are consistent with the media playback speed. The speed of the original ×2 CDROM is 300 Kbytes/second peak (2,400,000 bits/second), a far cry from the 55,296,000 bits/second needed by our video example above.

A video library stored in a multimedia database or in a flat file must be accessed for transmission to its destination. Given the large size of these files, the retrieval software has to buffer up the data and attempt to stream them toward the destination. The access software tries to keep its transmit buffer filled to guard against variations in the disk access speed and in the data transmission rate.

Real-time transmission of video data requires careful attention to network bandwidth, latency, quality of service (QOS), and jitter. When data are sent at 30 fps, there is 33.3 milliseconds between frames. Allowing a 10% jitter means that frames must be delivered every 33.3 ms plus or minus 3.3 ms or the user will notice. For one-way video, average network latency is not so critical, but for two-way conferencing, latency must be well under 1 second or the spontaneity is lost. The bandwidth of the network between the video transmitter and receiver must be adequate for the video data rate. A dedicated 384-Kbps full-duplex circuit delivers very acceptable video. The

QOS to support video requires a constant bit rate with no data loss. Dedicated circuits can provide this. So can ATM networks. When a video frame is delayed and does not arrive within the jitter window, it is discarded. It makes no sense to play a late frame. The playback software will likely repeat the last frame, instead.

At the video receiver, data are buffered to ensure that a smooth supply of data is available to the playback unit. Video is reconstructed by assembling the available video, sound, text, MIDI, graphics, and other tracks from the available received data. This involves the inverse of compression. Each frame is reconstructed at the desired resolution and bit depth.

Video playback requires an application such as QuickTime MoviePlayer, the QuickTime Netscape plug-in, or O/S-level support for embedded video in a document. The application provides playback controls to let the user stop, start, move forward or backward, change the size of the playback window, and even make simple edits to video stored in a local file. The playback application typically receives, reconstructs, and plays back a video stream. Conferencing applications like White Pine CU-SeeMe also include a recording component that interfaces with the video capture device and microphone to digitize, compress, and transmit locally generated video to the remote-user desktop computer. See Table 13-1.

Major technical issues in video conferencing include multiple video streams, slow receivers, network packet loss, contention with data traffic on the network, and taking advantage of the emerging reservation protocol (RSVP) and router priority queues. Later in this chapter we'll address these issues in more depth.

Architectures for video conferencing include point-to-point (two-party), multipoint (three or more parties), multicasting (one-way broadcasting), and the use of conferencing bridges and reflectors to support user coordination.

Streaming Video Servers

A digital video server is equipped with a mass storage system containing video files, software to access and transmit the data, and network adapters. Since the user wants to view the video in real time, it is necessary only to send the data at the rate that the receiver can handle them—in a steady stream that takes up only the bandwidth necessary to accommodate the data. It makes no sense to try to send the data any faster because this will not benefit the user and takes up precious bandwidth that can be used to support additional video streams.

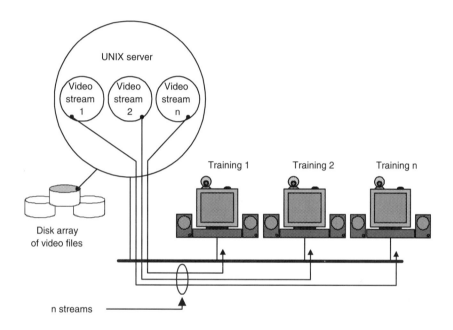

Figure 13-1   Traffic control at the video server
  A simple streaming digital video server is shown delivering n concurrent video streams across a local area network to local video-capable desktop computers. The video server is reading ahead and buffering in memory portions of each video file to ensure a steady supply of data. Concurrently, it is metering out fixed-bit-rate video streams to each destination. The server is aware of the local topology and will not al-low more video streams than can be reliably delivered across the Ethernet LAN.

Streaming better shares the available LAN and WAN bandwidth by reducing the nondeterministic (random, bursty, misbehaving) component of the video to a better-shaped, steadier, more predictable utilization profile. This predictability lets the streaming controller software govern and limit how many concurrent video streams the network can handle without degrading video performance. Naturally, this will work only when the controller understands the network topology between the video server and the users.

Transport for video traffic does not require guaranteed delivery, so the transmission control protocol (TCP) is not the correct choice for several reasons. TCP tends to burst data between the transmitter and the receiver until the receiver's receive window is filled. TCP has no mechanism for metering out the data at a fixed rate. Video data rates need to be steady. TCP also provides buffering services that are not necessary. Finally, TCP will retransmit lost data, but the timers are variable and far too long to meet the needs of video service. A video stream would stall while TCP works out the retransmission. Even the TCP ACK packets would simply get in the way, since acknowledgments are not needed in video streams.

User datagram protocol (UDP) is therefore the preferred transport for video data. It still provides the necessary multiplexing features to support multiple video streams, and it can support multicasting since it's connectionless. Some video server products use non-IP-based protocols, limiting their usefulness to environments where proprietary protocols are tolerated and limiting the scope of the conference to a LAN, since routers won't forward non-IP packets without CPU-expensive bridging turned on.

Broadcast Video Servers

Whereas digital video servers deliver digital data, broadcast video servers deliver broadcast-quality NTSC standard analog video over CATV coaxial cable. The video sources are derived from MPEG-2 encoded digital video stored on hard drives. The MPEG-2 decoding is performed in hardware. This is the core technology for video-on-demand (VOD) services, and the HP Broadcast Video Server addresses this market segment.

Broadcast video (Figure 13-2) has unique properties. Video frames are interlaced so that 60 fields per second are transmitted, alternating odd lines in one frame and even lines in the other. This prevents flicker. MPEG-2 supports interlacing; MPEG-1 does not.

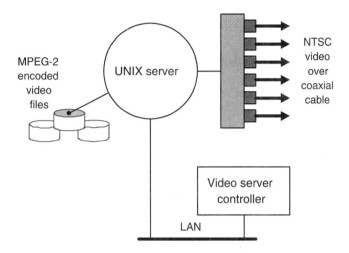

Figure 13-2   Broadcast video server architecture
A broadcast video server streams digital MPEG-2 encoded video from the hard
drives to the MPEG-2 decoding hardware, which converts the digital data to analog
video signals for transmission over coaxial cable. The video server controller is the
remote control that allows the service provider to select a new video title file, assign
an output cable number, schedule the streaming operation to begin, and make an accounting entry into the billing system.

CU-SeeMe Video Conferencing

Cornell University produced a public-domain video conferencing package
and named it CU-SeeMe. The desktop software is available for Macintosh
and Wintel platforms, and a UNIX reflector is available for multiparty
conferencing and broadcasting. The package supports low-cost cameras like
the Connectix QuickCam and provides the necessary codecs for audio and
video compression and decompression. White Pine Software offers a
commercial version of this software with added functionality.

CU-SeeMe provides many conferencing features. An ASCII "talk" window
is used by users to exchange simple text messages in real time. Users
without a camera can still "lurk" on a reflector and view ongoing
conferences or broadcasts (Figure 13-3). There is even a "push-to-talk"

feature that silences the microphone until the user wishes to speak. Available codecs allow the user to select video and audio data rates consistent with their data link speed, which for dial-up users is typically 22.8 to 33.6 Kbps.

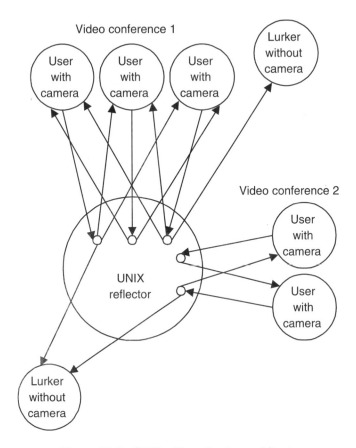

Figure 13-3 CU-SeeMe reflector architecture

A UNIX CU-SeeMe reflector is shown supporting a three-way video conference and a two-way video conference. One lurker is monitoring one of the three-way participants in conference 1. The other lurker is observing one of the participants from each of the video conferences. Judging by the number of video streams that the UNIX reflector has to handle, the system administrator has to carefully balance CPU and network utilization against the number of lurkers and video conferencing users that the reflector is permitted to support concurrently. Multiple reflectors with multicasting between them can create a scalable video conferencing solution.

Given a 100 by 100 pixel window and 4-bit video (16 grays) a frame rate of about 0.84 fps is possible at 33.6 Kbps, ignoring protocol overhead. The need for compression is clear, since users want to talk to as well as see each other. When CU-SeeMe is used over the Internet, the variable congestion and delay properties of the connections can reduce the video conferencing experience significantly.

The CU-SeeMe software includes a preferences file with a list of reflector systems located on the Internet. For multiway conferencing, a UNIX reflector box is used. Client systems connect to the reflector system and choose one of the existing conferences. The reflector will replicate a copy of all the other user video streams and direct it toward the one user, and it will also take the one user's video stream and duplicate it for the other users to see. Each user can decide which of the other users they wish to see on their screen.

For completeness, many other desktop video solutions are available, including PictureTel, Connectix VideoPhone QuickCam, Baraka Intracom's Mediafone, Intel's ProShare, StreamWorks, VDOLive, Progressive Networks' RealVideo, InSoft's CoolView, AT&T Vistium Personal Video, IBM's Person to Person, EyeTel's Communicator III, InVision's DeskTop, MRA's VidCall, Northern Telecom's Visit Video, and Specom's TelePro.

Starlight Networks Video Server

Starlight Networks produces a software products for HP-UX systems that acts as a special file system redirector (see Figure 13-4). This redirector is multimedia aware; it can distinguish a data file from a multimedia file such as a video clip. This distinction is critical, because the applications that read multimedia content have completely different requirements than applications reading data files. The major difference is the rate at which they need the data to be delivered.

As we saw earlier in this chapter, multimedia applications require only a steady stream of data to operate. They don't require the data to be delivered as quickly as possible, nor do they require the whole network bandwidth.

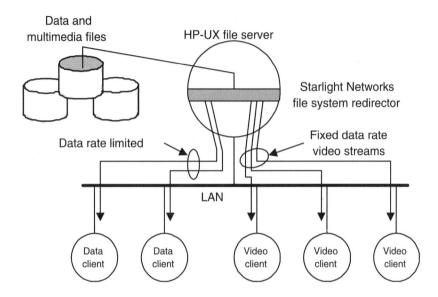

Figure 13-4   Starlight Networks file redirector support for multimedia
The anatomy of the Starlight Networks file system redirector shows how the server
is able to guarantee the performance of multimedia data streams in the presence of
the much more bursty data streams. The data files are sent to their respective clients
at a smooth but maximum rate, while the video streams are sent at the constant bit
rate needed by the streaming video clients. This arrangement reduces the burstiness
of the LAN traffic and allows data and video to coexist. When there are no video
streams to service, the file server is able to send data at the maximum rate permitted
by the shared-medium LAN.

Applications that open data files normally attempt to read the data as fast as
they can go, heedless of the network bandwidth consumed. For example, the
FTP client may not need to, but it still tries to do a network file transfer as
quickly as possible, and the *ftpd* daemon complies.

The Starlight Networks software can limit the rate at which data are metered
out, while at the same time sending out several multimedia streams across
the local area network. As long as the software can assume that the data and
the multimedia streams share the same LAN, it can satisfy the performance
constraints of the data and multimedia file transfers. This functionality is
contained totally in the network file system redirector on the HP-UX file
server. The clients are not aware of it.

Engineering Digital Video Solutions

Existing data networks can often support digital video to some extent, but they were often not built with video in mind. Indeed, many networks are constructed to deliver reliability first, offer connectivity second, and provide bandwidth third, with issues like quality of service and response time often being a distant fourth.

Without doing much analysis, it is possible to deploy video conferencing by taking advantage of software features that can limit the number of video streams to what the network can handle and by using smart servers like the Starlight Networks described above. Video performance on a LAN is better than on a WAN, since LAN available bandwidth exceeds that of a WAN by a hefty margin. But how many people need to video conference over a LAN, when they can just as conveniently assemble in one meeting room on the campus and interact directly?

Video conferencing over the WAN requires more engineering insight. Video conferencing software has less bandwidth to juggle, and the flow of data packets will be more of an issue. For example, a 1500-byte data packet takes 7.7 milliseconds of time to cross a T-1 circuit. This exceeds the 3.3-ms maximum jitter 30 fps video will tolerate before users notice the degradation.

Some simple things can be done to reduce the maximum packet size on the WAN. HP-UX has a *subnetconfig* command that lets the administrator reduce the maximum packet size for destinations not on the local subnet. The router can be configured to reduce the MTU of its serial ports. The router serial port is then configured with a high-priority queue for packets with UDP ports corresponding to the multimedia traffic.

For broadcast-mode video, IP multicasting is preferred because it avoids cloning video streams for each receiver, which can consume considerable bandwidth. IP multicasting requires router support. The digital video source simply transmits to the IP multicast address assigned to it, and the local router is configured to send a clone of this stream to the other routers in its list. Users at the remote sites simply "tune" their video-receiving software to this IP multicast address. Any number of local users can view the multicast video with no increase in network traffic. MBONE is an example of this technology (see Figure 13-5).

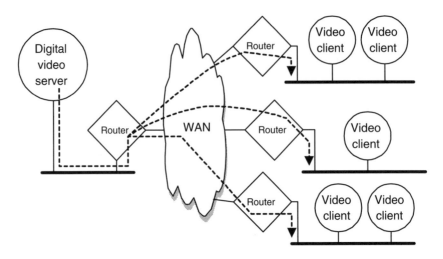

Figure 13-5   Multicasting in a routed network

A digital video server is using IP multicasting to transmit a single video stream onto its LAN. The local router replicates the stream to three remote routers, which in turn feed the IP multicast stream onto the LAN, where any number of video clients can "tune in." This architecture eliminates the need for local video support, since the routers can be administered from a central location. Not shown here are data packet sources or multiple router hops, both of which could vary the video stream in unpleasant ways.

When the opportunity to redesign the WAN occurs, the option of dedicating several 64-Kbps DS0s for video, perhaps several more for voice, and the remaining channels to data can be exercised. A second T-1 circuit can even be put in to support the video (see Figure 13-6). A digital access cross-connect switch (DACS) can be used to do this. Many companies provision one dedicated video circuit and create a video conference room that can be booked in advance by parties that need it. At the appointed time, the necessary DS0s are "nailed" to support the video conference and released when the meeting ends. The data traffic simply has a little less bandwidth to itself during the conference.

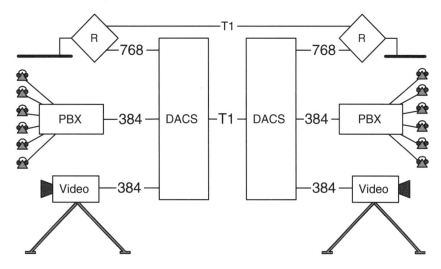

Figure 13-6   Dedicated video circuit bandwidth
A WAN design that dedicates up to 6 channels for video, up to 6 channels for voice,
and at least 12 channels to data by combining them using a DACS. A separate
24-channel T1 circuit carries data as well. The routers group the 768K and the T1 circuit into one logical data circuit, doing load balancing across them for best performance. The DACS are programmed to give unused voice or video channels back to
the data channel.

The ultimate in network engineering for video is to use a network simulation
tool to model the proposed network design, superimpose the reasonable
worst-case data and video traffic, and validate that the solution can meet its
performance objectives. Considerable what-if analysis can be done without
the risk of a "build it and see" or "we'll just add more bandwidth than we
need" approach. The what-if analysis might include the following:

> Compare reflectors and multicast models
> Check several alternative network topologies
> Find the best location for the video servers
> Establish bandwidth requirements for acceptable performance
> Determine where the knee is in the response-time curve
> Choose the best video conferencing product

A digital video solution's performance is measured using end-to-end or
round-trip delay, jitter, and packet loss. Network simulation tools like

CACI's COMNET III, Mil3's OpNet, and The Alta Group's Bones Designer calculate these performance metrics in their data analyzer modules. A typical simulation scenario will evaluate several standard network designs (say ISDN, dedicated lines, switched Ethernet, and ATM) by distributing the video sources and sinks among the topologies, varying the number of active users over a range, and plotting the performance metrics for each topology. The best network design will be easy to pick out of the simulation results.

A Manufacturing Application for Web and Video

In a manufacturing environment, new equipment, materials, procedures, and users require that current easy-to-access multimedia data be available from any desktop computer (see Figure 13-7). A UNIX web server equipped with a good search engine, a well-laid-out web page hierarchy with navigation bars, and QuickTime video clips compressed for web viewing can provide factory floor workers with training footage on the use of milling equipment, lathes, metal forming equipment, or safety procedures

The video clips may be stored on a separate CD-ROM drive that's part of a small array connected to the UNIX file server. To store huge amounts of video, an array of DVD-5 4.7-gigabyte DVD-ROMs can store video on the MicroUDF file system format. If the movies are recorded as standard MPEG-2 DVD movies, then the user's desktop computer will need an MPEG-2 hardware decoder. If the MicroUDF file system just stores standard QuickTime movies, no extra hardware is needed.

Figure 13-7   Manufacturing video training and web technology
This is a sample web page delivering a quarter-screen (320 by 240) millions of colors training video showing the use of a drill press. Notice that the QuickTime movie includes a text track that carries the same information as the audio track. The movie controller allows the operator to stop, start, reverse, fast forward, and otherwise manipulate the movie.

References

Adobe Systems, *Adobe Premier, Classroom in a Book*. Upper Saddle River, NJ: Hayden Press, a division of Prentice Hall, 1993, ISBN: 1-56830-052-2.

Gertler, Nat, *Multimedia Illustrated*. Indianapolis, IN: Que Corporation, 1994, ISBN: 1-56529-936-1.

Rustici, Robert, *CU-SeeMe Internet Videoconferencing*. New York: MIS Press, 1995, ISBN: 1-55828-490-7.

Stern, Judith L., *QuickTime, The Official Guide for Macintosh Users*. Indianapolis, IN: Hayden Books, 1994, ISBN: 1-56830-129-4.

Szuprowicz, Bohdan O., *Multimedia Networking*. New York: McGraw-Hill, Inc., 1995, ISBN: 0-07-063108-5.

Internet Service Providers

Introduction

Internet service providers (ISP) offer home users and businesses alike access to the that big cloud called the Internet. In this chapter we review the nature of the ISP business, address the major role of UNIX networking, and diagram the structure of the Internet. ISPs maintain web server farms, offer hosting services, provide DNS and IP routing, support SMTP and news feeds, and provide telnet and FTP services complete with authentication support. We will also discuss what web technology is, introduce Java on UNIX, give some insight into the new PNG and FlashPix file formats, and briefly review the history of the web servers.

The Nature of the ISP Business

In addition to providing simple connectivity to the Internet, ISPs also offer a set of services to its customers. Consider the single-user home customer (Figure 14-1). A standard package provides the following:

> Telephone support
> Account management
> Billing
> Configuration assistance
> Reliable DNS
> IP routing
> Dial-up terminal access
> Dial-up PPP access at 22.8 to 33.6 Kbps
> Dial-up 56 Kbps access
> ISDN access (64K and 128Kbps)
> Shell account (on a UNIX system)
> POP3 mailbox and SMTP support
> Personal web page disk space and support via a web server
> Personal CGI script support (Perl and shell scripting)

The home user can have a Wintel machine, a Macintosh, or a Linux/UNIX system as long as it supports the necessary PPP standards and runs the necessary TCP/IP applications for Email, telnet, FTP, and WWW access. The user's system is effectively a node on the internet with full access; no firewalls are in the way.

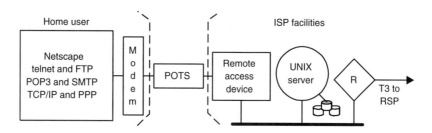

Figure 14-1   ISP PPP service architecture

A typical ISP provides a toll-free telephone number that terminates on a remote access device that supports PPP and cooperates with the UNIX server to authenticate the user ID and password. IP datagrams sent from any application on the home user's system pass directly to the router to the regional service provider (RSP). The UNIX server may host the user's home directory, POP3 mailbox, and web pages, which are accessible via telnet and FTP. The same UNIX machine may also run the web, FTP, SMTP, and DNS servers. Larger ISPs may provide a second UNIX system containing the user home pages, which are NFS mounted to the main web server.

Corporate clients, including educational institutions, require a permanent high-speed connection from their ISP, typically in the form of a fractional or full T1 point-to-point line, a frame relay circuit, or a primary rate ISDN connection. The ISP will provision the circuit, install and manage (and retain ownership of) a router, and allocate a public class C IP address. Routing information to and from this class C network is forwarded to the Internet's routers, and a domain name is associated with this network. The ISP may even offer a firewall to its customer, for those not inclined to deal with them.

ISPs often offer hosting services. A physically secure facility on the ISP premises houses the customer-furnished computer and is responsible for managing it. The ISP provides Internet connectivity, power, IP routing, DNS support, and physical security. This is an excellent way to create an Internet presence without dealing with the expense of extending the Internet to private facilities. It also offers a way for private companies to locate redundant DNS machines off site.

UNIX and the Internet

The TCP/IP suite came very early to UNIX. Historically, UNIX machines often acted as IP routers as well as servers for DNS, news, SMTP Email, telnet, archie, veronica, gopher, and FTP. Web technology first appeared as NSCA's famous Mosaic product, taking the form of an X-Windows client application. This suite of TCP/IP protocols and applications naturally migrated to desktop computers, and today the Wintel and Macintosh platforms enjoy unparalleled Internet functionality.

UNIX is a good choice for the development of Internet technologies because it enjoys a 32-bit architecture and a linear memory model. Contemporary UNIX hardware and software are 64 bit capable, such as HP-UX 11.x and later. The presence of a TCP/IP stack in no way affects applications as a result of the linear memory model. For systems with insufficient physical memory, the UNIX virtual memory system lets users run programs that would consume many times the available memory; but since many applications run well with only parts of them in memory, UNIX still performs admirably under heavy memory pressure. This makes UNIX suitable for heavily loaded web servers.

The protected memory model has always been a part of UNIX; it was not added later, and so a UNIX system continues to function even though applications may attempt to access illegal memory locations. This adds to the stability of the platform. UNIX has true preemptive multitasking. Even the X-Windows system multitasks, so a UNIX system can perform well under heavy CPU loads. And UNIX can run in symmetric multiprocessing (SMP) hardware to build up very large scalable computing solutions.

UNIX also enjoys a robust inode-based file system that doesn't readily fragment, and supports multiuser environments intrinsically. UNIX will even allow different users to execute applications in a secure manner at the same time. Indeed, UNIX has a long history of security features. In fact, a glance at Table 14-1 confirms the security architecture of UNIX as the best in all the land:

Table 14-1   Viral immunity of the major computer platforms

Operating System	UNIX	Macintosh	Wintel
Approximate number of viruses	0	100	10,000

For all these reasons, UNIX can accommodate multiple protocol stacks, multiple network adapters, and multiple users and remain stable under heavy resource pressures. UNIX is an ideal choice for Internet server applications. UNIX earned its place as a commercial-quality operating system many years ago and continues to be the choice for mission-critical corporate applications. UNIX continues to be the platform of choice for Internet applications and is the preferred O/S for ISPs.

The Internet's Architecture

This section will be out of date by the time it hits the presses so rapid is the expansion and investment activity of the Internet. The reader is encouraged to visit *http://www.boardwatch.com*, Boardwatch magazine's web site, where Internet topology information is featured. See Figure 14-2 for a generic architecture drawing of the Internet.

Basically the Internet is a big IP network based mostly on Cisco routers. Millions of IP networks are interconnected in a hierarchy that uses routing protocols such as classless interdomain routing (CIDR) and BGP-4 to maintain the routing tables. ISPs upload (readvertise) their routing tables to the Internet routers at least daily. The backbone links are a mixture of T3 (45 Mbps) and ATM OC3 (155 Mbps). ATM makes up about 45% of the links.

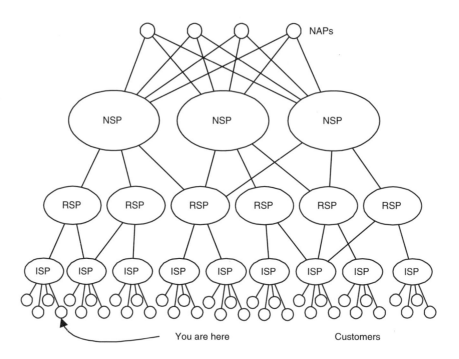

Figure 14-2   The Internet's four tiers

The Internet's architecture shows the multiple tiers beginning at the network access points (NAP). A network service provider (NSP) must connect to all four to qualify for the title. NSPs typically build large, high-speed WANs across the country and allow the regional service providers (RSP) to connect. The ISPs connect to the RSPs. ISPs can connect with multiple RSPs, which in turn can connect to multiple NSPs to improve reliability and performance. Note that some ISPs and RSPs are known to create private connections directly between them, an arrangement called peering, in order to reduce network latency or increase reliability.

Web Server Farms

A web server receives HTTP requests from web clients for files containing HTML, images, sounds, movies, and others types of data. It is obligated to locate the file and transmit it to the client. All this sounds very basic, but a popular web site may sustain a million "hits" a day. Is that a lot? Suppose each that hit involves a 2-Kbyte transmission (2 Kbytes = 2048 bytes) and that the activity occurs over 10 hours. The average data rate is about 455,111 bits/second, something a 512-Kbps fractional T1 circuit could handle with ease and which a single SCSI disk drive could manage with ease.

But averages can be deceiving. HTTP requests are rarely spaced uniformly in time. There are periods of peak activity around 3 P.M. daily on domestic U.S. OC3 links. Web pages often contain many images, so a single web page can lead to dozens of file transfers at the maximum rate of the network connection. Web traffic is very bursty, so our 1million hits a day on the average may actually result in bursts of ten times this figure.

Web servers do more than simply honor HTTP requests. They also execute CGI scripts, operate search engines, handle FTP and Email, and service active shell sessions. Web servers are increasingly running Internet Commerce applications. Pioneers in this area include the Amazon.com Internet bookstore and First Security Bank. More recently, Egghead Computer began selling its product exclusively through its web site. Apple Computer in 1997 claims it sold $12 million worth of products through its web site in its first month of Operation, and in 1998 that rate exceeded a $1 million per day. Dell Computer is believed to sell between $2 million and $3 million a day of Wintel systems through its web site. The bottom line is that Internet servers have to do a lot more work these days to support Internet Commerce. There is a strong need for a scalable web server farm.

A single UNIX web server can be made only "so big." Basic compute resources like RAM, disks, LAN adapters, and number of CPUs can be added to increase the web server's performance, and some expert system tuning (such as using *inetd* to launch *httpd* versus a fixed number of *httpd* daemons) can stretch a web server performance. At some point, additional web sever systems will be needed to meet the growing workload. This suggests that some form of load balancing will be needed to keep all the servers about equally utilized. Several methods are available.

Many DNS implementations can be configured to return the IP address for a name from a round-robin list. For example, if there are ten servers all to be known as www.company.com, the DNS will hand out the IP address for 192.6.173.1 for the first DNS lookup, hand out 192.6.173.2 next, then

192.6.173.3, and finally 192.6.173.10, before returning back to 192.6.173.1 and repeating the process. This will keep all ten web servers equally loaded.

HP's Network Connection Policy Manager (NCPM) is better suited to this task because it load balances on the basis of existing utilization metrics. Whereas the round-robin DNS approach will pass a request to a heavily loaded system while a lightly loaded system is available, the NCPM will return the IP address of the least utilized system so that it gets the next hit.

Manual tuning of web server content is still a powerful and often necessary tool. If a hot news story is posted on a site, the server with that web page will see a serious increase in demand. Perhaps the content should be moved to a faster server, and large images and embedded multimedia should be temporarily removed. There is also good reason to keep the size of individual web pages down, say to under 50 Kbytes, to ensure a more consistent download time.

When we have multiple web servers, how do we manage the content? Should each server contain a fraction of the total content, with the main server linking to these other servers? Should each server have a duplicate copy of the data? How scalable are these approaches? Let's take advantage of our networking, UNIX, and NFS expertise and review the following network and systems architecture.

Before implementing the single-FDDI solution (Figure 14-3), scalability issues may force us to reconsider the LAN topology supporting the UNIX servers. The single shared-medium FDDI ring may not sustain all the web and NFS traffic, especially if the servers are also running search engines. More T3 lines may be brought in to handle anticipated increases, and more web and FNS servers may be added to handle future loads. A solution that retains the advantages of FDDI is given next (Figure 14-4). But why do we still use shared-media FDDI when we could use FDDI switches, cheaper fast Ethernet switches, ATM, or even fibre channel? Reasons for retaining FDDI are as follows:

> Physical reliability of the dual-ring architecture
> Excellent performance under extreme load
> Large MTU (4500 bytes)
> Mature technology
> FDDI links can span large distances
> FDDI is already in use and we understand it

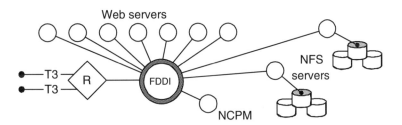

Figure 14-3   Using NFS with web servers
A web server farm on a 100-Mbps FDDI ring fed by two 45 Mbps T3 lines takes advantage of a pair of NFS servers to give all servers identical access to content. The
NCPM machine does the web server load balancing. Most web traffic is in the outbound direction, so the FDDI and dual T3 lines are fairly well matched. FDDI performs very well at high utilization and its 4500-byte MTU makes for efficient NFS
file transfers.

Suppose we are asked to design an "extreme web farm" that has tremendous
scalability, that will accept multiple OC3 and T3 WAN links, and that will be
very reliable. What architecture would be appropriate to meet these
requirements? We'll assume some type of switching LAN is needed, then.

In this architecture, at least two LAN adapters for the routers and NFS
servers ensure high availability (Figure 14-5). They also provide about the
right bandwidth. Each web server can access two NFS servers directly, and if
100-BASE-T adapters are used, the bidirectional 200 Mbps roughly
balances the 320 Mbps available from a SCSI-3 40 MBps disk subsystem.
As the solution scales, it is tempting to add network adapters to the routers
and NFS servers to provide full connectivity, but this can add considerably
to the expense, may not provide significantly increased reliability, and may
not be practical if their I/O cages can't accommodate the extra network
adapters.

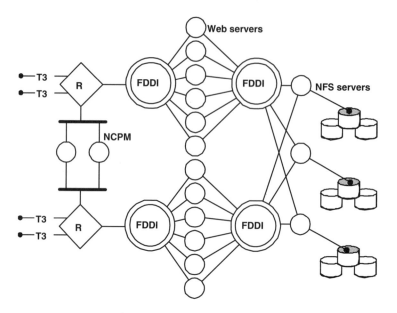

Figure 14-4   A scalable web server and NFS server architecture
This scaled-up web farm has an additional router and two more T3 circuits connected
to another RSP. The load-balancing NCPM service is now running a secondary DNS
server and is connected to Ethernet ports on the routers for additional reliability. To
handle the extra LAN traffic, we've added a second FDDI adapter to each web
and NFS server and created three more FDDI rings. All web servers have access
to all NFS servers.

Hosting Services

A company wants a publicly available web server setup but doesn't want it
on the corporate network because of security issues and because of the
performance impact it will have on the link with their ISP. An off-site
location is preferred for the web server, which has no sensitive information
on it. An ISP offering hosting services can overcome all the security,
performance, and location issues and even provide proper DNS support for
the company's web server, so Internet users trying to access *http://
www.company.com/index.html* will reach the correct system.

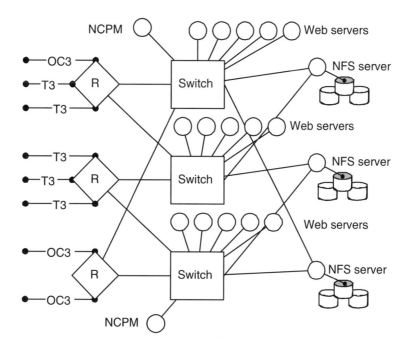

Figure 14-5   Switching architecture for web and NFS servers
Our highly scalable web farm is shown with three routers connecting to the RSP.
Each router is connected to two of the three switches. Each switch is a subnet. The
web servers have been given single LAN adapters and belong to just one subnet. The
NFS servers are given two LAN adapters, on the same subnets as the corresponding router. The NCPM DNS machines are single-homed and two of them
are sufficient. Note that the loss of a single NFS server, a switch, or even a router
leaves the entire web farm functional. The switches should be at least FDX
100-BASE-T or faster LAN technology.

Note that it's not a requirement that the corporate web pages reside
physically on a hosted system. ISPs maintain sizable UNIX machines that
are quite capable of hosting hundreds of home pages. An ISP's home-based
customers are typically given around 5 megabytes of disk space for personal
web pages and for an extra service charge, they will even register a domain
name. See Figure 14-6.

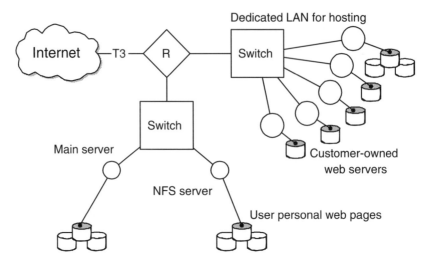

Figure 14-6   ISP hosting service
ISP web server hosting service provides a separate high-performance switched
subnet for customer-owned web servers. Small businesses may share disk space on
the NFS server, take advantage of a custom domain name, and appear for all intent
as a separate entity on the Internet. Users manage their web page content directly on
the NFS server. The main web server NFS mounts the personal web pages.

DNS and Routing

The domain name service (DNS) is a lightweight client–server protocol used
to look up computer names to get an IP address (see Figure 14-7). It also
supports inverse lookups—looking up the name of a system when you know
the IP address. Another major lookup is the mail exchange (MX) record used
by SMTP forwarders to send Email toward its destination. DNS is absolutely
essential to the workings of web technology because there are millions of
systems with unique names and IP addresses. Many are dynamically
assigned to individual home computers as Internet users log in and out of the
net. This large volume of dynamic information cannot be maintained in a
centralized flat file form. It has to be distributed and organized so that those
people who control a group of systems and IP addresses can put up an

authoritative DNS server to serve this information to the Internet. In summary, DNS is essential to the Internet because of the following:

There are too many names and IP addresses to manage centrally.
IP addresses and computer names are dynamically allocated.
Flexibility is needed in organizing the name space using domain names.
SMTP needs DNS to find mail forwarders.
It provides support for POP3 Email.

An ISP provides an authoritative DNS server that the Internet can access so that the ISP web pages, the user web pages, and the hosted systems can be accessed by name. This is typically done when users click on a URL or send Email. Private companies also set up DNS servers for Internet access to their web servers and for internal use as well.

DNS is a client–server protocol based on standards. There is a server called the domain name server and a client called the resolver. Each has configuration files that control it. UNIX resolvers look in a file called */etc/resolv.conf* to find the IP addresses of the name servers, the local domain name, and search domain names. The name server daemon *named* reads a configuration file called */etc/named.boot* for authoritative name and IP address "database" files and pointers to other authoritative DNS servers and to root name servers.

ISPs also advertise routing information on each router interface connected to their regional service providers. All networks reachable via these routers are advertised. Several years ago, a small crisis was avoided when the size of the IP routing tables grew so large that router memory overhead became excessive. It does not make much sense to have a unique route for every network reachable on the Internet. The solution to the crisis is classless interdomain routing (CIDR), which aggregates and allocates contiguous groups of class C addresses. This aggregation makes possible a significant reduction in routing table size.

SMTP and News

ISPs also provide Email and Internet News services to their customers. SMTP in the form of the UNIX *sendmail* daemon gets the mail in and out of

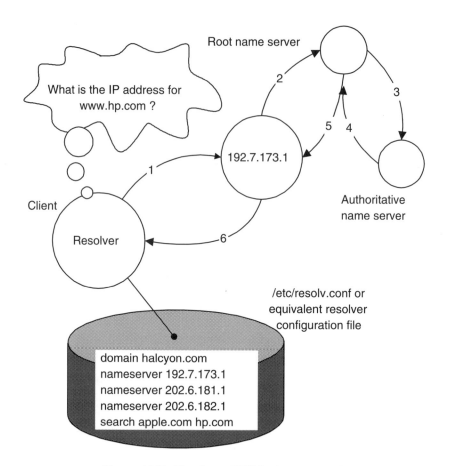

Figure 14-7   Tracing a DNS lookup request

This is the sequence of events initiated by the client system when it asks for the IP address of the *www.hp.com* system. The client's local resolver notes that a name server at 192.6.173.1 is available and sends it the request (1). This name server does not have the information in cache, is not authoritative for the hp.com domain, and has no direct knowledge of which name server is, and so it passes the request to a root name server (2).The root name server knows an authoritative system and sends the request to it (3). The authoritative name server reply (4) is sent back to the root name server, which in turn passes it to the local name server (5), which passes the information to our client (6). All the nonauthoritative name servers will cache the information looked up.

the server. Users with shell accounts may read the mail with the *elm* mailer, which reads mail directly out of the user's mailbox. Dial-up users will probably use an Emailer that supports POP3 to retrieve the mailbox contents to the user's desktop computer hard drive, where the mail can be read at leisure. Thus, a POP3 daemon is standard fare on the ISP's server.

Unwanted Email messages called spam became a serious concern beginning around 1997. Large mailing lists are created, clever subject headings are invented, and often bogus source addresses are included, and a flood of messages is sent to unsuspecting user mailboxes. Some ISPs offer to filter out messages from known spam addresses, but this is an ongoing battle. Most Email programs include filters that can be set to filter out spam. The downside of the spam filters is that legitimate but unsolicited mail may be mistaken for spam.

Long before there was a web there were Internet news and the network news transport protocol (NNTP). This is basically an Email system with some automated list keeping support. Users typically send ordinary SMTP Email to the list servers, which sort and thread the messages, allow for an optional moderator to keep things civilized and orderly, and forward the messages to participating news servers. Many ISPs keep local news groups in support of their users. For example, North West Nexus (*http://www.halcyon.com*) maintains several news groups at *news://news.halcyon.com.* See also the DejaNews web site at *http://www.dejanews.com.*

Internet news groups can be quite lively, and many of them allow users to send attachments, which are typically uuencoded. This places pressure on the ISP server's disk space, and the influx of messages places some pressure on the incoming Internet links.

The ISP is obligated to run the Network News Transport Protocol (NNTP) to exchange news with remote news servers. The ISP news server subscribes to certain news groups from the remote news servers and archives the data so that customers can access them using their personal news readers.

Authentication: Telnet and FTP

The ISPs supporting shell accounts basically give users an account on their UNIX server, which is accessed via a modem-connected terminal, or *telnet*, or FTP, depending on the user preference and capabilities. UNIX is a multiuser system, and hundreds of users can be logged into their accounts concurrently on a typical day.

Let's review how *telnet* logs you into a UNIX system. The internet daemon *inetd* listens on a group of well-known port numbers, which are listed in */etc/inetd.conf* and which are read at the time *inetd* is invoked or restarted with the *inetd -c* command. One of these well-known ports is 23, the *telnet* port. When a user invokes the *telnet* client program, the client connects to port 23 of the target system. When *inetd* detects this, it notes (from *inetd.conf*) that the *telnetd* program is supposed to get the connection, spawns a copy of *telnetd*, passes the socket descriptor to it, and waits for the next socket connection.

telnetd spawns a copy of *login*, which requests the user login and password in raw mode and then executes a copy of the user's login shell (per the */etc/passwd* file). The login shell will execute the system-wide */etc/profile* or equivalent and then execute the *$HOME/.profile* or equivalent. Finally the user is given the command prompt by the shell program. Full command line access to UNIX is now available, a wonderful feeling after being constrained by a graphical desktop operating system for most of the day.

Command line access to UNIX means that the user can read mail using *elm*, put and get files with *ftp*, surf the web using *lynx*, and even search for files using *archie*. The typical ISP customer will use its shell account for educational purposes and to maintain its web pages.

The ISP may choose to enable UNIX password aging. This feature can force the user to change passwords after a certain time and prevent it from changing the password again for another interval.

The ISP will probably want to support anonymous FTP into their system as a courtesy to its users. Normal FTP services require an account on the system, which means that the user needs an account name and valid password. Such a user is allowed to change directories anywhere in the system and copy files to and from them consistent with their access rights. Anonymous FTP recognizes two additional user names, *anonymous* and *ftp*, and allows any password at all to be entered. Some systems require a password that looks like a valid Email address. An anonymous FTP user does not have full system access; rather, it is rooted at some directory of the system manager's choosing, such as */home/ftpuser*, and attempts to perform stunts like

```
cd /etc
get passwd
```

will result in the anonymous FTP user accessing the bogus */home/ftpuser/ etc/passwd* file and not the true */etc/passwd* system password file. To prevent abuse of this service, ISPs may configure the directory permissions such that legitimate users are allowed to put files into the anonymous FTP area, and anonymous FTP users are only allowed to get files.

Web Technology

The Internet has been around for years. It was initially built by the government and now the backbone is entirely commercially supported. Originally, the TCP services used on the IP Internet were NNTP, SMTP, FTP, and *telnet*. Anonymous FTP archives could be searched via *archie*, an archives and indexing engine that periodically harvested the directory structures of anonymous FTP sites and created a searchable database. The author has fond memories of his first *archie* search for security information using just the keyword "secur" and getting such a treasure trove of information that it cost a full week of time, hundreds of megabytes of disk space, and several reams of paper. This was when much information was stored in compressed PostScript files.

Once Mosaic on UNIX was commercialized by Netscape Communications and made available for desktop computers, the concept of storing information on distributed web servers and linking it all in some organized, customized way using network-linked hypertext exploded. Over half the Internet traffic is due to web protocol. Today, the Internet service provider provides a web server for their customer home pages, all major and most minor companies have a web presence, and anybody with a hundred dollars can register his own domain name.

Tools for authoring web content as WYSIWYG (what you see is what you get) are abundant. All major word processor and publishing packages, such as Corel Word Perfect™, ClarisWorks™, and Adobe FrameMaker™, provide an HTML export feature. Stand-alone packages, such as Netscape Composer™, Adobe Page Mill™, and Claris Home Page™, also abound.

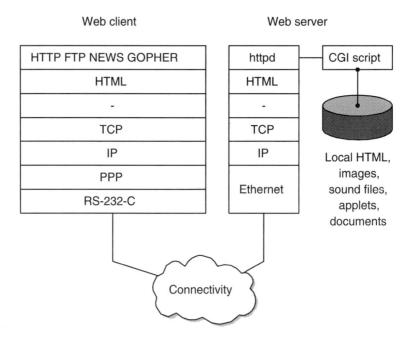

Figure 14-8   The OSI view of web technology
The architecture of web technology seen from the OSI model point of view is a simple two-tier client-server application driven by client requests for HTML and subsequent client requests for in-lined images, sound files, and applets. If the HTML contains a form, then a CGI script executes, and tier three applications execute. The user may register a product, make a purchase, or invoke a search engine via a broswer form. The CGI script typically completes by returning a page of HTML to the user, which the browser dutifully displays.

The basic web technology, browser, HTML, HTTP, the web server, and some CGI scripting, worked well (see Figure 14-8), but commercial interests have expanded the capabilities of web technology by extending the HTML language, evolving HTTP, including plug-ins to extend the ability of the browser to display exotic multimedia content, and allowing cascade-style sheets and extensible HTML (XML); even JavaScript™ and Pure Java™ applets can be inserted using the *applet HTML* tag. This extends the flexibility and capability of the web browser interface. Still, there are low-bandwidth and terminal-based scenarios that require a nongraphical interface, and the program *lynx* fills that need.

Further extensions into secure Internet commerce came to light with the invention by Netscape of the secure sockets layer (SSL) to support encrypted data transmissions between the browser and the web server. This paved the way for companies like Amazon.com™ to set up shop on the Internet.

UNIX and Java

Java was invented by Sun Microsystems. It is available for all major computer platforms. It is well suited to the UNIX environment because of its support for multitasking, multiprocessing, and threads, an open widowing system (X-Windows), inherent O/S security, RISC-enhanced CPU performance, and a linear virtual memory model with 32- and 64-bit native addressing.

Netscape Navigator 3.0 and above support Java. The Java virtual machine (JVM) implementation is within the browser itself, and no explicit O/S support is needed for it. Since Navigator is an X-client, this means that Java applets are X-clients capable of projecting their window to the X-display that the user is browsing at. Since the X-display can be a UNIX workstation, an X-terminal, a desktop computer (Wintel and Macintosh), or a network computer, users in any environment can run Java applets with Navigator. This is unequaled openness.

Java applets are byte streams of compiled Java code stored in files located at the web server and referenced by the HTML that takes advantage of their capabilities. Netscape's JVM loads and executes them. An applet is required to execute in a strictly controlled secure environment by the JVM, and the applet is discarded when it terminates. Note that Java applets are quite a different thing than JavaScript, which is a web scripting language with different syntax and capabilities.

A Java application is stand-alone, compiled, native code written within the Java language, compiled with the Java compiler, and linked with the UNIX loader to create an application. A Java programming tool kit can be purchased for HP-UX.

So what? Well, Java is designed to give developers the means to write code once that will run anywhere. This has the potential to level the playing field for hardware and operating system platforms alike. A list of Java's features include

Portable
Object oriented
Cross-platform
Vendor independent
Compiled and interpreted programming language
Multithreaded
Standard
Secure
Open

FlashPix, Fractal, and PNG File Formats

The original web browser, Mosaic, could only display Graphics Interchange Format (GIF) files. Later, browsers could display embedded JPEG (joint pictures expert group) files. The transmission of images embedded in web pages accounts for a large proportion of Internet traffic between UNIX web servers and web browsers. Image files account for a large amount of disk storage on web servers. The new applications for web technology, such as image libraries, consumer photo development delivery, and Internet printing, require new file formats to meet their requirements. GIF and JPG file formats are no longer adequate because of their limitations and shortcomings, which include the following:

Both file formats are low resolution, nominally 72 dpi.
Magnifying the images creates blocky, jagged images.
File size increases by the square of the resolution.
GIF is limited to 256 color images.
GIFs lossless compression limits compressibility.
GIF's LZW compression algorithm is patented by Unisys.
JPG compression is lossy and it creates compression artifacts.

Enter three new file formats: portable network graphics (PNG), fractal image format (FIF), and FlashPix™ (FPX). PNG combines the best of GIF and JPG, but retains the shortcomings of traditional bitmapped images. FIF files take advantage of a computationally expensive algorithm that looks for repeated patterns in a raw image and encodes their position and orientation, significantly reducing the compressed image size. Such files can be magnified and still retain their sharpness. FlashPix stores multiple resolutions so that a web page will display a 72-dpi version while a printing application may use the 266-dpi version. A section of the file can also be displayed at the desired resolution without downloading it totally and then cropping. All three file formats can be created using plug-ins for Adobe Photoshop. Flashpix information can be found at

http://image.hp.com
http://www.kodak.com/flashpix
http://www.flashpix.com
http://www.livepicture.com

UNIX Web Server Software

UNIX web servers originally came in two flavors, the national supercomputer association (NSCA) and the CERN versions. The Apache server came next, and commercial-grade server software for UNIX came from Netscape Communications in the form of the Netscape Commerce Server, followed by the Netscape SuiteSpot™ products. Personal web servers are now bundled with all popular desktop operating systems.

Hewlett–Packard is fully behind the Internet Commerce industry, not only by reselling and supporting Netscape's HP-UX server products, but also with solutions like HP Virtual Vault and VefiPhone software. Firewall products are also available.

Managing the Network

The ISP technical team has to manage the network electronics, the UNIX servers, the firewalls, content, and the services provide to the customers. Performance has to monitored: bandwidth utilization, load balancing, outages, alternative routes, and packet loss.

HP's Internet Service Manager runs on an HP-UX management system with IT/Operations (IT/O) and provides agents to manage these systems:

> NT server or workstation
> HP-UX
> AIX
> SGI
> SUN

which run Netscape Enterprise Server, FastTrack Server, News, Proxy, and Mail. The Raptor Firewall™ is also monitored. Even operational HTML link auditing is provided, and related events are introduced to the IT/O event correlator. Internet Service Manager addresses the business needs of the small ISP.

References

Check out the bimonthly _Internet Service Providers_ issues of Boardwatch magazine for a directory of ISPs, performance information, ISP backbone topologies, and the Internet's architecture.

CHAPTER 1 5

Engineering Environments

Introduction

E ngineering computer environments are demanding. Tools are in use almost continuously. Design, rendering, computation, and high-volume outputs are common. Large data volumes move frequently and for long periods of time. This places rigorous demands on the computer systems and the network. Stability and high availability are paramount, and the use of UNIX and RISC workstations is traditional in the engineering computer environment. Engineering LANs are usually dedicated, with connectivity to the corporate network by bridges, switches, or routers.

In this chapter we'll review software development, geographic information systems, file and print sharing, and X-Windows solutions in the engineering environment.

Software Development Environments

Large software development projects have a complex work flow that can be divided into the three phases of code development, application testing, and integration testing (see Figure 15-1). Code development involves entering and editing text with smart editing tools, performing syntax checks, compiling small pieces of code to evaluate functionality and performance, and checking code in and out of a repository. Application testing compiles and links large amounts of source and object code into executable code that is put through a battery of functional tests. At intervals in the development cycle, all applications are brought up to date and tested as an integrated unit.

The code development phase is not as demanding on systems and LANs because the work is naturally very user interactive. Compiles are small and take less than a few minutes. Syntax checks don't verify megabytes of code, and use of the source code control system is not intense. This makes UNIX workstations an excellent choice for developer desktops. Using a software development tool like ClearCase allows the software source code to be kept on one or more shared NFS servers.

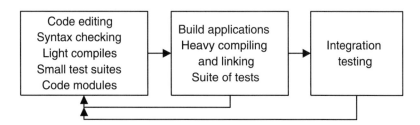

Figure 15-1   Software development work flow
Work flow in a software development project begins with the developer working on code. The results of many such tasks are periodically combined into an application build-and-test phase. Less frequently still, all applications are integrated and tested as a unit.

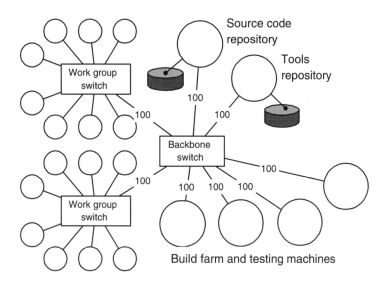

Figure 15-2   A highly scalable development architecture
A software development environment with a UNIX desktop per user connected to work-group switches minimizes Ethernet contention and gives each user about 10 Mbps to the backbone switch. Clients use NFS to mount their development tool binaries and source code repository. All NFS servers are given a dedicated 100-Mbps, full-duplex Ethernet connection, which doubles maximum throughput and eliminates collisions.

Application building and testing is more demanding, and for large projects a build farm of UNIX compile engines is appropriate (see Figure 15-2). Alternatively, since ClearCase supports distributed builds, an application build could be farmed out to dozens of UNIX workstations under the control of one *Makefile*. Application or O/S builds may take hours at first and run overnight later in the development cycle.

Integration testing requires a dedicated environment that emulates the production environment. Indeed, many such environments may be built for testing purposes. Integration testing of a given environment may take days at first, and over a week late in the project cycle.

GIS, AutoCAD, and Simulators

Geographical Information Systems (GIS), the AutoCAD engineering drawing, design, and rendering tool, and simulator applications are often found on UNIX workstations in cooperative network environments. Users of GIS typically work at a UNIX workstation or an X-terminal to access property boundaries, utility rights-of-way, roadways, buildings, and other special landmarks in graphical format (see Figure 15-3). GIS systems are used by governments to manage public resources. The surface-water department may use GIS data to develop new surface water-retention systems to handle runoff from new development. The revenue department may locate and update its assessments by using GIS data to locate properties with similar features. The Department of Ecology (DOE) may use GIS data to verify the impact of a proposed timber harvesting project on the stability of nearby slopes. The Building and Land Department (BALD) may use GIS to validate developer data regarding soil stability, stream-flow rates, and slope angles. In the spirit of cooperation, governments and utilities are beginning to share their GIS data. After all, the cable television, telephone, gas, electric power, drinking water, and sewer utilities use the same GIS data to show where their inventory is located, and they often need to know about each other's inventory before planning and installing more of their own.

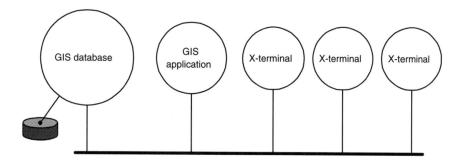

Figure 15-3   GIS applications and X-Windows
A simple GIS solution uses a database to contain data that will be searched, modified, updated, displayed, and printed or plotted. Users may take advantage of a desktop UNIX system running the GIS application, or they may use X-terminals to access the GIS application across the LAN. Users may be located anywhere on the network, and they may use any desktop computer running X-terminal emulator software.

AutoCAD is an industry standard engineering drawing tool with 3D rendering capabilities and is used to prepare engineering drawings for buildings, houses, works projects, mechanical parts, and architectural views. AutoCAD is used very interactively to prepare drawings, it is very I/O intense when preparing output, and it is very CPU intense when rendering (see Figure 15-4).

Simulators range from discrete event network simulators to finite element analysis programs. They are computationally intense during the simulation phase and may work cooperatively with many other UNIX systems performing part of the simulation work. Full-scale simulations may run for hours, although the network activity is often very low during this interval, since most of the data are kept in memory. For simulators that must read a lot of data from networked databases or from remote system disks via NFS, we'd expect a lot more network traffic and design the LAN to support this requirement.

A very nice discrete event simulator that HP has used in the past is PlanNet from the Alta Group (now you would buy Designer). A single user-license permits the licensed HP-UX workstation to cooperatively allow additional compatible workstations to act as NFS clients to mount the PlanNet binaries and user simulation models from the user's workstation (see Figure 15-5).

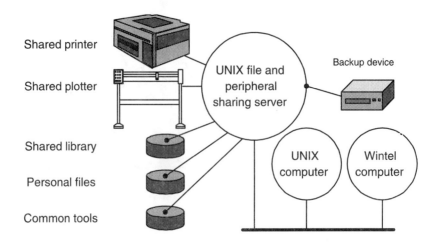

Figure 15-4   AutoCAD in a mixed UNIX and Wintel desktop environment
The UNIX server controls all networked and direct-connect printers and plotters and makes them available to the UNIX workstations via the *lpr* protocol. Wintel computers should also use *lpr*, but the print feature of *pcnfs* or AdvancedServer/9000 may be used instead. The AutoCAD parts library may be accessed using NFS from the UNIX computers, and this is also the recommended access method for the Wintel computers. AdvancedServer/9000 may be used instead. With this arrangement, if users follow the practice of storing all personal files on the server, then they can take advantage of an automated daily backup of the UNIX server.

For network models that are parametrized (say we vary the number of active users from 10 to 100 in steps of 10), ten simulations must be executed. Suppose that we have three additional workstations available, then four simulations can be running at the same time. When one of the four workstations completes a simulation, it is assigned the next. It turns out the best way to arrange this is to run the long simulations first, and successively shorter ones after that until the last and shortest simulation is left.

UNIX File, Print, and Plotter Sharing

UNIX file and peripheral sharing in the engineering environment typically involves UNIX, Wintel, and Macintosh client systems. Users often run

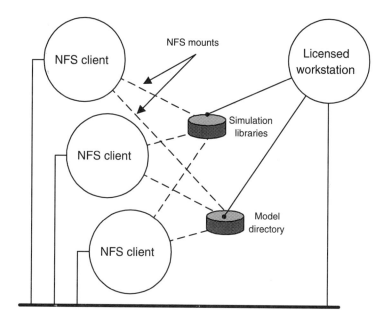

Figure 15-5   Using NFS to speed up a PlanNet simulation
Three NFS clients are shown mounting the binaries and model directories of a
workstation running a single-user license for the PlanNet network simulator. All four
systems will execute simulations under control of the licensed system. This approach
can quarter the time needed to complete a series of parameterized simulations. There
is very little network activity during the simulation, except at each 10% point when
results are saved to disk for later analysis and every 10 seconds when the licensed
workstation polls the clients for a status update.

applications on their favorite desktop computer and want to use the large file
system on the UNIX server for storage, and use the spooling features for
large unattended print and plot jobs.

File sharing in an engineering environment is typically implemented using
industry standard protocols such as NFS, because it also provides the
necessary user authentication on the client system that is consistent with the
UNIX environment (see Figure 15-6). Non-UNIX systems have simplified
file systems that don't properly support multiuser multigroup permissions.
In practice, the desktop NFS client prompts the user for its user ID and
password and authenticates with the UNIX server before any file system

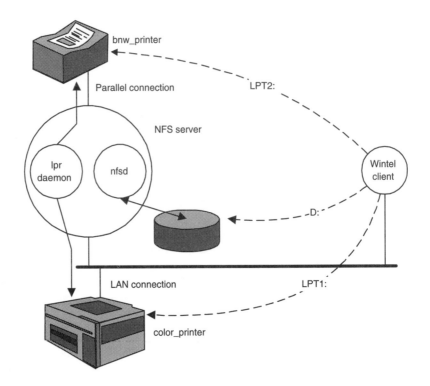

Figure 15-6   NFS and the Wintel client
A Wintel client is shown using NFS to attach to a network drive and can read and
write to the file system using the *D:* drive letter. The UNIX directory to which *D:* is
mapped is owned by the user and is protected from other users that may be sharing
directory space on this network drive. At the same time, the client uses the *lpr* protocol to redirect its *LPT1:* and *LPT2:* printer ports to color_printer and bnw_printer.
UNIX, Wintel, and Macintosh clients can participate in this file and print sharing environment using the standard NFS and *lpr* protocols over TCP/IP.

mounts are accepted. The *pcnfsd* daemon running on the UNIX server
implements this multiuser security feature.

NFS server and client tuning may be necessary in a mixed-platform or a
large environment. The HP-UX default file system block size is 8192 bytes.
The NFS client should mount the UNIX file system using this value for the
rsize and *wsize* parameters to maximize performance. As long as client

systems are connected with the appropriately sized LAN to the NFS server, life is good. Under conditions of excessive utilization, packet loss, or excessive network delays, as when NFS is used over a WAN, it may be appropriate to adjust the *rsize* and *wsize* tunable parameters and others such as *timeo*, *retrans*, and the number of *biod* and *nfsd* daemons.

The UNIX server runs a standard print spooler. All applications running on the server generally pipe their output to the *lp* spooler program. For example, an X-Windows user may print a window screen shot to the printer with the command:

xwd -frame | xpr -device ps -gray 4 | lp -opostscript

Between UNIX systems, the *lpr* protocol is the standard for system-to-system print sharing, and the *lprdaemon* daemon process listens for incoming remote spool requests to be printed on attached parallel, serial, and network printers. The *lprdaemon* may be invoked using *inetd* to support multiple, concurrent inspooled operations. Contemporary Wintel and Macintosh systems also support printing using *rlp*. This means that the engineering environment can standardize on a single, routable standard network printing protocol.

Since we have recommended NFS for file sharing, it's also possible to take advantage of *pcnfsd* running on the UNIX server. *pcnfsd* can accept print data from the desktop Wintel and Macintosh client at the UNIX server. The client system sends redirected print data over the network to the *pcnfsd* process running on the UNIX server. There *pcnfsd* collects the data until an end of file is sensed or a time-out occurs. Then it sends the data to the appropriate printer queue for outspooling.

In either case, the UNIX print spooler will print a banner page for each print job to identify the user. This is essential in a multiuser environment to avoid lost output when a user inadvertently picks up its own output plus that from other users. Banners are generally avoided when printing to slower ink jet printers, to transparencies, and to large-format plotters.

There may be issues in mixed printer environments because some users print in color, some in black and white, some to PCL, and other to PostScript. The newer HP printers will autosense the data type and print correctly either PCL or PostScript data. Monochrome PCL and PostScript printers will also convert color to gray scale. Older printers may not autosense correctly and have been known to dutifully print out 500 pages of PostScript language instructions in ASCII form instead of a 10-page report containing complex tables and graphics data. This can be alleviated to a considerable extent using HP SharedPrint software on the UNIX print server. SharedPrint examines the beginning of the print job for specific character strings for clues about the data and will attempt to find a filter process to convert that data to a form that the real printer can handle.

This SharedPrint feature proved very handy in the preparation of the manuscript for this book. The publishing industry uses PostScript, so the author used Adobe FrameMaker to prepare the manuscript and output it in PostScript form. With only an ancient but sturdy HP LaserJet III PCL printer at hand, but with SharedPrint running on the controlling HP-UX workstation, SharedPrint correctly interpreted the PostScript language into PCL so that the author could proof the PostScript output at home.

X-Windows Solutions

The X-Windows system is the standard GUI for UNIX systems. All HP-UX series 700 workstations with graphical displays use X-Windows. The common desktop environment (CDE) provides a task bar, window manager, productivity tools, and terminal emulators. X-terminals and X-terminal emulators support user sessions with the full CDE environment. For economy reasons, many engineering environments install several high-end workstations or nongraphical UNIX servers and allow users to use the X-Windows graphical environment to share this powerful resource over the LAN. The advantages of this include a single point of administration, easy backups, and economy of scale. No special client–server software is needed.

Engineering software that uses X-Windows includes FrameMaker for large and complex document preparation, BONeS Designer™ for network simulation, AutoCAD™ for engineering drawing, Photoshop and XV for image editing, Wingz™ for spreadsheets, Ghostview for viewing PostScript files, Netscape Navigator for web access, and SoftBench™ for software development (see Figure 15-7). For example, suppose that three FrameMaker licenses are installed. As each successive X-Windows user runs a copy of FrameMaker, the available license count on the server decrements until it's zero, after which subsequent users must wait for a license to become free. Engineers can also collaborate using HP's SharedX extension to X-Windows, available on all HP X-terminals and UNIX workstations.

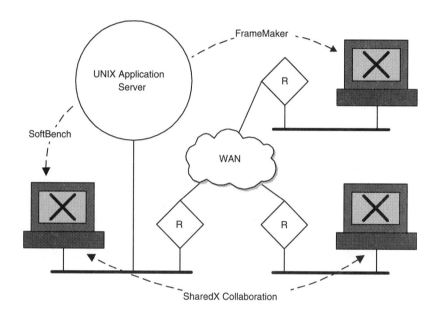

Figure 15-7   The X-Window UNIX application server
A centrally located UNIX application server is loaded with X-Windows application binaries. A remote FrameMaker user is preparing a manuscript across the WAN. The user's document itself is located on the UNIX system; in fact, so is the user's entire home directory and environment. A user local to the file server is using SoftBench and sharing the display with a remote user to collaborate on a software development project. Each user could be provided with a printer attached to the LAN at its site so that its remote application can print locally.

X-Windows supports all types of screen sizes, color depths, performance, memory, and window managers. It can also handle different keyboard mappings at the client side (such as DEL versus backspace), different numbers of mouse buttons (which can vary from one to three), various fonts (through mapping and substitution), and languages (via native language support or NLS). HP's X-terminals even support multimedia such as MPEG movies and sound.

X-Windows basically allows any user to run a UNIX applications from any point on the network provided there is IP connectivity, some measure of bandwidth is available (it will most certainly work over WAN links), and provided the user has a valid login on the UNIX server where the application executes.

In a pinch, a UNIX workstation may be used as an X-terminal by logging into it in nongraphical mode and typing the command

    X -query server_name

which runs the X-Window emulator program *X* and sends an XDMCP login request to the system called *server_name*. CDE provides this feature directly at the login window.

Quite a few myths about X-Windows exist. Most cite performance problems, but X-Windows sends drawing commands over the network, and the graphics are drawn using the CPU power of the X-terminal. Usually, when large amounts of graphics images are displayed, LAN utilization will increase, but this is expected and is not caused by X-Windows. X-Windows drawing programs take advantage of TCP streaming and buffering to aggregate mouse and button activity. Measurements of heads-down users running a variety of X-Windows engineering applications show that peak utilization of only 2.5% of a 10-BASE-T LAN is possible per user.

See Chapter 11 for more information about the X-Windows system.

The Wireless Industry Does UNIX

Introduction

Wireless is a term that has changed meaning in recent years, as have other technical words like broadband (cable TV technology) and hacker (a person skilled with computers, communications, and electronics). Wireless used to refer to AM/FM radio and television signaling, and people owned wireless sets and listened to "the wireless." When cable-oriented LANs could not address new portability and mobility needs, wireless LANs came into being. Lately, the cellular radio industry's marketing arm got busy and positioned itself as the wireless industry. Even the cable TV industry got into the act and started selling "wireless cable TV" in the mid 1990s.

A variety of applications for UNIX systems takes advantage of both infrared (IR) and radio frequency (RF) wireless services to communicate. UNIX systems can manage and support wireless networks, customer care systems, data centers, cellular digital packet data (CDPD) networks, fraud detection, and satellite constellations.

Customer Care Applications

The term customer care is a wonderfully warm contemporary 1990s term for customer support, help desk, or response center. Computer support systems and applications are needed in the service centers to support the cellular service areas or markets. Data centers consolidate the bulk of the computer and network equipment into safe, reliable, 24 by 7 operations. The support systems provide object-oriented databases with words and pictures, so the customer care agent can pull up any information to answer a customer question.

For example, a cellular customer may call in with some question about her Motorola flip phone. The agent pulls up a list of possible Motorola models, asks a few clarifying questions about the equipment, and determines that the customer has a Motorola DPC-650 (Piper) model. The agent can pull up multimedia information about all aspects of the cellphone, words, pictures, and animations and share these with the customer.

Given the large amounts of multimedia data that a service center has to keep up to date and access regularly, there are LAN and WAN capacity and design issues. Caching data at the desktop or at an intermediate tier can help reduce network traffic pressure.

Developing customer care applications is a demanding short-turnaround activity because customer satisfaction in the wireless industry is critical. The necessary applications to support customers have to be up and running quickly. This calls for a rapid prototyping environment, so developers use tools such as SmallTalk™, NextStep™, Java, and HTML running on UNIX platforms. The features of a "fat" client versus a "thin" client pit the requirements of low desktop hardware costs, LAN performance, high availability, and good overall performance against each other.

Many IT organizations don't want to place two desktop computers on an agent's desk, so the need to run Wintel productivity applications and customer care applications on the same client system must be satisfied. The benefits of X-terminals and third-party products like Ntrigue™ that wrap Wintel applications windows inside X-Windows become compelling reasons to adopt the thin-client approach.

System performance for the customer care agent is important so that the customer calling in gets the information he needs quickly, conveniently, and with satisfaction. The desktop system has to have sufficient RAM to be able to run all necessary applications concurrently. The CPU must be fast enough to keep the GUI highly responsive, and the network response time must be kept low even at peak call-in times.

CDPD IP Networking Overlay

Cellular digital packet data (CDPD) is a low-speed (nominally 19,200 bits/second) IP network overlaid on top of the cellular voice network. It takes advantage of idle time in the voice channel to send digital data from the cellular device to the base station, where the data portion enters a traditional all-IP network. In the Seattle, Washington, area, it is common to see a lone person with a laptop computer sipping an espresso at a small table at Starbucks™ Coffee, reading Email and surfing the Net. Always present is a small cellular antenna emerging from the CDPD modem inside the laptop computer.

CDPD network service providers offer a proxy gateway service into the Internet, but they also will bring a T1 connection into a business facility so that a company's mobile users have access to their corporate resources such as UNIX mail servers and SAP business software. This connection is quite secure and behaves somewhat like a virtual private network (VPN). See Figure 16-1.

The CDPD cellular IP overlay network has certain features that must be considered before a mobile connectivity solution to central UNIX resources is designed. These are bandwidth, latency, connectivity breaks, noise, congestion, IP numbering, routing, security, and application development.

The peak speed of CDPD is 19,200 bits/second, and after factoring in TCP handshaking, IP network propagation time, network congestion, and application response time, it should be fairly clear that CDPD is not suited for applications that move large amounts of data or require instantaneous response times. It's ideal for messaging applications like Email (with small attachments), Web surfing (with image fetching turned off), and three-tier client–server applications like SAP.

CDPD's layer I connectivity is less reliable than traditional wire-based LAN technologies because of radio frequency (RF) noise, connection drops, gaps in coverage, and roaming transients. Traditional TCP-based applications that depend on a continuously available physical layer will not work properly under such conditions. Third parties such as Oracle have special software development kits suited to the CDPD environment.

Security is always an issue in the wireless environment. It is well known that sensitive voice mail should not be listened to on a cellular telephone because third parties may be using scanners to monitor cellular frequencies. There is no way to secure the publicly available radio frequencies, so some form of data encryption is necessary over such links to protect sensitive information.

IP numbering and routing on a CDPD network are simplified if a single class B IP network number can be used for all portable systems, which may be assigned fixed IP addresses. Since the CDPD network is privately managed

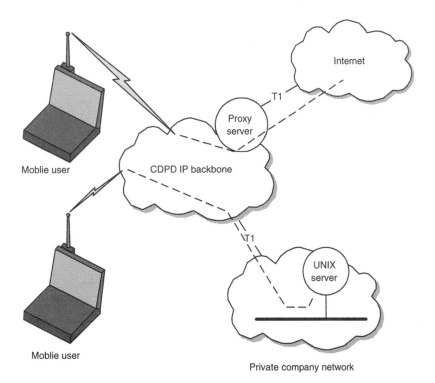

Figure 16-1   Mobile laptop computers and CDPD networking
The mobile user at the top of the figure is sipping an espresso at Starbucks while surfing the Internet. The laptop computer being used has a standard TCP/IP stack and
runs standard TCP applications like Netscape and FTP. The modem setup strings are
appropriate for a CDPD modem. The bottom mobile user is taking advantage of the
service provider's virtual private network service to access a corporate UNIX system.

and isolated from the Internet with a proxy server, the service provider is at
liberty to choose any IP numbering scheme for maximum convenience.
However, since contemporary portable computers all support DHCP and
PPP, it is not necessary to assign fixed IP addresses at all, and the dial-up
process can obtain an IP address at connection establishment time.

The Ricochet Wireless Network

Ricochet™ (*http://www.richochet.com*) has created a wireless network out of RF microcells based on small antennas hanging from lamp posts. A blanket of interconnected microcells currently (1998) covers portions of the Seattle area of Washington state, the San Jose area of California, and the Washington, D.C., area. No doubt some of those Starbucks Coffee customers in Seattle surfing the net while drinking an espresso are using a Ricochet wireless modem in their laptop computers.

Cellular Fraud Detection with UNIX

A cellular telephone has the following attributes:

> ID (in a chip)
> RF signature
> Telephone number
> Cell site currently checked into
> Customer profile (roaming, services)

Fraud is committed when the ID chip is cloned and an otherwise valid telephone number is programmed into the cellphone. As far as the cellular network can tell, the cellphone is valid because nobody has reported stolen equipment.

The key to identifying fraudulent cellphones is their proprietary and unique RF signature. Special RF equipment at the cell site routinely measures legitimate customer equipment RF signatures and stores them in a central database.

When a cellular call is attempted, the chip ID, calling telephone number, and RF signature are compared in real time against the database (Figure 16-2). Service is denied and an entry is logged if the following occur:

> The chip ID does not match the telephone number.
> The RF signature does not match the chip ID.
> This cellphone's last location is too far from its present location.

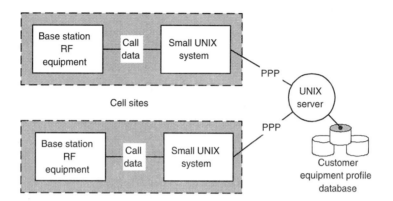

Figure 16-2   UNIX cell site controller
The small UNIX system uses the interface to the base station RF equipment at the
cell site to extract the RF signature, cellular equipment profile, and calling information and packages the data for transmission to the central UNIX server. This server
quickly consults the customer profile database, checks the call data, and returns a go
or no-go indication to the cell site.

To perform this fraud detection in real time, a dedicated (and properly sized)
data circuit from each cell site connects to a central UNIX server where the
database resides. Many cell sites terminate on the server, so the incoming
call attempts will arrive at random intervals in a bursty manner. The server
response time will vary, of course, with the instantaneous call rate. The
reasonable worst-case call rate can be used to size the server CPU, RAM,
and disk speed.

Data Center Design

Data centers for the wireless industry have the same requirements as other
industries. These include reliability, security, and performance, while
providing mission-critical business functions.

Power to the data center has to be reliable, so a standby diesel generator and
a fuel source must be provided and kept ready in case of extended public

power outages. An uninterruptible power supply (UPS) with a battery backup filters power and provides continuous AC power until the diesel generator can be activated. Equipment not powered this way is often provisioned with a small stand-alone 300- to 600-ampere hour UPS such as those from APC™.

Air-conditioning equipment not only maintains a cool environment in spite of the heat-generating computer equipment, but it also increases its reliability. But removing the heat in turn consumes power, which is in short demand during a power failure.

UNIX systems are usually powered by their own UPS and monitored with an RS-232 port between them that allows the system to perform an orderly shutdown before power fails totally. Higher-end UPSs are SNMP-manageable and connect to the data center LAN.

The data center may house the distributed network and systems management systems to leverage the highly available environment that it provides. The data network used to support the cellular service business tends to be centralized at data centers. The voice and CDPD networks are managed as a separate entity by another group.

Diverse physical points of presence (POP) will enter the facility to provide continuous connectivity to all remote sites that use the data center's services. Services provided by the data center generally include network management, application server and database support, periodic data backups, naming and directory services such as DNS, WINS, and DHCP, printing, remote access, and even a secure Internet gateway.

Disaster recovery or, more politely, business continuity planning, is a critical aspect of a corporation's long-term survivability. Disasters include security breaches, fire, flood, earthquake, strike, sabotage, and other types of misery that might be visited on the data center. It is common to maintain at least two data centers, each of which can peer for the other. In the rare case that a data center outage occurs, corporate users switch to the surviving data center, possibly in a degraded performance mode, pending the restoration of their usual data center.

To maintain a high-availability LAN at the data center, a redundant design is adopted that includes multiple WAN links into the site, preconfigured and

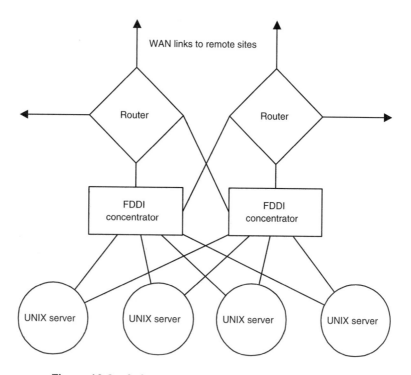

Figure 16-3   A data center high-availability LAN design
A small data center's high-availability LAN may take advantage of two independent
LANs, each a unique IP subnet, to which all mission-critical devices obtain connectivity. This diagram depicts two dual shared-media FDDI rings. Connectivity with
the WAN is assured because two independent routers each carry half the circuits. Pre-
sumably, the WAN itself is a redundant IP backbone with at least two circuits between hub sites, so a single line failure will not cause an outage. Note that, for
performance or political reasons, FDDI concentrators may be replaced by FDDI,
100-BASE-T, or ATM switches configured using VLAN to maintain the redundant
IP subnet functionality.

tested network equipment like concentrators, hubs, switches, routers, and
communications servers (see Figure 16-3).

Business functions of a data center for a wireless company include billing
software, collecting call progress data, combing these data and combining
airtime and toll charges of each call, handling billing data with carrier
partners, and fraud detection.

Satellite Constellations

A satellite constellation consists of a large number (in the 50 to 400 range) of low-Earth-orbit (LEO) satellites that carry a payload to provide communications services. Ground stations form the communications gateway between the orbiting grid and data communications equipment of the network service provider. To keep this network operational, we must address the following:

> Real-time control to steer and orient the satellites in their orbits
> Control of the data flow within the orbital mesh
> Failed satellites and their replacement
> Network management at each Earth station
> Long support life of support equipment
> Simulation for capacity planning and what-if analysis
> Power management for night-side orbital intervals

The computer systems necessary to manage satellite constellation networks must have extremely high reliability, be capable of real-time control, provide high computational performance, and be available from multiple vendors to avoid the high cost of lock-in. Enter the legendary stability, scalability, supportability, and performance of UNIX.

Wireless LAN

At the end of the wireless communications dimension opposite the satellite constellation is the lowly wireless LAN (see Figure 16-4). Wireless LANs offer a solutions to a wide range of applications, including the following:

> Mobility (such as Surfing at Starbucks Coffee)
> LAN in historic building
> Large manufacturing area and warehousing
> Point of sale terminal
> Real-time medical patient data entry terminal
> SCMODS (ref: <u>Blues Brothers</u>™ movie)[1]
> Mobile teams of professionals

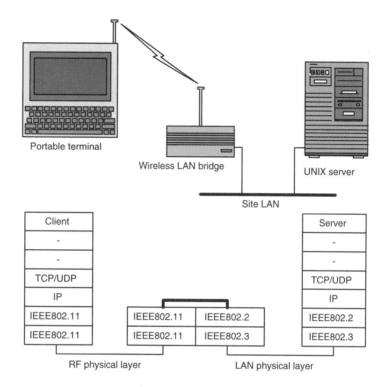

Figure 16-4   The OSI view of wireless networking
The physical and logical aspects of a wireless application distributed between a portable wireless terminal and a LAN-based UNIX server. This example supports medical professionals as they visit patients at their bedside, enters real-time medical data, reviews stored data, and makes notes that will be stored on the server. The portable unit acts as a portable GUI, and the server acts as a shared information repository. The productivity gains that this application imparts is that end-of-shift data entry note transcription is avoided, data accuracy is increased, and data are always current.

The IEEE 802.11 wireless standard offers a standardized physical and link layer to help ensure interoperability among compliant wireless products.

---

1. State County Municipal Offender Data System.

References

Nemzow, Martin, *Implementing Wireless Networks*. New York: McGraw-Hill Book Co.,1995, ISBN: 0-07-046377-8.

Glossary

AARP   AppleTalk address resolution protocol. When a Macintosh doesn't know what network numbers are valid at start-up time, it broadcasts an AARP probe packet to find a valid node address in the start-up network number range.

ABR   Available bit rate. In ATM LANs, this is the lowest quality of service that a device may request. No bandwidth guarantee is made by the ATM switch, and the device may suffer cell loss when the ATM LAN has to guarantee delivery for higher QOS devices.

ACL   Access control list. This mechanism is used to extend the simple owner/group/world read/write/execute permissions of the standard UNIX file system to increase the flexibility of file access. For example, a file may be given an ACL that gives only certain users in various groups write permission.

ADSP   AppleTalk Data Stream Protocol. AppleTalk applications may use this byte-oriented service to transmit streams of data reliably.

AFP   AppleTalk file protocol, the remote file access protocol used between Macintosh clients and file servers.

AM   Amplitude modulation. A carrier's amplitude is varied in proportion to the amplitude of the data signal, as in AM radio. Quadrature amplitude modulation, is a modem modulation scheme that varies both the carrier signal's amplitude and phase.

ANI   Automatic number identification. This is part of the SS7 protocol. ANI is offered commercially to telephone customers as caller ID, whereby the caller phone number and name are displayed at the receiver.

ANSI   American National Standards Institute. The United States member body of the International Standards Organization is ANSI.

APC   American Power Corporation, a manufacturer of uninterruptible power supplies suitable for small computer systems.

API   Application programming interface, is a documented set of function calls that programmers use to perform useful tasks. For example, the Berkeley socket library is a set of APIs to let programmers write code to move data between networked applications using TCP/IP standards.

ARM   Application response measurement, a set of APIs to instrument an application for automated performance data collection during operational use.

ARP   Address resolution protocol, a broadcast mechanism used on local area networks to determine the MAC address corresponding to the LAN adapter of a local system with the requested IP address. The MAC address is stored in an ARP cache for reuse.

ASCII   American standard code for information interchange, a seven-bit standard way to represent characters.

ASIC   Application-specific integrated circuit, an integrated circuit built for a specific purpose, as opposed to a general purpose.

ASN.1   Abstract syntax notation one, a standard used to describe the way SNMP MIBs are written.

ATM   Asynchronous transfer mode, a high-speed switching technology based on 53-byte cells.

AUI   Attachment unit interface, the Ethernet/802.3 physical 15-pin D-connector standard for connecting transceivers to network devices.

Automagically   Refers to a feature or process that occurs automatically, as if by magic.

AV   Audio-visual, an environment that takes advantage of visual and audible elements. A video conferencing connection is an AV application. AV is an older term that has been supplanted by the general-purpose term multimedia.

AVI   Audio video interleave, a simple file format for video on Wintel platforms.

BASE   Baseband refers to the modulation technique used in the IEEE twisted pair standards such as 10-BASE-5, 10-BASE-2, 10-BASE-T, and 100-BASE-T.

Base64   A method for converting binary files to ASCII form suitable for Emailing using SMTP. UUENCODE and BinHex are similar methods.

BER   Bit error rate, the rate at which bits are transmitted in error on a communications circuit. Errors are often caused by electrical or magnetic interference at the physical layer of the OSI model. A bit error rate tester (BERT) is an instrument that measures bit error rate.

BGP   Border gateway protocol, a routing protocol frequently used between multihomed autonomous systems (AS) that connect to the Internet.

BinHex   Binary to hexadecimal, a conversion method that allows one or more binary and ASCII files to be converted into ASCII form for transmission by SMTP. It is popular on Macintosh computers.

BLS   B-level security, a standard set of features for defining security levels.

BNC   Baby N-connector, the small coaxial connector used by the 10-BASE-2 thin-LAN standard.

BRI   Basic rate interface, the 64 Kbps channel of an ISDN circuit.

BSD   Berkeley software distribution, a term generally referring to the Berkeley variant of UNIX.

CACI   A software company specializing in network and system simulation products used in capacity planning.

CAD   Computer-aided design typically refers to a high-end drafting package used to document architectural building plans and network topologies.

CATV   Cable television, an analog method for distributing television channels with 6 MHz channel allocations using 75-ohm transmission facilities that terminate in RG-59 coaxial cable at the end user drop.

CBR   Constant bit rate, an ATM service that guarantees delivery of fixed-bit-rate data such as audio and video data.

CCNA   Cisco certified networking associate, a person that passed a test blessed by the Cisco company, a well-respected manufacturer of network electronics such as routers and switches.

CCR   Current cell rate. In ATM switches, this is the rate at which 53-byte cells are being switched.

CD   Compact disk, a plastic disk that stores digital data used to represent audio tracks or a file system. It holds about 650 Mbytes. The DVD standard holds about 4.7 Gbytes in the same form factor.

CDE   Common desktop environment, a standard look and feel for UNIX X-Windows graphical workstations developed by HP, SUN, and IBM. It sports a trash can, a file manager, a desktop, and multiple work spaces.

CDPD   Cellular digital packet data, a method to transmit IP data from portable computer equipment such as laptop computers and digital personal assistants.

CER   Cell error ratio, the ratio of ATM cells with errors to the total cell count.

CERT   Computer emergency response time, an organization that supports computer users, especially in the area of security breaches.

CGI   Common gateway interface, a programmatic interface between hypertext on a web page and the UNIX environment. For example, form data can be processed using a CGI script written in Perl and added to a mailing list program.

CHAP   Challenge handshake authentication protocol, used to pass the user account name and password to authenticate a dial-up PPP connection. The name and password are not sent in the clear.

CIDR Classless interdomain routing, a routing protocol that takes advantage of the allocation of contiguous blocks of class C IP addresses to simplify routing information. Its invention avoided problems associated with large routing tables on the Internet.

CIR Committed information rate, a guaranteed minimum bit rate on a frame relay permanent virtual circuit for which the customer is charged a service fee and at which the service provider guarantees delivery.

CISC Complex instruction set computer, one that has large, complex, variable-length instructions stored as ROM microprograms, which require multiple clock cycles to decode and execute, and which require a large number of transistors, resulting in a very hot chip that is often cooled by a fan. Performance is gained by massive parallelism and pipelining. Examples include the Intel line of X86 chips and the Motorola 68xxx line.

CLEC Competitive local exchange carrier.

CMS Color management system. Ensures that color images seen on a display, printed on paper, input by a scanner, and stored in a file maintain their integrity when moved to another computer with a different display, scanner, or printer. CMS is an essential element in the publishing industry.

COTS Commercial off the shelf refers to products, typically software, that can be purchased in the marketplace as a final polished supported product that will perform all the required functions without any modifications whatsoever, using only standard and supported configurations and installation options.

CPU Central processor unit, an integrated circuit with the basic intelligence behind all computer equipment. Examples include the Intel X86 line, the Apple/Motorola Power PC, HP's HPPA, and the HP-Intel Merced chip.

CRC Cyclic redundancy check is an additional 16- or 32-bit check field calculated by the network adapter from the encapsulated data to protect the integrity of the transmission. The receiving adapter recalculates the CRC field from the received data, checks it against the transmitted value, and either discards the frame (as Ethernet adapters do) or requests a retransmission (as HDLC links do).

CRT Cathode ray tube, a term often used to refer to a computer monitor screen. In televisions, we call it the picture tube.

CS Collection station, an HP OpenView network management station responsible for discovering, managing devices in its management domain, and maintaining a configuration database. The CS polls these devices periodically. A collection station may forward event and topology information to an OpenView management station.

CTD Cell transfer delay, the amount of time it takes an ATM cell to traverse the switched network. This will include the "wire time," multiple hops, and queuing delays at congestion points.

CTI Computer telephony integration, a set of tools and products for integrating telephone technology with computers. Applications include automated calling units that allow a bank to automatically call customers and, if they answer, to transfer the customer to a live agent within a second.

DAS Dual attach station, a device that connects to both of the FDDI rings and therefore has a very reliable LAN connection.

DCE Distributed communications environment, a set of standards that emerged from the Open Software Foundation for doing multiplatform client–server networking in an open standards-based manner controlled by no vendor; **or,**

DCE Data communications equipment, typically an ASCII terminal connected to a modem, a router connected to a DSU/CSU, or a computer connected to a hub or switch. The modem, DSU/CSU, and hub/switch are referred to as the data communications equipment, and the ASCII terminal, router, and computer are the data terminal equipment.

DDP Datagram delivery protocol, a protocol for delivery of datagrams without connection-oriented services such as multiplexing, buffering, retransmission, or reliability.

DEC Digital Equipment Corporation, a company founded by Ken Olsen. DEC blazed the minicomputer frontier with its PDP and VAX systems. It is now a wholly owned subsidiary of Compaq, a PC clone maker.

DEL The delete or backspace character varies from system to system. It may be the Del key itself, the Backspace key, or control-H. It is a plague at the presentation layer of the OSI model.

DEN Directory enabled networks support directory services such as Novell Directory Services (NDS) or lightweight directory access protocol (DLAP).

DES Data encryption standard, an internationally accepted standard for encrypting data using symmetric, private, 56-bit keys intended to make business transactions safe but interoperable.

DFS Distributed File System, a derivative of the Open Software Foundations Andrew File System, which provides an open standard for remote file access across networks.

DHCP Dynamic host configuration protocol, a standard to allow a device to determine its IP configuration from a DHCP server instead of a local configuration file. This method considerably simplifies the administration of an IP network in the presence of frequent moves, adds, and changes.

DLT Digital linear tape is a quarter-inch-wide tape used for high-capacity backups. A DLT array holds many such tapes and cycles them in and out of the drive mechanism automatically under control of the backup software.

DMZ Demilitarized zone, the LAN segment between the bastion host and the ISP's router. It is vulnerable to attack from the Internet because it is directly connected to it.

DNS Domain name system, a hierarchical, scalable, distributed standard for host name-to-IP address resolution. It allows sites responsible for their own IP address and system names to build an authoritative name server, and it allows other name servers to find them transparently to the end users.

DSAP Destination service access point, a 1-byte field in the IEEE 802.2 frame format that identifies the upper-layer protocol contained in the frame.

DSL Digital subscriber line, a copper circuit between the central office and the customer premises operated digitally.

DTE Data terminal equipment. In the RS-232 world the data terminal equipment is the terminal, printer, plotter, or computer serial port. The modem is the data communications equipment. In the Ethernet world, the data terminal equipment is the networked X-terminal, printer, scanner, or computer, and the hub or switch is the data communications equipment.

DTP Distributed transaction processing occurs when a client passes a user query to an upper-tier application server, which in turn may process it and in turn make another query to its upper tier, perhaps a database server.

DVD Digital video disk, a standard file format for a CD-ROM with much higher capacity than the earlier 640-megabyte technology. Movies stored on DVD disks are meant to be played back by stand-alone DVD players driving a standard television or by movie playback programs on desktop computers (which may require hardware support to decode the movie's MPEG-2 encoded frames).

EAROM Electrically alterable read only-memory is an integrated circuit that contains instructions and data.

EC Electronic commerce is a catch-all phrase depicting the migration of point-of-sale transactions to Internet-based transactions. This includes advertising, accepting orders from customers in a secure way, allowing customers to check on the status of their order, and so on. These systems must be up on a 24 by 7 by 365 basis. Customers span the globe and speak many languages.

EDI Electronic data interchange is the transmission of documents by electronic means using standards.

EIA Electrical Industries Association, a group that defines electrical transmission standards, such as the familiar EAI RS-232-C.

ELM Electronic mail, a standard UNIX mail reader.

EMC A vendor of large-capacity high-availability disk arrays.

EMI Electromagnetic interference. Any electrical or magnetic waves emanating from unshielded conductors may induce voltages in sensitive equipment and disrupt its operation. This may happen to computer equipment, generally causing the operating system to crash and data to be lost. It also happens to radio, television, wireless, and audio equipment.

EMP Electromagnetic pulse, usually of very high amplitude, generated when a nuclear weapon explodes, which can destroy sensitive electronic equipment, especially semiconductors.

EPS Enterprise parallel server, a cluster of HP9000 HP-UX computers capable of handling very large applications with very high performance.

ESP Extrasensory perception, a sixth sense possessed by some gifted people that endows them with information not available to ordinary people.

Extranet When a private corporate network must also service customers and business partners over the Internet, the special network arrangement has this new 1990s term associated with it.

FAT File allocation table. A simple means of allocating blocks of data on a disk using a 16-bit integer to represent the allocation block number. This method is inefficient for large disk volumes, since many small files are allocated the full allocation block. The FAT-32 file system addresses this inefficiency. The FAT file system is found mainly on Wintel computers.

FAX Facsimile, a method for scanning paper documents, transmitting them over standard telephone lines, and printing them at the receiving end. A FAX machine, typically with a built-in dialer, is used at each end. FAX technology uses CCITT group 3 compression to improve throughput.

FCA Fibre Channel Association is an organization intended to promote the fibre channel technology.

FC-AL   Fibre channel arbitrated loop is an implementation of fibre channel that daisy chains up to 127 devices on a single loop.

FCS   Frame check sequence is an additional field attached to the frame by the link layer protocol, which is calculated from the payload data. The receiver checks the FCS field against the data field as an integrity check. The term FCS is sometimes used in place of the term cyclic redundancy check (CRC).

FDDI   Fiber distributed data interface is a time-tested fiber-optic LAN and MAN technology operating at 100 megabits/second. It features a dual counterrotation architecture that is self-healing, providing high availability.

FDX   Full duplex refers to a data communications channel that can simultaneously send and receive data.

FIF   Fractal image format employs a pattern-based compression method that finds variations of similar patterns in an image that differ only in position, orientation, scaling, and stretching. A nice illustration is an image of a field of ferns, which has a single shape that is found almost everywhere in it, and which can therefore be highly compressed. Decompression is much faster than compression.

FLDB   File location data base is the centerpiece of the Distributed File System, which provides a global name space for clients to access their files. The file location database is usually replicated to ensure high availability of the file system.

FM   Frequency modulation imparts information to a fixed frequency carrier signal by varying its frequency linearly with the applied signal. This makes the signal relatively immune to interference and fading.

FPS   Frames per second refers to the video frame rate of a digital video stream. A frame rate of 30 frames/second is considered high quality. The bandwidth required to transmit a digital video signal increases in direct proportion to the frame rate. Compression techniques are necessary to reduce this data rate to a reasonable level.

FPX   FlashPix is another file format that contains multiple file resolutions in multiples of 2. In conjunction with a proper image web server, this allows a remote web user to indicate a position on a low-resolution image, whereupon the server transmits a higher-resolution subimage. The user sees this as zooming in to get new detail. FPX format is popular with digital cameras.

FTP   File transfer protocol is the classic Internet protocol that allows a user to log into a remote machine using either a personal or an anonymous account, navigate and view the remote file system, upload and download ASCII and binary files, and even create and delete directories. It is embedded in all popular web browsers.

GEO   Geosynchronous Earth orbit (22,300 miles above Earth) positions an object in a fixed position over the equator, because its period of rotation matches that of Earth. This is useful for fixed-antenna Earth stations such as communications satellites and direct TV broadcasting satellites.

GID   Group ID. Users on UNIX systems are assigned a group name that maps to a numeric group ID used to govern file and directory access. The command *id* returns the user and group ID.

GIF   Graphics interchange format is an image file format popular on the Internet. It supports a 256-color palette, LZW lossless compression, interlacing, and multiple images per file (used to make animated GIFs).

GIS   Geographical information systems are computers with an application for the storing, cataloging, accessing, and printing of geographical features such as property lines, easements, gas lines, communications circuits, land elevations and cover, rivers, streams, dams, buildings, roads, and highways.

GUI   Graphical user interface. UNIX systems provide an X-Windows-based common desktop environment (CDE), a set of tool bars and utilities to support common activities like reading mail, web browsing, application launching, and file management. Applications running in the X-Windows environment must present a window with buttons, scroll bars, text, and graphic viewing areas, plus tools for manipulating information. This graphical user interface is accompanied by a standard set of window manipulation-features for positioning, scaling, iconifying, and closing the window. Each window is obliged to offer a menu bar or button bar to let the user open and close files and perform other tasks related to the functioning of the program. For example, Adobe Frame Maker on UNIX has a graphical user interface to allow author the to write books.

HDLC   High-level data link control, a layer 2 protocol often used on router serial circuits to reliably transmit data. It can detect errored frames and request retransmission, making it a connection-oriented protocol.

HDX   Half-duplex describes a data communications channel that can only communicate in either the forward or the reverse direction at one time.

HIPPI   High-performance parallel interface is a copper twisted pair, point-to-point, simplex, serial standard running at 100 or 200 megabytes/second. Variable-length IEEE802.2 encapsulated frames support multiple network layer protocols such as the venerable TCP/IP.

HPPA   Hewlett–Packard precision architecture is the marketing term for HP's RISC-based computer systems, such as the HP3000 and HP9000. The term PA-RISC is also used.

HP-PB   Hewlett–Packard precision bus is an early generation of HP's I/O subsystem used in the HP9000 family.

HSC   High-speed controller is the name of HP's fast I/O bus technology.

HSSI   High-speed serial interface, such as the 45 Mbps serial WAN line of a router T3 circuit.

HTML   Hypertext markup language is a text-based language for laying out web pages. Web browsers render HTML by displaying text, images, buttons, forms, and other objects such as sound clips and streaming videos. Any piece of text or graphics can posses a link to another location on the Internet, which the user simply single-clicks to navigate there.

HTTP   Hypertext transport protocol is the protocol used between web browsers and web servers to transmit pages of HTML, images, sound clips, or movies.

IBM   International Business Machines, a major computer vendor known for its proprietary MVS operating system, SNA networking, and the EBCDIC character set.

ICMP   Internet control message protocol is defined in RFC 792 to support IP functions such a remote loopback testing (*ping*), ICMP redirects for dynamic end-station routing table updates, and parameter requests for network management.

IEEE   Institute of Electrical and Electronics Engineers, a global standards body that drafted the famous IEEE 802.3 10-Mbps LAN standard.

IETF   Internet Engineering Task Force, a volunteer organization that provides technical support for the development of networking standards that directly affect the functioning of the Internet. The members write, moderate, approve, and publish requests for comment (RFC) documents, which may be found at *http://www.internic.net/rfc* and other mirror sites.

IMAP   Internet message access protocol.

IMSP   Internet message support protocol.

Internet   An IP network consisting of multiple high-speed private backbone networks connected at network access points. The public gains access to it via Internet service providers.

Intranet   A private corporate network suddenly becomes an intranet when web-based services run on it. There is no other difference.

IOPS   Input–output operations per second is a standardized performance metric for the network file system measured with the Laddis benchmark. An IOP represents about 4 kilobytes of data transferred between the client and server systems.

IP   Internet protocol, defined in RFC 791, is a standard for an OSI layer 3 network protocol that provides 32-bit classful addressing.

IPC   Interprocess communication is a mechanism that allows multiple processes to exchange messages reliably. The applications typically make use of a standard set of APIs to facilitate communications.

IPX   Internet packet exchange is a proprietary network protocol invented by Novell and used in their Netware products.

IR   Infrared, a range of frequencies just below that of the visible light spectrum and used for wireless line-of-sight communications and in fiber optics.

ISDN   Integrated services digital network provides data and voice transmission services to businesses and homes over 64-kbps basic rate channels. Two basic rate channels may be bonded together to create a 128-kbps data channel. ISDN supports a packetized data service and a dedicate virtual circuit service suited to voice and digital video.

ISO   International Standards Organization.

ISP   Internet service provider offers individual subscribers and businesses access to the Internet. The ISP offers dial-up PPP, frame relay, ISDN, or dedicated access, maintains a domain name server (DNS), and in turn connects to regional or national service providers, which form the backbone of the Internet.

IT   Information technology, an all-encompassing term used to describe a collection of technologies used provide access to information, including LAN, WAN, computers, and software.

IT/O   IT Operations, an HP product that provides the tools, methodologies, and processes needed to manage a network of computers.

ITU   International Telecommunications Union, an international standards body.

JDK   Java developer kit, a collection of software, tools, applications, and documentation to support an application developer in writing java applets and programs.

JFS Journal file system, an implementation that provides fast recovery of the file system after a UNIX system crashes. Normally, the UNIX buffered file system is checked using the standard utility *fsck*, but this is very time consuming and isn't guaranteed to recover all the data.

JPEG Joint pictures expert group, which defines a standard for compressing bit-mapped millions-of-colors images with user-defined levels of lossiness. These pictures often look better than GIF images and are usually much smaller, making JPG files popular in web pages.

JVM Java virtual machine, the Java byte code interpreter.

L2TP Layer 2 tunneling protocol encapsulates one link layer protocol inside another.

LAN Local-area network, a collection of cable segments interconnected using hubs, switches, bridges, and routers that extends over a relatively small area, such as a building. Distances are limited to a few kilometers, and even those distances require fiber optic-cables and repeaters. Examples of LAN physical media are Ethernet and FDDI.

LANE LAN emulation is required to fool IP into thinking that an ATM LAN adapter accepts reasonable (1500-byte) frames as the maximum transmission unit (MTU), as opposed to the 53-byte cell of native ATM.

LANIC LAN interface card is an input–output adapter in a computer or router, which usually implements layer I and II of the OSI model. The adapter has buffer memory to hold frames, a microprocessor, and ROM. The adapter computes the frame check sequence, recognizes special MAC addresses, and implements all the function associated with the particular LAN standard.

LAT Local area transport is a link layer protocol developed by Digital Equipment Corporation (DEC) to allow terminal servers to communicate with the DEC VAX computer.

LATA Local access transport area.

LDAP Lightweight directory access protocol, a standard for looking up information such as Email addresses and the location of networked resources.

LEC Local exchange carrier.

LED Light-emitting diode, a two-terminal semiconductor that emits light when an electrical current flows through it. LEDs are used for equipment indicators and for driving fiber-optic cables.

LEO Low Earth orbit, one which is 500 to 1000 miles above Earth.

LFS   Local file system is the distributed file system server's physical logging system that can restore the server quickly after a crash.

LLC   Link layer control is a layer 2 protocol that identifies the nature of the payload carried within a frame.

LVM   Logical volume manager is an HP-UX tool for partitioning and managing a group of physical disk drives into one or more logical volumes, each containing a file system.

LZW   Lempel Ziv Welch, a lossless compression technique used to compress image files, typically in the GIF format. It is patented by Unisys, which licences it to developers of graphics programs.

MAC   Media access, a functional layer defined by all LAN standards for giving link layer access to the physical layer for transmission of a frame.

MAE   Macintosh application environment, a mature product from Apple Computer that emulates the complete Macintosh Operating System (Mac OS) on a UNIX system (HP-UX and SUN computers) within an X-Windows environment. Users can load, run Mac applications, and share UNIX resources.

MAN   Metropolitan area network, a network that spans the geography of a metropolitan-sized area such as a city or campus. Fiber-optic cables are typically used to support such distances.

MAPI   Mail API, a standard for integrating electronic mail with applications.

MAU   Media attachment unit, the IEEE's name for the Ethernet transceiver that implements the physical layer electrical and mechanical layers of the OSI model. The MAU connects the network device to the LAN cable; **or**

MAU   Media access unit, the IBM term for their token ring interconnect hardware.

Mb   Megabits usually means millions of bits (1,000,000) in data communications circles. Sometimes it means 1,048,576 bits, the square of 1024.

MB   Megabytes usually means millions of bytes (1,000,000) in data communications. Sometimes it means 1,048,576 bytes, the square of 1024.

MEO   Medium Earth orbit, one about 8000 miles above Earth.

MIB   Management information base, a description of the data an SNMP-managed device is able to return information about. This includes configuration information (such as the type of LAN adapter) and performance data (such as the number of bytes sent on a LAN adapter).

MIC   Media interface connector, used to connect FDDI cable. It is rectangular, keyed, and connects two fibers.

MII   Media-independent interface, the 100-BASE-T connection standard between the transceiver and the network device.

Mil3   Produces network simulation tools that integrate with HP OpenView and NetMetrix.

MIME   Multipurpose Internet mail extensions, a method for transmitting non-ASCII files as SMTP messages. SMTP only supports single-part 7-bit ASCII text, and MIME headers identify the attachments using headers that SMTP ignores. It is up to the user's Email program to parse the Email message MIME headers and reconstruct the attachment files.

MIPS   Millions of instructions per second, a simple performance metric for CPU chips. It's also been called "meaningless indicator of performance" because MIPS is such a simple metric.

MIT   Massachusetts Institute of Technology, an institute of higher learning and the developer of the X-Windows standard.

MOM   Manager of managers, a network management station that in turn manages information from a lower tier of network management stations. The lower tier will filter information and pass only high-level data to the MOM.

MOSS   MIME object security services.

MPOA   Multiprotocol over ATM, a standard for transmitting multiple network protocols over an ATM network.

MPEG   Moving pictures expert group, a video compression standard capable of both temporal and spatial compression. MPEG-2 requires hardware decompression. That is why a DVD CDROM player needs an MPEG-2 card in order to view videos on a desktop computer.

MPP   Massively parallel processing, an architecture for interconnecting upward of hundreds of CPU chips to create a high-performance supercomputing device.

MS   Management station, an HP OpenView system that accepts event and topology information from lower-tier collection stations (CS). The MS has a high-level view of the network, while the collection stations have a detailed view of a limited subset of the network.

MSS   Multiprotocol switched services.

MTA   Message transport agent, that part of an Email system responsible for moving messages from the originating user Email agent (UA) to the destination UA.

MTBF Mean time before failure is the average amount of time a device remains operational before experiencing a failure. This value is usually the mean of a Poisson distribution.

MTTR Mean time to repair is the average time it takes to detect a failure, replace the device, and restore service. The repair time can be reduced by stocking a hot preconfigured spare on site.

MTU Maximum transmission unit, the largest number of bytes a LAN adapter can accept from the upper layers. The LAN adapter will then wrap a frame around these data for transmission. Ethernet's MTU is 1500 bytes, and the framing adds 18 bytes for a maximum frame size of 1518 bytes.

MUA Mail user agent, an Email program such as *elm*, *pine*, or Netscape Mail.

MX Mail exchange, a special record provided by the domain name system (DNS) that allows an SMTP mail system to determine the correct system to forward Email to. For example, Email sent to *user@system.company.com* should not be sent directly to *system.company.com*'s IP address when it's behind a firewall. Rather it should be sent to *mail.company.com*, which is what the DNS would return when a DNS request for its MX record is made.

NAP Network access point, a location where network service providers (NSP) interconnect their networks. These are located at San Francisco, Chicago, New York, and Washington, D.C.

NC Network computer, typically a diskless computer that boots from a server and gets all its applications and files from it. This reduces administration and hardware costs.

NCPM Network connection policy manager, a DNS-based load-balancing product from Hewlett–Packard.

NCS Network compute system, a set of programming standards that allows an application to distribute its functions across a TCP/IP network of like-equipped systems to increase performance and reliability.

NDIS Network Driver Interface Specification, a standard for supporting multiple network protocols such as IP, IPX, and NetBUIE over a single LAN adapter on a Wintel computer.

NetPC Networked Personal Computer.

NFS Network file system, an industry standard for file and print sharing supported by UNIX, Wintel, and Macintosh vendors.

NHRP Next hop routing protocol, a method for performing layer III switching.

NIC   Network interface card, another word for a network adapter or LANIC.

NIS   Network information service, the part of the network file system that provides a consistent domain view of user and group IDs, host files, service files, and other maps as appropriate.

NLS   Native language support, a set of utilities to allow application developers to isolate the language-dependent strings in their code to make it easy to use that code in other countries that don't use English.

NMA   Network management architecture, a way of structuring how networks are managed by a product. An example is HP OpenView Network Node Manager.

NMS   Network management station, a computer executing network management applications, such as HP OpenView Network Node Manager.

NNM   Network node manager, an SNMP-based hierarchical network management product.

NNMGR   Network node manager.

NSP   Network service provider, a company with a national backbone that connects to the four network access points (NAP) in San Francisco, Chicago, New York, and Washington, D.C.

NT   A Wintel proprietary operating system.

NTSC   National Television Standards Committee, a standard format for video used in the United States, describing the number of scan lines, the horizontal and vertical scan rates, and the encoding of timing, intensity, and color information.

OAM   Operations and management.

OC3   Optical carrier 3, a standard for transmitting data at 155 megabits/second over fiber-optic cable, typically used in ATM and synchronous optical networks (SONET).

ODI   Open Data Link Interface, an alternative standard to NDIS on Wintel platforms for supporting multiple networking protocols on one LAN adapter.

OLTP   On-line transaction processing, a system for executing user units of work called transactions while the user waits for the results.

OS   Operating system, a comprehensive collection of programs for coordinating the execution of applications by providing services such as file and peripheral I/O, authentication, memory management, multitasking, multithreading, preemption, and security.

OSI Open systems interconnect, a model from the International Standards Organization that defines the functionality of networked applications in a seven-layer model.

OSPF Open shortest path first, a standard routing protocol that considers the number of hops and the bandwidth of each hop in the routing metric. It also updates routing tables using link state changes and supports the notion of areas across which routing information flows in a controlled manner.

OSS Operations and support systems.

PAgP Port aggregation protocol, a Cisco Systems protocol that can aggregate multiple fast Ethernet ports on a switch to create a virtual higher-speed link. This can be used to provide higher-speed links into a switched subnet from a router. It can also be used to increase the link speed into a file server from an Ethernet switch.

PBX Private branch exchange, a small telephone exchange owned and operated by private companies for supporting the internal telephones as well as providing access to outside lines.

PCI Peripheral component interconnect is a standard I/O specification used in desktop and UNIX systems alike. PCI has wide industry support, and high-performance adapters for SCSI disks and video adapters are commonplace.

PCL Printer control language, a complete page description language developed by Hewlett–Packard for its printers.

PCR Peak cell rate.

PDF Portable document format, a file format invented by Adobe Systems for the cross-platform distribution of documents. The major advantage is that the end user of the spreadsheet, presentation, report, mathematical scratchpad, or other, need not own a copy of the authoring software to use that document. The Acrobat Reader is all that the end user needs, and it's free; **or**

PDF Product description file, an HP-UX product file that describes the properties of all files contained in a specific product. This lets the system administrator verify that no on-line product files have been tampered with.

PEM Privacy enhanced mail, Email that supports privacy features such as encryption.

PGP Pretty good privacy is public-domain message encryption software generally used to protect Email from being intercepted by unwanted third parties.

PINE Pine is not *elm*, another Email program with more features than *elm*.

PNG   Portable network graphics, a new image format for storage and compression of millions-of-colors images. It combines the benefits of GIF and JPG without the uncertainty of the Unisys patent on LZW compression used in GIF file formats.

POP   Point of presence is a place where a network service is available. For example, an Internet service provider may offer a dial-up service by making available a local telephone number.

POP3   Post Office Protocol version 3 allows dial-up users to securely access their electronic mail boxes and copy messages to their desktop computer for off line reading and replying.

POTS   Plain old telephone system, a cutesy term referring to the analog telephone system's front end, the last mile, or the local loop, which is generally an analog communications system. Beyond the central office (CO), the telephone network is digital.

PPC   Power PC, a RISC CPU chip developed by Apple, IBM, and Motorola (AIM) that powers the Apple Macintosh computers.

PPP   Point-to-point protocol, a standard means for routers from multiple vendors to exchange packets containing multiple network protocols. However, it is commonly used between desktop computers and Internet service providers to support automatic dialing (of alternative numbers), login, authentication, negotiation of PPP parameters, exchange of IP addresses, and optionally, the exchange of name-server IP addresses.

PPTP   Point-to-point tunneling protocol provides a secure path through an insecure network (such as the Internet) between two networks that are otherwise separate. It may also be used to provide secure access to a corporate network from a desktop computer connected to the Internet.

PRI   Primary rate interface, a 1.544 megabit/second ISDN line.

PS   PostScript, a page description language developed by Adobe Systems. PostScript includes font technology, screening, color separation, and color management. PostScript is interpreted by a raster image processor (RIP) to create a high-resolution color bitmap for output to laser printers, ink jet printers, and image setters. PostScript is the industry standard for printing.

PVC   Permanent virtual circuit, a logical connection that's permanently established and requires no setup or tear down. An example is a point-to-point leased line. A frame relay network provides a PVC between two routers defined by the two end-point data link channel identifiers (DLCI).

QOS Quality of service, a metric that includes throughput, latency, timing jitter, and cell loss. QOS is supported by ATM networks to allow concurrent transmission of time-sensitive data, such as streaming digital video, and nontime-sensitive data, such as Email and file transfers.

RAID Redundant array of independent disks is a technology that combines multiple independent disk mechanisms into a single logical unit in order to provide increased performance, greater flexibility, and high availability. The technology includes mirroring, parity, redundancy, and striping mechanisms.

RAM Random access memory, the semiconductor chip storage medium from which the central processing unit receives instructions and data.

RAS Remote access server, a computer or special communications equipment equipped with modems designed to accept connections from remote desktop computers in a secure, reliable, albeit low-performance manner.

RBOC Regional Bell operating company.

RF Radio frequency, electromagnetic signals between approximately 1 and 1000 megahertz.

RFC A request for comment is an Internet engineering task force document, which may define a standard, report a technical result, or make a recommendation.

RFP Request for proposal, a document distributed by one party to multiple vendors to solicit a formal proposal for services.

RIP Routing information protocol, a standard, simple, low-overhead protocol for the exchange of routing tables between routers and participating end systems.

RISC Reduced instruction set computer, a design paradigm that simplifies the instruction set of a CPU to reduce the complexity of the chip design. The resulting chip runs faster and cooler than its complex computer instruction set (CISC) counterpart. Examples of RISC chips include the IBM/Apple/Motorola PowerPC (PPC), Hewlett–Packard Precision Architecture (HP-PA), Digital's Alpha, and Sun's Scalable Processor Architecture (SPARC).

RMON Remote monitor, an industry standard for remotely monitoring a shared media LAN segment, with a promiscuous probe supporting the RMON management information base (MIB). Ethernet statistics, traffic source–destination pairs, automatic thresholds, and packet capture are available. The RMON-2 standard extends the information available from layer 2 to layer 7 of the OSI model.

RMP Reliable multicast protocol.

ROM   Read-only memory, semiconductor memory that stores a fixed program to allow a computer to find a boot device and start up from the code stored there. The HP-UX systems can search for boot devices and allow the user to select one.

RPC   Remote procedure call, an application programming interface (API) that allows a program located on one computer to issue a function call, whose parameters are wrapped in a request packet and sent across the network to a server process where the actual function code resides and executes. Results of the remote function execution are returned in a reply packet.

RSP   Regional service provider, a level 3 provider of Internet services, located between level 4, the Internet service provider, and level 2, the national backbone provider. RSPs often provide DNS services.

RSVP   Reservation protocol, a standard intended to support time-sensitive multimedia traffic in the presence of data over routed IP networks.

RTMP   Reliable multicast transport protocol; **or**

RTMP   Routing table maintenance protocol, a protocol in the AppleTalk suite responsible for keeping the routing tables current in an AppleTalk network.

SAAL   Signaling ATM adaptation layer

SAM   System administration manager, an HP-UX system administration front end that greatly simplifies common tasks.

SAP   Systems, Applications, and Products in Data Processing is a comprehensive suite of business applications from the German company SAP AG; **or**

SAP   Service advertisement protocol, a broadcast or multicast service that file servers (especially Netware) use to advertise available resources such as printers and disks.

SAR   Segmentation and reassembly, a function of the Internet protocol (IP) that fragments packets larger than the underlying LAN media maximum transmission unit (MTU) for transmission, and that reassembles them at the destination system. The reassembly process deals with fragment reordering, but cannot recover lost fragments.

SAS   Single attach station, a device that connects to only one of the two FDDI rings.

SATAN   Security administration tool for analyzing networks, a UNIX-oriented set of utilities that probes networked systems for well-known weaknesses as an aid to improving their security configurations.

SCR   Sustained cell rate, a metric used in ATM.

SCSI   Small computer systems interface, a parallel daisy-chained interface that allows a computer to access hard disk drives, CD-ROMs, tapes drives, scanners, and such. A single SCSI bus can accommodate any mixture of these uniquely addressed devices consistent with the operating system's ability to support them.

SDK   Software development kit, a product containing manuals, libraries of code, and tools to support the rapid creation of new applications by programmers.

SET   Secure electronic transaction.

SGI   Silicon Graphics Incorporated is a manufacturer of high-performance UNIX systems used in graphics, 3D rendering, and video arts.

SLA   Service-level agreement, a contract between a service provider such as an IT department responsible for managing networks and computers, and the end users. Metrics may include uptime, response time, throughput, and reliability of service. These metrics are typically collected over a one-month period and reviewed with the user representatives.

SLIP   Serial Line IP, a standard for encapsulating IP packets over an RS-232 circuit. SLIP is a predecessor to PPP.

SMB   Server message block, the basic protocol used by LAN Manager, Samba, LM/X, and AdvancedServer/9000 to provide file and print services for Wintel client computers.

SMP   Symmetrical multiprocessing, an operating system feature that allows it to use multiple processors efficiently using load-balancing mechanisms that don't favor one processor to execute kernel code.

SMTP   Simple mail transport protocol, an Internet standard for transmitting and forwarding single-part 7-bit ASCII messages.

SNA   Systems network architecture, IBM's former name for its data communications products.

SNMP   Simple network management protocol, an RFC-compliant protocol that provides only the *get*, *getnext*, *set*, and *trap* operators between a management station and a managed device agent.

Socks   A secure circuit relay protocol through which client systems inside a private network obtain a secure connection to Internet-based servers.

SONET   Synchronous optical network, the fundamental fiber-optic technology and signaling techniques used by the telcos, which is used for ATM networks.

SPARC   Scalable processor architecture, SUN Microsystems RISC CPU chip.

SQL   Structured query language, a standard means to request information from a database.

SRM   Scalable reliable multicast.

SS7   Signaling system 7, the standard used by the digital telephone network to establish, reroute, manage, and control voice and data calls.

SSL   Secure sockets layer, an API developed by Netscape Communications to support the secure exchange of sensitive customer information between the web browser and its server. This is a necessary feature of secure Internet commerce.

SSN   Secure server network, a LAN segment connected to a bastion host in a firewall configuration, access to which is governed by the bastion. This LAN is more secure than the DMZ LAN facing the Internet.

STP   Shielded twisted pair, a LAN wiring standard that adds shielding around pairs of twisted insulated wires to improve its transmission properties. Shielding reduces electromagnetic interference and susceptibility.

STS   Synchronous transport signal, the fundamental 51.84-megabit/second clock speed for SONET and ATM.

SVC   Switched virtual circuit, a logical connection across a network that is established prior to data transmission, maintained for the session, then torn down at termination. ISDN supports this.

TAXI   Transparent asynchronous transmit and receive interface, a FDDI-like interface definition for ATM.

TCO   Total cost of ownership, an estimate of the annual cost of supplying a service to a user. For example, the TOC for a networked Wintel computer includes the cost of the hardware, software, installation, help desk support, service, downtime, formal training, informal training, and "futzing."

TCP   Transmission control protocol, a transport layer standard defined in RFC 793 used to provide reliable, flow-controlled, multiplexed connections between communicating systems.

TFTP   Trivial file transfer protocol, a very simple protocol typically used to upload and download network electronic device configuration. X-terminals, routers, hubs, switches, and bridges often support it.

TIF   Tagged image format, a cross-platform image file format capable of holding color space conversion data, multiple layers, and alpha channels.

TTL   Time to live, an 8-bit field in the IP header defined by the sender and reduced at least by one by each intervening router. If there is a routing loop, the last router decrements the TTL to zero, discards the packet, and notifies the sender with a "TTL exceeded" ICMP message.

TTRT   Target token rotation timer is a value agreed on by all members of a FDDI ring for the time it takes for the token to circulate around the ring.

TV   Television.

UA   User agent, typically in the Email sense, this is the user's Email program. Examples include *mailx*, *elm*, *pine*, *advmail*, Netscape Mail, cc:Mail, and Zmail

UBR   Unspecified bit rate, a quality of service (QoS) in ATM networks for which the connection will accept any bit rate available. This service is suited for data transmissions.

UDP   User datagram protocol, a version of TCP that does not provide and therefore does not have the overhead associated with reliable transmission and multiplexing. UDP is used by applications such as SNMP and NFS.

UID   User ID, a numeric and alphabetic identifier unique for each UNIX user.

UPS   Uninterruptible power supply, a device that filters public power, stores it in a battery, and delivers clean continuous AC power even during failure of the public power grid. The UPS may be SNMP managed, and servers often collect data from their UPS via an RS-232 cable so that an orderly shutdown may be performed when the UPS battery runs low.

URL   Uniform resource locator, a way to address a web page or service on the Internet. For example, *http://www.hp.com/openview* is a URL that specifies a hypertext document on system *www.hp.com* in folder *openview*.

UTP   Unshielded twisted pair, a cabling system used in LAN technologies such as the IEEE 10-BASE-T and 100VG-AnyLAN. The cable pairs are twisted to reduce radio-frequency interference and reception of electrical and magnetic noise.

UUCP   UNIX to UNIX copy, a standard protocol between UNIX systems to copy files. It was used historically to move Email over dial links among a loosely knit but vast community of UNIX systems.

UUENCODE   UNIX to UNIX encode, a technique that transforms binary files into 7-bit ASCII format suitable for transmission by SMTP. UUENCODE is also the name of the program that does this, as well as the inverse operation, UUDECODE.

VAN   Value-added network.

VAR   Value-added reseller.

VBR   Variable bit rate, a quality of service in ATM networks characterized by a fluctuating data rate.

VC   Virtual circuit, a logical connection through a switched network that moves data along it between two end systems.

VCC   Virtual channel connection, a connection via a virtual circuit.

VLAN   Virtual LAN, a way to create multiple LANs within a group of Ethernet or ATM switches to which devices may be assigned based on their MAC address, switch port number, network protocol, or application. This avoids a major configuration management issue with flat switched networks, that is, broadcast control.

VOD   Video on demand, a service by which a customer specifies that he wants to see a movie at a specific time, and a digital video server at the service provider's facility is primed to deliver the analog video stream on a predefined scrambled channel

VPN   Virtual private network, a means to use the Internet to create a secure tunnel between multiple private networks.

VSAT   Very small aperture terminal, usually a small satellite dish antenna.

VUE   Visual user environment, a desktop paradigm for UNIX systems built on the X-Windows system. It includes a task bar, a trash can, and automated tasks. Most of VUE's elements were contributed to the CDE standard.

WABI   Windows application binary interface, a product from Sun that emulates the Wintel windowing system to allow users to run their favorite Wintel applications without owning a PC.

WAN   Wide-area network, a network such as T1, T3, ATM, OC3, SONET, frame relay, and ISDN characterized by its ability to cover global distances, well beyond the reach of LAN technology. The fiber and cable infrastructure is owned by carriers.

WINS   Wintel name service, a naming service for PCs.

WRQ   Walker Richer Quinn, the Seattle, Washington, company famous for its terminal emulation programs and more recently for its X-Windows emulator Reflection/X.

WWW World wide web, a term used to describe a collection of hyperlinked web servers accessed from desktop computers running web browsers for the purpose of disseminating and sharing information of all kinds.

XDMCP X-Windows display manager control protocol is used to give X-Windows users the means to log in to a UNIX system. A daemon process such as *xdm* listens for XDMCP requests from X-terminals and provides a login window for user authentication and access.

XDR External data representation, used by the network file system (NFS) to deal with differences in file system semantics between clients and servers running on different platform, such as PCs, Macintosh, and UNIX systems.

ZIP Zone information protocol, used by AppleTalk to propagate, manage, and access zone information across an AppleTalk network.

Index

PostScript, 201, 267
power, data center, 277
PPP, 73, 76, 92
preference for NFS, 164
primary link, 32
print spooler, 267
printer traffic, 55
privacy issues, 160
product description files, 138
PROFFS, 155
protected memory, 168, 240
proxy ARP, 109
PVC, 37

Q
QOS, 223
QuickTime, 223
QuickTime MoviePlayer, 224

R
radio frequency, 272
RAM disk, 61
raw disk partition, 56
redundant links, 36
reflector, 228, 229
reliability, 30
reliability analysis, 28
reliable IP backbone, 36
remote access, 141
remote administration, 204
repeaters, 81
requirements analysis, 3
resources, 179
response time, 20, 180
Ricochet, 38
Ricochet Wireless, 276
RIP, 35
risk analysis, 13, 133
root, 139
round-robin, 243
routers, 60
routing, 108

routing table, 34, 108, 249
RSP, 242
RSVP, 224

S
safe sets, 210
SAP, 42
SAP/R3, 22, 74
satellite constellations, 280
scalable architecture, 51
scale, 8
SCSI buses, 56
security
    account management, 138
    analysis, 132
    application, 140
    B-level, 137
    communication, 132
    correction, 132
    DCE model, 136
    definition of, 129
    detection, 132
    event, 130
    opportunity, 132
    privacy, 132
    UNIX auditing tools, 141
    wireless environment, 274
serial components, 28
server message block, 176
server scaling, 51
server, well-balanced, 179
service denial, 131
shared memory, 61
SharedPrint, 268
SharedX, 198
SharedX whiteboard, 199
simulation tools, 15, 233
simulator, 265
    Designer, 182
    Mil3 OpNet, 182
simulator applications, 262
slow-start, 62

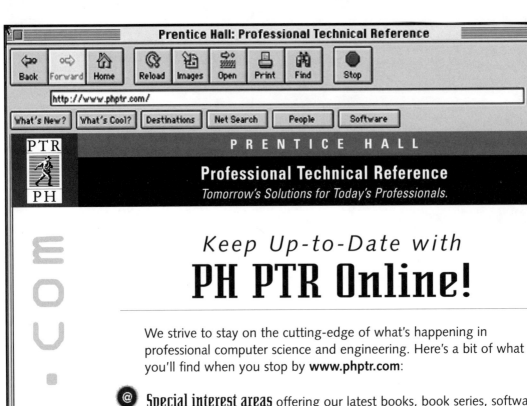